PILGRIMAGE TOURISM IN NEPAL

PILGRIMAGE TOURISM IN NEPAL

YAJNA RAJ SATYAL

ADROIT PUBLISHERS
Delhi-110 053

Published by
ADROIT PUBLISHERS
C-8/2, Yamuna Vihar, Delhi-110 053
Phone: 3266030, 3242552

Distributors
AKHIL BOOK DISTRIBUTORS
4675/21, Ganpati Bhawan, Ansari Road,
Darya Ganj, New Delhi-110 002
Phones : 3266030, 3242552
e-mail: akhilbooks@yahoo.com

ISBN : 81-87392-29-0

Layout by
Sudhir Kumar Vatsa

Laser Typeset by
Nidhi Laser Point
e-mail: nidhi_vatsa@hotmail.com

Printed in India on behalf of M/s Adroit Publishers by
Arpit Printographer, B-7, Saraswati Complex,
Subhash Chowk, Laxmi Nagar, Delhi-110 092

PREFACE

Since ancient times many religious minded people not fearing for hardships on the way who travel on pilgrimage braving multiple dangers. The principle motives impelled them to travel—religious sentiment. Nepal, described as the abode of gods and goddesses since ancient times by mythological accounts and versions in religious texts, religious sentiment persuaded people to make long pilgrimages to places of venerated worship travelling roadless mountain rigged paths not caring the limits of human endurance. Nepal was so famous for religious and pilgrimage sites. So, the religious minded people are even now visiting the pilgrimage places in large numbers to pay homage to gods and goddesses of their choice for veneration in different parts of the country.

Nepal has got big potentials in natural and cultural resources. To lovers of ancient art and culture, Nepal is really stronghold and store house of ancient art and architecture untouched by any foreign invaders at any time of her long and glorious history. So, Nepal has been able to preserved the oldest pilgrimage places with the oldest idols of gods and goddesses, sculptures, art architecture and paintings and decorations of the past. Archaeologically speaking, Nepal is one of the oldest nation in the world. The ancient relics and remnants bear testimony to the fact that Nepal has been the safe custody of the earliest Asian civilization and culture. Nepal has so much religious touch, mythological background and ideal philosophical thought which has created trust and confidence and devotion to her places of pilgrimage. It has always been one of the most important pilgrimage sites for Hindus as well as Buddhist in the Central Himalayas. So the various Hindu and Buddhist temples and stupas are preserved and are of an astonishing richness in the pilgrimage sights in the different parts of the country. Nepal has a most active blend of Asian cultures with as abundance of, monasteries and temples which makes it a land of devotees with sacred places of religious pilgrimages.

Lastly, every efforts are being made for the assessment of pilgrimage tourism in Nepal, but the subject matter is complex interactions are warmly requested from all to make this book more comprehensive and rich for the future.

The Author

Contents

1 Abode of the Gods

"Among the Mountains, I am the Himalaya"—Lord Krishna in Bhagvad Gita signified the sanctity of Nepal as one of the holiest places on earth. The Himalaya, or the "abode of snow" is referred to as the home of Lord Shiva and his consort, Parvati. Goddess Parvati presented as the daughter of the Himalaya, the majestic mountain range in the world. The Himalaya has a particular importance to the followers of Hinduism since time immemorial. The Mythological period covering the *Satya, Treta* and *Dwapar Yugas*, or ages, also contains numerous references regardings the temples, shrines and holy places of the country. Many reflections are expressed in the ancient Hindu and Buddhist texts about the holiness of Nepal as the land of spiritual blessing and tranquillity.

The book containing the rules of the language defines Nepal as "Ne Munina Palitam Nepalam", the land protected by sage Ne is Nepal. Many sages and seers preferred the serene environ and quiet natural atmosphere of Nepal as the best place for their meditation. To the Hindus, it is the holy land of Lord Pashupatinath. Many philosopher-saints like Viswamitra, Kapila, Yajnavalka, Balmiki and Raja Janak found endless spiritual inspiration while penancing by the sacred banks of Koshi, Gandaki and Karnali rivers or in the pristine Sagarmatha (Mt. Everest), Dhaulagiri and Annapurna Himalayan mountains. Their in-depth observations, and analysis of concrete phenomena regarding Hindu religiosity still dominate the intellectual arena. All these great thinkers attained perfection in their spirituality here. The hermitage of all of them was in the tranquil recesses of Nepal.

Nepal's physical location and character is regarded as extraordinary and picturesque. Barely rectangular in shape, it is a beautiful country located in the southern slopes of the mid-Himalayas, the formidable range of eternal snows. The nearest sea coast is about 1,127 km. from its border. It is bounded on the north by the Tibat, Autonomous Region of the People Republic of China, on the east by Sikkim and West Bengal, on the south by Bihar and Uttar Pradesh and the west by Uttar Pradesh of *India*. The major part of the country is of high mountains and rolling hills.

Nepal displays an unique variety of geographical regions ranging from the tropical lowlands to the Arctic plateau. Between these lie the Middle hills, inhabited thousands of years ago. It is this traditional region of Nepali culture and history, at whose heart lies the exotic valley of Kathmandu, embracing an exceptional culture and religious and scenic wealth.

The Himalayan mountain range across northern Nepal topped by 8848 m. Sagarmatha (Mount Everest), highest peak in the world together with some eight snow peaks of over 8000 m. and about two hundred 4877 m. peaks. In the fringe of the range dwell famed Sherpas who have climbed earth's highest snow peaks.

The climatic condition in Nepal is governed by its topography extremities. Tropical, temperate and tundra types of climate and respectively encountered in its Terai belt, midland hills and the alpine region.

The Kathmandu Valley at 1310 m. has an equable climate. But it is much colder at higher elevations. The summer is wetter than in winter. The monsoon period begins from June and lasts till September. The climate is warm and humid in summer, moist and temperate in monsoon, and cold and rain-free in winter.

Nepal is the only Hindu Kingdom in the world. Hinduism and Buddhism constitute two major religions of Nepal. There are many castes and creeds but no rigidity. Religion is an integral part of Nepali life. The Nepali people observe various forms of Hinduism such as Shiva, Baishnava, Buddha, Sakta, Nath in both tantric and non-tantric forms. Shiva and Vishnu both have occupied an unique position in the religious belief of people. There is religious tolerance everywhere. Everything is based on compromise and understanding. The Nepali people are a happy creed of men, proud of their glorious past and sure of the great future that lies ahead of them.

From the rolling places of the Terai bordering India, skIrting the foothills up the serried ridges of the mountains enclosing lush valleys, through to the soaring majestic heights of the Himalayas, Nepal offers within her short compass such a big variety of attraction which is unique and spectacular. Nepal is a wonderful, world of Variety. Enchanting scene of the architectural wonder, golden pagodas beneath the stupendous natural environs everywhere with a snowy Himalayan mountains on the distant horizon. Kathmandu city is for tradition, art and architecture. Nepal's capital city has many cultural treasures such as the famed Kathmandu Durbar Square, temples and stupas, half a century in building, is a attractive combination of many architectural styles. Kathmandu Durbar Square is a complex of varied attractions for marvellous art and designs as well as for experiencing some of the greatest sites of South Asia's cultural heritage. It attains traditional artistry and the rich cultural heritage of Nepal. The exorcism of historical remains consisting of palace buildings and temples in the Durbar Square offer elaborateness of artistic detail and beauty treatment which has no rival in Asia. Kathmandu's greater importance lies in the fact that it is the artistic as well as cultural capital of Nepal. Nepal by these singular beauty of art and architectural marvel is regarded as one of the few countries in the world where seven world heritage sites are situated within 20 kilometres of radius.

Kathmandu Durbar Square or most popularly known by the name of Hanuman Dhoka Palace is famous as the most attractive part of Kathmandu, full of temples, palace buildings and courtyards constructed during Malla Period (12th to 18th century). The main gate of the palace is known as the Hanuman Dhoka, the golden gate of Monkey God, guarded by two lions. The palace complex is divided into many courtyards as Nasal Chowk, Mohan Chowk, Basantpur Chowk, *etc.* After passing the Hanuman Dhoka, close by stands the triple-roofed Taleju temple on top of a multi-tier plinth built in 1549 by the King Mahendra Mall in dedication to goddess Taleju. The temple is projected in the form of the mystic Yantra. Its architecture is a fine example of the world famous Nepali pagoda style. It dominates the skyline of the Kathmandu City with its brass plated roofs and the gold gilt finial. The roof ends are lined with small bells. These are also a number of other interesting and historic temples and objects of arts in the vicinity. Some of the most important ones are Gigantic figure of Kal Bhairab (God of terror). The large temple opposite the Hanuman gate is the Jagannath temple built by Mahendra Malla in 1563. This two tiered temple has very elaborately carved roof-strufs famed for their erotic carvings. There is another magnificent temple of Deotale built by Shiva Singh Malla in the sixteenth century. Almost beneath the Deotale temple, lies the large golden mask of Sweta Bhairab fierce in appearance erected in 1796 by the King Rana Bahadur Shah to drive off evil spirits and ghost. Then equally famous two temples namely Shiva Parvati temple, Trilokya Mohan Mandir are unique in their arts and architectures. Adjacent to these temples, there is three-story building with carved windows. It is in the form of Bahal (courtyard) and is the dwelling of the Goddess Kumari, the living goddess. This is an imposing residential building in Pagoda style with carvings, very ornate and elaborate on its windows and window frames. Another equally famous temple is two roofed pagoda temple Kasthamandap built in 1596 A.D. by King Laxmi Narasingha Malla. It is believed to be made of the timber of a single tree "Kathmandu" derives its name from this wooden structure.

The second religions shrine showing a typical example of the stupa architecture. It is situated on top of a hillock three km. west of Kathmandu amidst a lovely and quiet environ. This stupa holds a big sanctity for the Buddhist as well as the Hindus. The stupa quadrangle holds many miniature stupas, shrines, sacred pillars and so on. There is a pagoda temple of Harati, the Hindu Goddess of smallpox and other epidemics. It is the oldest Buddhist shrine in the Kathmandu Valley.

The most important double-roofed pagoda temple of gold-gilt brass dedicated to God Pashupatinath—Hindu God Shiva is another holiest shrine in Nepal. It is guardian deity of Nepal and is situated on the western bank of the Bagmati river about five km north east of Kathmandu. It contains the lingam of Pashupatinath. This holy place is a mosaic of other temples and shrines. On the occasion of the annual festival of Shivaratri (February/March) the temple is visited by thousands of devotees including large number of Indians from different parts of India to make homage to Shiva, the Lord of all creatures. This holy place is full of numerous other temples and shrines. There is an amazing collectors of stone sculptures (dating from the fifth century) of deities along the bank of the Bagmati river.

Boudhanath Stupa is another Buddhist Stupa which is eight kilometres east of Kathmandu and about two kilometres to the north of the temple of Lord Pashupatinath. This stupa is one of the largest Buddhist Chaitya in the world. It is built on an octagonal base. The dome and its base are adorned white and coloured with yellow paint in the form of petals to signify the lotus. It has about eighty small recesses each bearing the image of Buddha. The wall around the Stupa is studded with hundreds of prayer wheels. It is considered to be built by Licchavi King Mana Dev in the fifth century A.D. Around the stupa are various smaller shrines and monasteries. This Stupa assumes a gay solemn appearance at all Buddhist festivals when Buddhists visit from all over the country, India, Bhutan, Tibat etc. to take part in the sacred rituals.

Bhaktapur city, another city of devotees by name in the Kathmandu Valley is full of temples and shrines. According to a legend, this city is shaped like a conch shell (one of the emblems of the God Vishnu) and was founded by King Ananda Deva in 889 A.D. This city lies fifteen Kilometers to the east and is linked by highway.

The glory of Bhaktapur city or Bhadgaon is famous by the Durbar Square with numbers of shimmering pagoda temples with figures of different Gods and Goddesses and religious symbols. The Batsala Temple, the Pashupatinath temple, Dattatraya temple and many others are the show-pieces. Batsala Temple is dedicated to Goddess Batsala Devi with carved stone walls and pillars in Shikhara style. Then imposing temple of Taleju Bhavani at Taleju Chowk, built by Hari Singha Deva in 1324 A.D. There is also the Lion Gate bearing the images of Hanuman, Bhairav and Narasingh Narayan which is lifelike stone works. This gate is embellished with figures of goddesses of Kali and Garuda and other mythical creatures with marvellous intricacy. The temple of Lord Pashupatinath built by the King Sumati Jayajita Mitra near about 1682 A.D. This temple is the replica of the famous temple of Pashupatinath located beside the Bagmati river in Kathmandu. Beyond the Durbar Square to the Taumadhi tole containing the famous Nyatapola temple which is an impressive five-sotrey pagoda. This temple is set on a stepped platform of five plinths, erected at the time of King Bhupatindra Malla in 1708. This is one of the tallest pagoda style temples in Kathmandu Valley and is famous for its massive structure and excellent workmanship. This temple is dedicated to a deity of the Tantric cult. Close to the Nyatapola Temple is another temple of Bhairav (God of Destruction). There is another famous temple of Dattatraya built by King Yakshya Malla in 1427 A.D. from the trunk of a single tree. Wakupati Narayan temple is dedicated to Garud Narain. Near the Dattatraya Temple is a monastery known as Pujari Math. This monastery is world famous for lattice windows weaving carved peacocks.

Changu Narayan Temple is the oldest pagoda-style temple of the valley, the rare artistic heritage from the Lichavi period. It is considered to have been built by King Hari Datta Varma in 325 A.D. It is a two-storied pagoda of the usual Nepali architecture with the sanctum of bronze portraying Lokeshwore mounted on Vishnu who stands on Garuda. Very beautiful and intricate ancient stone sculptures bearing images of Narashimha Narayan, Satya Narayan, Vishnu Roopa and many others are scattered in the quadrangle and just outside Changu Narayan Temple.

After Changu Narayan, Patan city or Lalitpur city of beauty is about five kilometers southeast of Kathmandu. Patan city and its ancient Durbar Square is a cluster of pagoda temples and stone statues. Many pagoda temples dedicated to Lord Vishnu and Lord Shiva is scattered in the quadrangle of the main city area of Patan. Adjacent to the Mul Chowk and dominating the palace complex because of its size is the Deotale built by King Siddhi Narasingha in 1641. It is five-tiered and is dedicated to Taleju Bhawani. The most striking temple at the edge of the Durbar Square is the unusual octagonal stone temple of Krishna built by King Siddhi Narasingha Mall in 1637. Scenes from the great epics of the Mahabharat and Ramayan have been engraved around the lintels above the colonnade. The temple is of Shikhara style and a bronze figure of Garuda, the mount of Lord Vishnu stands in front of it. Near to Krishna Mandir, there are two other temples known as Bishwanath temple and Bhimsen Mandir. Patan is rich is Hindu temples and Buddhist Vihara or monasteries. In the vicinity of the complex, there is the famous Mahaboudha temple which is well-known for thousand of carved figures of Lord Buddha. Hiranya Varna Mahavihar, Rudra Varna Mahavihar, both Buddhist monasteries of exquisite arts collection of images and statues in metal, stone and wood.

Temple of Machendra Nath and Min Nath is situated at Tabahal and was built in 1408 A.D. It is also known as Avalokiteshwor and Adinath Lokeshwor. The Ashoka Stupas are at the four corners of Patan.

After these temples and stupas in the Kathmandu Valley, there are Balaju Garden famous for the 22 Mdkara-headed stone water spouts. It is situated five km west of central Kathmandu.

Buddhanil Kantha is situated seven km north of Kathmandu, a place of pilgrimage for Hindus. There is the statue of Lord Vishnu, lying in the pool of water in the bed of snakes. This is one of the masterpiece of stone sculpture of the Lichhavian period of fifth century A.D. The colossal image of Lord Vishnu seems to float in water of the pond.

Dakshinkali Temple is situated at about twenty kilometers south-west of Kathmandu city. This is one of the very important places of pilgrimage regarding Hindu Kali Goddess. Pilgrims visit this temple to offer their prayers and animal sacrifices to the alter of goddess.

Kirtipur is an ancient township eight kilometers south-west of Kathmandu city on the top of a hill. This historic town has many old shrines and temples. There is an ancient temple of Bagh Bhairab with beautiful carvings.

Bajra Barahi is situated about ten kilometers south of Paten city. It is located in a small woodland park adjacent to the village of Chapagaon.

Surya Vinayak—It is a shrine of Ganesh, the elephant-headed god. It is located at south of Bhaktapur city in a sylvan setting to catch the first rays of the rising sun (Surya)

Another equally famous temple of elephant headed girl is Jalavinayak situated near the Chovar gorge. This temple was constructed in the Malla period.

Ashok Vinayak is also known by the name of Maru Ganesh or Kathmandu Ganesh (elephant-headed God). He is worshipped while starting a new entrepreneurs or business.

Karya Vinayak in Bungamati, Chandra Vinayak in Chabahil are other images of Ganesh. Tuesday is propitious day to honour Ganesh.

There are Akash Bhairav, Bhadrakali and many more Gods and Goddesses in the Kathmandu Valley. Col Kirkpatrick described Kathmandu Valley in 18th century as "There are as many idols as there are men and as many temples as there are home."

Outside Kathmandu Valley and all along the west and east regions of Nepal, there are many famous temples and shrines of Gods and Goddesses. Places full of religious images of Gods are remarkable for their pilgrimages. These are described below :

Gosainkunda : This is famous place having a lake reknown for the Hindu pilgrimage. It is located at an altitude about 4360 m. This place can be reached through Dhunche, 132 kilometre north east of Kathmandu. This religions lake is surrounded by high Himalayan mountains on the north and south and by alpine landscape on the east and west. There are other smaller lakes known a Saraswati Kunda, Bhairav Kunda, Soorya Kunda and Ganesh Kunda etc. This lake has been associated with Lord Shiva.

Gorakhanath and Kali famous temples are located in the Gorkha township. The Gorkha township is the headquarter of the district of the same name. Gorkha is the birth place of the King Prithvi Narayan Shah, the Great, the founder of modern Nepal, hence it is the ancestral home of the Shah Kings of Nepal. It landscape is lovely. Two well-known temples of Gorakhnath and Kali and many pilgrims visit to pay homage. It is situated 145 kilometers west of Kathmandu. The famous holy place of Manakamana is very near to it.

Manakamana : Manakamana Mai is situated in Gorkha District which lies 106 km west of Kathmandu. This temple of Manakamana Mai is situated at the top of a hillock and formerly it generally took several hours to reach the revered temple by several hours of arduous trekking. Now it has become more attractive by the installation of cable cars by a private company. The Manakamana Darshan (P) Ltd. The cable car route which is 3.1 km linking Cheres (between Kurin and Mugling) at Dare Chowk VDC — 3 of Chitwan district and Manakamana Mai. The cable car starts at the height of 2600 m. above the sea level and ends at 3,100 m. high is the longest in Asia.

Another famous temple of Lord **Muktinath** lies in the Mustang district. This is one of the important places of pilgrimage for the Hindus and the devotees visit this place to pay hosmage to Lord Muktinath during the Janai Poornima and Ram Navami festivals. This place is located at an altitude about 3749 m and is situated about 18 kilometers north-east of Jomsom. Flight is taken up to Jomsom and trek for a couple of hours via Kagbeni.

Varahakshetra is in the Koshi zone of Nepal near the industrial city of Biratnagar in the north-west of this city. It lies at the confluence of Sapta Koshi and Koka rivers. There is the temple of Baraha Bhagban (Boar incarnation of Lord Vishnu). Baraha or the boar is the third of the ten incarnations of Lord Vishnu. A great Mela takes place on Kartik Sukla Poornima (November-full moon day) in the vicinity of this temple.

Narayanghat is a small township near famous Narayani river (seven Gandaki rivers) in Chitwan Valley. This is also a place of pilgrimage. It lies south-east of Kathmandu. Chitwan is a District of Nepal situated about 120 kilometers south-west of Kathmandu. About 22 km. south of Kusande village on the Narayanghat-Butwal highway is Valmiki Ashram, the epic hermitage place of Ramayan famed sage Valmiki. Devaghat is located about eight kilometers north of Bharatpur of Narayani zone. This is situated at the confluence of the Kali and Trishuli to be Narayani river. This place is known by Harihara Chhetra. I has many temples and images consecrated to Vishnu, Shiva and Chakreshwori Mahadev.

In the high Himalayas, many places such as Helambu, Thyangboche, etc. are famous for their Buddhist monasteries.

Lumbini, the birth place of Lord Buddha, is one of the holiest and most sacred place on earth. It is situated in Kapilvastu District the western Terai of Nepal. It is about 300 kilometers south-west of Kathmandu. The centre of attraction at Lumbini is the sacred garden with Mayadevi Temple, the Ashoka Pillar signifying the place of birth of the Lord Shakyamuni Buddha. With the assistance of the United Nations and efforts of many nations, a major preservation and development are going on now to make this place really a masterpiece.

Lumbini, the birthplace of Buddha is in Nepal and so it is one of the world's great centres of the Buddhist faith and statues of the great teacher are to be seen everywhere.

Janaki Temple: This place is famous as the marble temple of Janaki. Janakpur is the birth-place of Sita, the consort of Rama the epic hero of the Hindu epic Ramayana. The lovely feature of this temple is its beautifully decorated cupolas, ceilings and tiles in the Indo-Persian style. Janakpur is in the Eastern Terai of Nepal and it is historical town. This place is associated with King Janak, the father of Sita. Ram Janaki temple is the centrepiece of this religious town and many pilgrims from all over Nepal and India visit here to pay homage to Sita Ram. Religious festivals, pilgrimages, trade fairs and other festivals are held here on Vivaha Panchami and Ram Navami days. This place of plgrimage is also linked with Kathmandu by air. Ram Janaki Temple, popularly known as Naulakha Mandir which refers built at the cost of Rs. 900,000.

The combination of temples, the artistic and religious creations of man and snow peaks of High Himalayas, the enduring products of God, lends to Nepal a charm and individuality which amply proves it as the abode of the Gods. The visit to religious pilgrimage sites of Nepal, seeing temples and images of Gods and Goddesses with a devotion and compassion provide an opportunity to enrich your sense and mind by invigorating deep religious sentiment within yourself. Nepal has quiet religious centre that is a world apart.

2 Religion in Nepal

The major religions of Nepal are Hinduism and Buddhism. Religion is an integral part of Nepali people. There is a religious tolerance and harmony existing between Hinduism and Buddhism from the ancient times. All deities whether it may be from Hindu or Buddhist people are worshipped by both the communities with equal reverence. There is full blending of Hinduism and Buddhism in Nepal and all the Gods and Goddesses are worshipped by Hindus and Buddhists alike. The special feature of Nepal is the religious homogeneity prevailing specially between the Buddhist and Hindu peoples, who, for long course of history have developed mutual love and respect for one another. Nepal has a tradition of religious tolerance: Hinduism and Buddhism are the two major religions of Nepal, which exist together in an amicable and harmonious atmosphere. Nepal's population are constituted almost 90 per cent of followers of Hinduism and more than 5 per cent of the total population are Buddhists and both co-exist together to comprise one concordant social system. This can be witnessed by seeing religious symbols and motifs of both religions which are placed in the places of worships. All the people of Nepal are generally religious and they observe traditional customs and rites.

Hinduism is the main religion of Nepal. The Nepali people observe various forms of Hinduism such as Shaivism, Vaisnavism, Buddhism. Nath sects in both tantric and non-tantric ways. Shiva as well as Vishnu both have occupied an unique position in the religious belief of the people. Hinduism is based on the holy texts of Vedas, Upanishads and the Puranas. It has basic trinity of three Gods, Brahma, the creator, Vishnu the Preserver and Shiva, the Destroyer and regenerator of all things. Besides, two of Vishnu's other incarnations—Rama and Krishna, the heroes of classical epics of Ramayana and Mahabharat also are worshipped by the Hindus. Other deities like Ganesh and Bhairab, etc. are also revered. The cult of Mother Goddess too holds a predominant place in Hindu pantheon.

Hinduism teaches to have faith in the Almighty Father, speak the truth, shun violence, prevent cruelty to animals, show benevolence to all, perform religious rituals, refrain from illicit sexual relations and lead a simple and pious domestic life.

Nepal is the only HIndu Kingdom in the world and has a tradition of religions tolerance. Hinduism and Buddhism are the two major religions of Nepal which exist simultaneously in an amicable and harmonious atmosphere.

Buddhism is another religion of Nepal. Nepal is the birth-place of Gautama Buddha the prince of peace. Buddhist beliefs and practices date back to Nepal since 543 B.C., the time of its founder Gautama the Buddha who was born at Lumbini in West Nepal Terai. He was a prince who renounced princely life of pomp and show in search of enlightenment and the real meaning of worldly life. He taught the eight-fold path of the salvation of human soul from worldly bondage and endless wheel of existence. The Eight fold path signifies Right Understanding, Right Resolve, Right Speech, Right Action, Right Living, Right Effort, Right Mindfulness and Right Meditation. Gautama Buddha was a prince who relinquished luxurious life in search of enlightenment.

Buddhism divided into two schools of thought in about 100 A.D.—Hinayana and Mahayana. Hinayana does not practice idolatry while Mahayana worships the idols of Buddha. The Nepali Buddhists are the followers of Mahayana School. One of the main beliefs of this doctrine is that man can liberate himself by "Bodhi" meaning essence. Very few other Nepali Budhists have adopted the Hinayana School of thought, choosing rather to follow Mahayana teaching. Buddhism known as Mahayana and Bajrayana have existed in Nepal from the ancient time.

The Mahayana canon contains a larger proportion of the esoteric wisdom than anyother religion and has always adherred more closely to the "Heart" as distinct from the "Eye" doctrine, the eternal life rather than the changinng form-off the message.

Tantrism is practiced both by Hindus and Buddhists in Nepal. Tantra is very dominant in the Nepali religious beliefs. A store house of tantric materials for the knowledge of Tantrism have preserved in Nepal. The first period coming to the end of the 12th century A.D. was marked by a fervent religious activities of the Tantric principles, a left handed cult with the elevation of sexual truth in worship.

Tantrism's origin is found in the ancient worship of the Shiva-cult, the followers of God Shiva who is the destroyer and regenerator of all things. The regeneration of the entire world depends on the procreational lesson of male and female. Absolute consciousness as Shiva is manifested as the male principle and power as Shakti is manifested as the female principle. In the second half of the first Millennium, Nepal came under the influence of a strange religious movement that incorporated ideas of sinister spiritual power, magic forces, necromancy and great variety of symbols. Named after it holy scripture the Tantra or "Warps"–it is known as Tantricism.

Tantricism welcome all devotees irrespective of caste, creed, sex or wealth. Bhairava who is regarded as manifestation of Shiva, the Hindu god is equally worshipped by Hindus and Buddhists in Nepal. Tantra, in its essence can be defined a "scripture by which knowledge is disseminated." In Nepal Shiva and Buddhist tantras have been mixed up giving birth to a new type of esoteric worship, influencing the socio-religious life of the Nepali people.

Tantrism has greatly influenced Nepali Buddhism by creating the path of Vajrayana "the Path of the Thunderbolt". The main object used in Vajrayana Buddhist rituals is a small thunderbolt like sceptre that is said to represent the infinite in three dimensions.

Buddhism, as it appears in Nepal belongs to third "school" which has often been called the third vehicle—Vajrayana or Lamaism i.e. a school strongly influenced by Tantrism.

In addition to Hinduism, Buddhism and Tantrism, a very small minority of Nepal adhere to Islam and Christianity. Muslims and Christians believe and practice in much the same way as their counterparts in the western and other countries.

Lamaism, as the Buddhism in Tibet used to be called is a mixture of the best and worst of Buddhism and much that lies between. At its best, it is a noble part of the Mahayana. Primitive Lamaism may be defined as a priestly mixture of Sivaite mysticism and Indo-Tibetan demolatry overlaid by a then varnish of Mahayana Buddhism.

La-ma means the "Superior one". It is a term which should be reserved for the heads of monasteries and the highest dignitaries but by courtesy is given to all of the fully ordained rank.

Before the seventh century the sole religion of Tibat was the Bon. The dominating figure as the Shaman, a sorcerer working on psychic levels to produce the right weather and the other needs of an agricultural population. This religion is a form of nature worship with sacrifice to vaguely defined gods of the earth and sky existed. These Bonpas are of two kinds using "Red-hats" as distinct from the "Yellow-hats" of the later Reformation and having degenerated into Bon Practices.

In the middle of the seventh century that Buddhism became a force in Tibet. King Srongtsen Gampo married two chief wives a princess from China and another from Nepal. Both were Buddhists and between them they converted the King to Buddhism. The king at once begin to preach and to build temples. Bon reaction was immediate, but the new religion has come to stay and Srongtsen Gampo is revered as the founder of Tibetan Buddhism.

By the Sixteenth Century, the various schools of Tibetan

Buddhism were reasonably well defined. The established Church, as it near is the Gelungpa or Yellow Hat Sect. Next comes the Kargyut-pat sect founded in the Eleventh century by Marpa. This maybe called the semi-reformed sect and its members supply a large number of the "entombed one" monks who shut themselves in caves on the hills for a time or sometimes for life-leaving but a hole through which their disciples bring them the minimum of food and water.

Another is Nyingmapa or Red Hat Order, the unreformed Buddhism of Padma Sambhava. Being now on the defensive against the Reformed Schools its members justify places hidden revelations which they claim to be the esoteric teachings of Sambhava. These discoveries are mostly concerned worth of the sect and add little to the religious worth of the sect. Beyond, these schools reformed, partly reformed and unreformed be the Bon-pa who though affected by Buddhism are the primitive nature worshippers of pre-Buddhist days.

The Nyingma-Pa Gompas in Nepal is Bodnath. In Bodnath, the Gonpa belongs to the non-reformed order of the "Nying-ma-pa" or "Red Hat Sect" which was first introduced in Tibet in the middle of the 8th century A.D. by Padma Sambhava, also called Guru Rimpuche. This Gonpa is headed by the chief abbot.

The Gelug-Pa Gonpa on the other hand belongs to the reformed order of the "Gelugpa" commonly called the "Yellow Hat Sect" founded around 1407 A.D. by the mystic Tsong-Kapa whose statue stands in the centre of the wall opposite the entrance. This order is headed by the Dalai Lama who, in other Lamaist Buddhists as their spiritual leader.

There are also the Sakya-Pa-Gonpa belongs to the "Sakya-Pa" order founded in 1071 by one of the Tibetan disciples of the Indian mystic Nagarjuna (2nd Century A.D.).

The Karma-Pa Gonpa—this is recently built Gonpa, it belongs to the "Karma-Pa" or Kar-gyud-pa community to which belonged both the famous Tibetan mystic Marpa and his disciple Milarepa (1038-1122).

These alone details in the Tibetan Buddhism are given

to be familiar with the streams of Buddhism as also noticed in Nepal by the influence of neighbourhood. Having lime-lighting Tibetan Buddhism in short, it is now almost important to know Tantricism and Eroticism. A visitor to Nepal is likely to encounter in old Hindu and Buddhist paintings and carvings seen on temple struts an art form that is referred "Erotic Art" in the outside world but which actually is the ancient art of Tantricism. Tantric Art, as it is known is a visualisation of the eternal cycle of creation, dissolution and preservation of the human race.

The harmonious balance between opposites evolved into a system of worshipping male and female force as manifested in the form of male and female sexual organs. This particular system of worship further crystallized in the form of Shiva-Lingum in perfect union with Shakti-Yonis, giving rise to the Shiva Shakti cult. In the Shakti sect, female sexual energy is worshipped as the Goddess Durga or Kali and Shiva is considered to be the guardian and protector. One finds a Shiva temple, close by will be a symbol or temple of Shakti. Shiva's power can not be fulfilled without the aid of Shakti.

Tantricism is a synthesis of spiritual and material potential. Tantra does not advocate withdrawal or renunciation from life but it is the fullest acceptance of one's family life.

Tantrism is practised both by Hindus and Buddhists in Nepal. Tantra is so much important in the religious beliefs that Nepal has preserved rich materials for the study of Tantrism.

Tantrism welcomes all devotees irrespective of caste, creed, sex or wealth. Bhairava, who is regarded as manifestation of Shiva, the Hindu God is equally worshipped by Hindus and and Buddhists in Nepal.

In the second half of the first millennium, Nepal attached with the influence of a strange religious movement that incorporatted ideas of unique spiritual power, magic fforces, necromancy and a great variety of symbols. Tantrism is named after the holy scripture related with particular Gods or Goddesses. Tantra means "Warps". The first period coming to the last phase of the 12th century A.D. was noticed by a remarkable religious activity of the Tantric type, a left handed cult with its focus and santity of sexual principles in worship. The unfying force in this fitness diversity is Tantrism. It unites Sakti, Shiva and Bhaisnava and popular as Bajrayana in Buddhist termonology and its influence is extended all the religious practices concerning to various sects. Bajra signifies immortality which is indiscriminable, indivisable, inseperable and incorporeal. The importance of Sakti sect rapidly increased with the development of Buddhism and Tanricism in Nepal.

Tantricism is a mixture of Hinduism, especially of Shiva worship and Buddhism, bringing about a union between the two religions. This syncretism is to be found even to-day in Nepal Buddhists, Visit Hindu temples and Vice-versa.

Tantra is not a black magic. The word can be defined as a "scripture by which knowledge is disseminated" in order to give all individuals the opportunity to attain the highest aim of life even by living a worldly life. In Nepal Shiva Buddhist Tantras have been mixed up giving birth to a new type of esoteric worship, thereby influencing the socio-religious life of the Nepali people.

Tantricism maintains that it is possible to make use of the powers of these terrible gods if one is initiated into certain magic practices. The expert is then able to conjure up deities at will and to invoke himself to their powers.

Characteristic features of Tantricism are mystic syllables (Bija), magic spell (Mantra), significant gestures, ponderings on the oneness of everything, meditation on the profound connections between microcosm and macrocism. The contemplation of images and the absorption into them is great importance. Strong emphasis is given on the female element and on sensuality.

In Buddhist and Hindu both in Tantricism to be a central Sadhaka must exercise of sexual contact under tantric "laboratory" conditions. The Hindu Tantric tradition makes some distinction between the Sadhana that is performed on a purely mental plane and that which involves actual handling of the ritualistic "ingredients" including women, meat and wine. Hindu usually refer to the latter as the left-handed to the former as the right-handed.

Buddhist Vajrayana refers ecstasy is reached when the Sadhaka immobilizes mind, breadth and the seminal fluid. The Buddhist variety of Tantricism is generally given the name "Vajrayana"—"Diamond Vehicle" after the Vajra (magic dagger) or "Thunderbolt". The word vajra is also used for the emptiness or nothingness which is Vajrayana regards as the absolute. In the sense, Vajrayana can become a way to salvation by means of the sacred enjoyment of love. As love-making thus receives an indirect sanctification and becomes an expression of salvation. Like the Hindu Gods, Buddhas and Bodhisatvas are allowed female complements which act as their Saktis or female powers.

In practice, the most remarkable features of Tantrism are the importance given to symbolism, occultism, magic, image-worshipping, yoga etc. supporting a "rules of action" in opposition perhaps to rules of thought since Trantric doctrine refers that "outside action, these can be no salvation". This action principally takes the shape of extremely complex and esoteric rites which progressively developed in what is now called Lamaism where greater importance is assigned to certain designs such as "mandalas" "Yantras" considered as symbolic representatives of the universe and used at the same time as instruments of concentration and meditation.

Magic formulas called "mantras" and tools such as prayer-wheels, player-flags, incense-burner, sounds produced by strange musical instruments, bells etc. ritual gestures such as Mudras which are, prescribed movements of the hands used to address to the many benevolent deities or malevolent demons for asking with them their magic power.

So, there are also Tantric strains both in Hinduism and Buddhism. One of the objectives of Tantrism which usually refers Sakti the female principle can allow the consumption of meat and liquor and the performance of esoteric sexual rites as well as sacrifices is to go about all of these in a compassionate manner but with detachment. In such a way both religions Hinduism and Buddhism use the same temples and worship the same deities and as tantrism developed , the Buddhist commonly adopted many Hindu ideas and gods.

Royal Kumari, the living Goddess meaning a vestal virgin and stands to signify "mother Goddess". In the Hindu Pantheon, traditionally is identified with either Goddess Taleju or Goddess Durga.

The Kumari, Kathmandu's living Goddess, her origins are hazed in legends. The Taleju Bhawani, Goddess has been considered an advisor and protector of the Nepali Nation since early times and she is referred to instigate the Kumari cult as reincarnation. Taleju was thought to have been brought to Nepal in 1323 A.D. by Hari Singh Deva, but it was not until 200 years that a temple was constructed to her.

Many stories of how the Kumari gained importance exit. One of the most popular versions runs that once upon a time, the goddess and the king were playing dice (Tripasa) still very popular in Nepal. It so happened that one day the king while playing with the goddess won the game. He became so excited that by mistake he hit the lap of the goddess. She immediately became very angry due to loosing the game and also had been greatly insulted by the king she would never appear before him again. Overcome, the king apologized profusely pleading for consideration. Thus the goddess agreed not to present herself in person as before, pleading for consideration. Thus the goddess, admitting his mistake agreed not to present herself in person as before and arranged to reincarnate herself in the form of a Sakya girl. So, the Kumari is choose from the Sakya family as through history up to the present.

The school of Shaktism, a branch of Tantricism takes the Kumari as the Shakti or consort of Kumara. Actually, for all Hindus of the valley, the Kumari is a representation of the goddess Durga. One of the most important festivals in Kathmandu the Indra Jatra festival is that devoted to the living Goddess which occurs is September. Living Goddess proceeds in a grand chariot and her chariot is followed by two others in which ride two small boys representing Ganesh a Kumar sons of Shiva.

Similarly, Machendranath (Red) is situated at Tabehal in Patan. The Pagoda of this temple was built in 1408 A.D. The three elegant storeys stands in spacious space. The God is considered to bring rain before the monsoon. The silver doorway of the temple is elegant and attractive. The God Machendranath is also known as Avalokiteshwor and Adinath Lokeshwor. In this courtyard Machhendranath is kept for half a year and the rest of the year. But this God visits his shrine at Bungamati. He is brought out during the month of May-June in an elaborate chariot. The celebration lasts for several days and finally a grand ceremony "Bhoto Jatra" is observed. Both the Hindus and Buddhists pay homage to God Machendranath equally."

There are two Machendra Gods–the Rato (red) Machhendra of Patan described above and the Seto (white) Machendra of Kathmandu. Some people believe that the twin Gods are actually one deity while others are of opinion that the two Machendra are sisters with both male and female attributes. The Buddhist scriptures, however describe them in the male forms.

The Hindus worship Rato Machendranath as Karunamaya—the God of mercy, whereas the Buddhists consider him with the fourth of the five Buddhas, Padmapani. Padmapani is generally called Arya Lokeshwor, Padmapani Bhodisattva or Lokeshwor for his powers of protecting and teaching the god themselves, including Lord Shiva.

There are many shrines in Nepal, many of them worshipped by Hindus and Buddhists alike with the result that there is an astonishing complexity of beliefs and public celebrations.

Mr. John Sanday, Expert of the United Nations Educational, Scientific and Cultural Organization (UNESCO) has rightly described about religion on Nepal as "The two main forms of Buddhism are that of Hinayana which was the earliest form and Mahayana Buddhism which developed from the former at about the beginning of the Christian era and was based more on the example of Buddha than on his specific statements. However, the form of Buddhism most practiced in the Kathmandu valley is that of Vajrayana, an off short of Mahayana and it is here the philosophical thought of the two religions of Hinduism and Buddhism is very similar. Vajrayana contrasts with Mahayana in its emphasis on tantric religious symbolism, but the two types do not differ their basic beliefs."

To conclude, as ancient as it is, the temples of Nepal display a religious tolerance which is remarkable contrasts to the communities of many parts of the world.

3 Nepal : The Land of the Temples and Shrines

Nepal is really a cultural museum where art treasures of time immemorial and monuments of historical and religious achievement are acquainted with warm sensibility. The arts and crafts of Nepal inspired by Hindu and Buddhist religions are of an astonishing richness especially in the valley of Kathmandu.

Kathmandu, the capital city of Nepal with Patan and Bhadgaon, the second and third cities in prominence fill up a rare ensemble of an architecture of great originality and quality. Various shrines, both pagodas and stupas and innumerable interesting monuments with carved doors, balconies and windows are within easy reach in the oval valley of Kathmandu which sprawls over about 580 square kilometers. Some of these places such as Hanuman Dhoka the ancient Palace Square in Kathmandu, Durbar Squares in Patan and Bhadgaon, the Buddhist Stupas of Boudhanath and Swayambhunath are well known and other places of interests like Chabahil, Sankhu, Changunarayan, Panauti, Pharping and Kirtipur deserve attention. While commenting on the valuable archaeological and religious collections of Nepali culture, Lieutenant Colonel Sir Clutha Mackenzle has actualised in his book, "Road to Kathmandu" in the following ways :

"Tiered pagoda roofs lifted themselves against the evening sky above them hung a faint silver line of the high snows. Brass dragons, multi-armed gods, fierce fanged tigers of the under world and from doors to linterils hundreds of ever watchful eyes of Buddha looked down upon us."

He rightly placed his observation on the pairs of eyes which actually catch a sight every where in the Kathmandu valley and in the hills, main entrance doors on many houses on cities and in the wayside, in villages and at the tops of mountain passes. They appear to observe passerby's as they go along and keep a contemplation on what you are doing and how you are carrying on with righteousness.

Nepal's temples and shrines form unique attractions. More so, Kathmandu valley is the land of temples and shrines. Kathmandu valley is set in the amidst of green mountains with snow capped peaks jutting out against the azure sky on the northern and eastern rims. The beautiful panorama of golden pagodas, brown temples, white edifices and red hamlets seen in romantic hills and dales is the most attractive feat of Kathmandu. Its shape resembles the sword of Goddess Devi. It is said to have been founded by Raja Gunkama Deva in 723 A.D. Here and in the two neighbouring cities, Patan and Bhadgaon, one finds magnificent modern palaces standing cheek and jowl with ancient picturesque temples and pagodas a contrast the like of which is rarely seen anywhere else in the world.

The Kathmandu valley is said to have been originally a lake named as Nagahrada and the dawn of the history of Napal begins with Manjushree's contribution. Manjushree, the supreme deity made the Kathmandu valley habitable. So the God Manjushree is being worshipped by the Buddhists as Maha Manjushree Bodhisatva, and the Hindus regard as Saraswati, the Goddess of Knowledge and Learnings. Saraswati is one of the consorts of Lord Vishnu, another being Laxmi, the Goddess of wealth and Prosperity. God Manjushree cut the gorge at Chobhar to drain water of the lake Nagharada and then Kathmandu valley became a place for settlement. The divine benevolences are the causes that make Manjushree being worshipped by both Buddhists and Hindus.

Within Kathmandu valley a small area, practically all the

principal temples and shrines of Nepal are situated. The temples and stupas are the chief glories of the country. In their walls are to be found some of the wonderful handy-works of by-gone ages with sermons in stone-carved by pious monarchs whose chief ambition seems to have been to leave behind them undying testimony to their burning devotion to arts.

The early history of Nepal is shrouded in mythological accounts. The chronicle mention the rule of the Gopalas, the Ahnrs and the Kiratees in early days. The authentic history of Nepal begins with the Changu Narayan Pillar Inscription of Lichhavis King Mana Dev I of the 5th century. The Lichhavis ruled over Nepal from 4th century to 12th century. Nepal achieved a high degree of progress in art and architecture, trade and commerce and religious beliefs and foreign relations.

The Lichhavis are considered to have migrated into Nepal from north India in near about 250 A.D. The undisputed and prominent of historical importance was Manadeva I of Nepal.

The most famous Lichhavi King was Amshuverma who ruled in Nepal and opened trade relations with Tibet. He gave his one of the daughter Bhrikuti in marriage to Tibetan ruler Tsrong-tsong Gompo. Amshuverma's daughter Bhrikuti was a devout Buddhist and who was instrumental in spreading the Buddhism in Tibet and China. From the account of the Chinese traveller Huen Tsang who had travelled India in the 7th century and to Nepal. He described Anshuverma as a wise and a King of various talents.

Narendradeva, another Lichhavi King initiated friendly relations with China and his successors laid the foundations of friendship with India by entering into matrimonial alliance with the Indian royal families. Accounts of a Chinese envoy testified to the economic prosperity and development of Nepal during Narendeva's rule. The palace of Narendra Deva described in detail by the Chinese envoy provides proof of the fact that pagoda style of architecture was evolved and developed in Nepal. It spread from Nepal to many eastern countries in subsequent centuries. The Lichhavis rule spanned a period of abut 630 years from 4th Century to 12th Century.

The famous palace named as Kailaskuta was the seat of Lichhavi rulers. There was another place named as Managriha and both these places were superb in architectural designs and full of arts and architectures. Amshuverma built the famous palace Kailasakuta which he was very proud. His family after him ruled from it. Managriha was built by Manadeva. The last ruler of this dynasty was Jaya Kamadeva.

After the Lichhavis rule came the Malla period which lasted from the 12th Century to 18th Century. The Malla Dynasty took over the leadership of the valley and became the Kings of Kathmandu as well as of the other surrounding towns and villages. The early Malla rule started with the Ari Malla in the 12th century. After ruling for two centuries in most organised and well managed ways the Malla rule and regime grew into a big state. Soon after towards the end of the fifteenth century, the United Kingdom of Nepal was divided into three Kingdoms by the sons of Yakshya Malla and with this the period of the medieval history of Nepal set in. This incident was more or less related with the establishment of the Chaubesi (i.e. twenty-four principalities) and with the Baisi (i.e. the twenty-two principalities) in different parts of Nepal disintegrating into small pockets of Kingdoms.

In spite of inter-state quarrels and mutual zealousness, the kings of these small principalities vied with each other to adorn their capitals with artistic and beautiful palaces, temples, shrines and other edifices which are considered to be the pride of Nepal at the present time. Besides, the Kings of these states were great patrons and lovers of arts and architectures. They also constructed a large number of temples, small and large in their capitals and organised the performance of various religious ceremonies and sacrifices.

Jayasthiti Malla was reigned the later Malla period in the Kathmandu Valley around 14th century with the various social and economic reforms. Then Yakshya Malla, the grandson of the King Jayasthiti Malla ruled to the end of the 15th Century in the Kathmandu Valley. After his death, the valley was divided into three independent valley kingdoms—Kathmandu, Bhaktapur and Patan—in about 1484 A.D. which were constantly involved in disputes and wars. Mutually debilitating wars gradually weakened them. But Pratap Malla (1640-1763) and more so Bhupatindra Mall (1696-1722) were among those King's of Kathmandu and Bhaktapur who not only extended considerably the territory and the political importance of these respective Kingdoms but also embellished its main cities and towns with innumerable temples, pagodas, stupas, palaces, fountains and public bathing places. They also promoted the development of handicraft in wood, stone and ivory carvings, etc.

The Malla rulers were weakened by their mutual quarrels and wars. King Prithvi Narayan Shah of the small principality of Gorkha of western Nepal made invasion of the Kathmandu Valley and the Malla rulers did not able to resist him. Ultimately he succeed in 1724 and united all the small and divergent warring principalities into a United Nepal. It took him almost 25 years of almost uninterrupted wars and political diplomacy. Then the Shah Dynasty ruled Nepal.

The Rana oligarchy (1846-1951)—the advent of the "Rana" regime which lasted until 1950. One hundred four years during which the king of Nepal, although still on the throne relegated to a purely nominal and depressed of all authority and power by the Ranas. Jung Bahadur Rana happened to emerge as the most powerful leader after a great Kot massacre of noblemen. He became the Prime Minister and appointed his brother and kinsmen to key posts. Thus Rana wielded all political power and imposed family autocratic rule in Nepal which lasted from 1846-1951 after the rise of Jung Bahadur Rana.

The autocratic Rana regime came to an end in 1951 following a popular uprising led by King Tribhuvan. On February 15th 1951, King Tribhuvan Bir Bikram Shah Dev took the reins of government, laid the foundation of democratic rule. His Majesty King Birendra Bir Bikram Shah Dev was the tenth of the line of Shah dynasty. The sad and untimely demise of his Majesty King Birendra Bir Bikram Shah Dev, new monarch His Majesty King Gyanendra Bir Bikram Shah Dev ascended the thron on June 4, 2001 and he is now ruling the country in keeping with the democratic traditions of the Shah Kings to providing the rule of the country as per the will of the people. The Ranas interested in the Arabian style of architecture and neoclassical styles prevalent in Great Britain of their time and many palaces were constructed copying these two styles. But they also constructed temples and shrines on traditional architectural styles. The rich tradition of traditional style of architecture survived the early Shah period but noticed to fade away during the Rana era.

Nepal is famous as the favourite places and shrines of Gods. Every city, town and even village are all full of temples, shrines and other religious edifices which tell a story of legend and every structure has some historical and an archaeological value.

As already referred that there are three cities in the Kathmandu valley, Kathmandu, Patan and Bhaktapur. It was very rightly observed by Mr. Kirkpatrick as "The valley (valley of Kathmandu) consists of as many temples as there are houses and of as many idols as there are men." So now it is better to start with the temples and shrines of Kathmandu. The ancient name of Kathmandu is Kantipur (the city of glory). It was established by the King Guna Kama Deva in 732 A.D. To be percise, it is better to describe the temples and start from Hanuman Dhoka (Durbar Square). The significance of Hanuman Dhoka refers an image of Hanuman, the monkey god, stationed at the main entrance of the place. This Durbar Square is full of old temples and religious palaces so it epitomizes the religions and cultural life of the people. This Durbar Square contains the Temple of Taleju built by King Mahendra Malla. Taleju temple houses Goddess Bhavani or Kali Durga or Shakti. It has been the private chapel of the Kings of Nepal for more than five hundred years. It is three storied Pagoda temple richly decorated. There is Kumari temple, home of the "Kumari" or living goddess, which is also a three-storeyed decorated with woodcarved balcony. It was built in 1757 by King Jaya

Prakash Malla. Another is Trailokya Mohan temple built in 1680 by Parthibendra Malla. This temple is dedicated to Lord Vishnu. The struts of this temple are carved with various images. Kastha Mandap was built from the wood of the single tree during the King Laxmi Narsingh regime. Kathmandu has derived its name from Kastha Mandap. The central image in this Mandap is of Gorakhnath. There are images of Ganesh, the elephant-headed god at each of the four corners. After Kastha Mandap, Bhagavati Temple the Nuwakot Bhagavati temple established by the King Prithvi Narayan Shah in a place of Mahipatidreshwar shrine with a empty spot and Nuwakot Bhagavati image was placed in the empty place brought by the King from Gorkha. Then, there is the image of Kal Bhairab or manifestation of God Shiva in his destructive mood. This is image of large single stone. It was set by the King Pratap Malla.

Ashok Vinayak is known as Maru Ganesh or even Kathmandu Ganesh and are popular for worshipping while starting a new enterprise and for its success. Similarly, the temple of Panchmukhi Hanuman inside the old palace, the Krishna Mandir, opposite the entrance to the Hanumandhoka palace, an enormous gilded face of Sweta Bhairav on the right hand corner outside the palace hidden under a big wooden lattice screen, etc. are many others. In such a way, the rule of the Malla dynasty (1200-1750 A.D.) was the period of the great architectural achievements in Nepal. The Malla Kings were great lovers of art and architecture. Countless buildings, temples, and shrines were constructed by the Malla kings and their artistic traditions continue to be one of the richest treasures of the cultural heritage in Nepal today.

With the death of Jayasthiti Malla (1382-1422) his grandsons divided the three kingdoms of Kantipur, Lalitpur and Bhaktapur which is now popular by their names as the cities of Kathmandu, Patan and Bhadgaon. So the Durbar Square complex of Tri-cities of Kathmandu, Patan and Bhadgaon are of intermixture of colour, of traditional architecture of pagoda roofs tier upon tier of great stone staircase surrounding paved courtyards between them.

Among the number of temples of this period can be divided into three broad types—Pagoda, Stupa and Sikhara. The pagoda is by for the most remarkable and greater in number and consists from one to five storeys in height made out of brick and wood, lavishly decorated with carvings, paintings and gilding. Nyatapola temple, constructed by the King Bhupatindra Malla in 1701 and 1702 in Bhadgaon is the biggest and most graceful example. Teleju temple built in 1564 by the King Mahendra Malla in Kathmandu is another example of pagoda style with the carved door frames, the metal torana, the row of figured struts, the gilt cooper roof with its decorative small bells and sparkling gajures. There are many pagoda style temples which are constructed by different Malla Kings in Kathmandu, Patan and Bhadgaon within the Durbar Complex and outside of it. Such temples in the Kathmandu Durbar Square are described above already and now the temples and shrines constructed around Durbar Square, Patan are described below.

The Malla Kings of Patan, specially during the reign of Sidhi Narasingh Malla and Sriniwasa Malla who reigned between 1620 and 1660 and between 1660 and 1684, the Durbar Square of Patan took its present form. The masterpieces of Patan is Hiranya Varna Mahavihar, the three-storeyed golden pagoda of Lokeshwar (Lord Buddha) was built by King Bhaskar Varma in the twelfth century A.D. Then comes Kumbheswar, five-storeyed pagoda style temple of Lord Shiva. This temple was constructed by King Jayasthiti Malla. The temple of Bagalamukhi to the right of Kumbheswar temple, is a tantric goddess who bestows blessings to anyone who pleases her by tantrically worshipping. Now, there is very famous terracota temple of Mahaboudha. Every brick of this temple contains an image of Lord Buddha, master pieces of the fourteenth century. This temple was built by Abhaya Rai, a priest of Patan. Another oldest Buddhist monasteries Rudra Varna Mahavihar and near it there is a temple of fine image of Lord Buddha. The world known temple of Krishna is famous for beauty of the Nepali temple craft. The three-storeyed stone temple has carved in bas-relief of the most of the important scenes from the Mahabharat and Ramayan. Equally famous another Jagat Narayan temple constructed in a tall Shikhara-style temple venerated to Lord Vishnu. The temple is in red brick and is situated on the bank of the Bagmati at Sankhamul and contains many stone images.

Ashokan stupas stand at four different corners of Patan giving this city as a city of monastic character. These Stupas are considered to be erected by Ashoka, the Buddhist Emperor of India.

Another temple of Machendra Nath, the Pagoda built in 1408 is situated in Tabahal. This temple belongs to Red Machendra Nath and is kept for half a year here and the rest of the year. He visits his shrine at Bungamati. The grand chariot festival of Machendra Nath is held during the month of May-June. The festival lasts for several days and finishes with a big ceremony of 'Bhoto Jatra'.

The Stupa is consecrated mainly to the Buddhist deities. Generally, the Stupa is an artificial dome-shaped memorial shrine. Stupa is an architectural structure in brick and stucco of different sizes, the biggest and most illustrious examples being those of Boudhanath and Swayambhunath in Kathmandu which are world famous for their magnificent architecture. The city of Patan abounds in many Buddhist monuments and shrines. All Malla Kings believed in religious tolerance and there was a blending of Hinduism and Buddhism and all deities were worshipped by both Hindu and Buddhist alike. The Malla kings constructed many Vihars and Buddhist shrines in their kingdom.

Among the innumberable temples and religious shrines, Bhaktapur (Bhadgaon) has the replica of Lord Pashupatinath of Kathmandu to the south east of the Durbar Square. Temple of Batsaladevi stands at the square with intricate carvings.

Nyatapola temple was built by King Bhupatindra Malla in 1702 A.D. This temple is of five storey pagoda standing on the five terraced base, on each of which sit a pair of figures-two famous wrestlers, two elephants two lions, two griffins and Baghini and Singhini the tiger and the lion goddesses. Each pair of figures is considered ten times stronger than the ones just below. This is one of the tallest pagoda-style temples in Kathmandu Valley and is famous for its size and supreme workmanship.

Sharing the same courtyard in common with Nyatapola, Bhairab Nāth temple, the three-storeyed temple is situated and resembles superb pagoda.

About four furlongs from the gate way of Durbar Square, the temple of Duttratraya is situated. It was consecrated by King Yakshya Malla in 1427 A.D. It is believed that this temple is constructed out of the trunk of a single tree. Just beside this temple is a monastery (Pujari math) with exquisitely carved peacock windows.

Bhaktapur is known as 'the city of devotees". It is a city of art, architecture, and temples and shrines.

Out of the Durbar Square complexes of Kathmandu, Patan and Bhadgaon, there are many temples and shrines dedicated to various gods and goddesses scattered all over the country. These are specified below :

Pashupati Nath is the temple of Lord Shiva and is situated five kilometers north-east of Kathmandu city on the bank of sacred Bagmati river. It has two tiered golden roof and silver doors and is famous for the superb arts. This is the holiest of all the shrines of Shiva in Nepal, the guardian deity of Nepal one of the holiest of Hindu shrines in the world. Lord Pashupatinath is visited by many of devotees each year from all parts of the world and every part of the country on the occasion of Shiva Ratri. The whole place is a complex of other temples and shrines. There is a crematorium outside the temple.

Guheshwori Temple is located near the Pashupati temple. This is the holy temple of Goddess Sati Devi (Parvati), Lord Shiva's consort : It is also situated in the bank of Bagmati river. There is no image in the temple. The whole architecture of the temple is in tantric Yantra signifying the female principle of procreation.

Swayambhunath : This is one of the most glorious Buddhist Stupas. It is said to be 2000 years old. The Stupa which form the main structure is made of a solid hemisphere of brick and clay supporting a lofty conical spire capped by a pinnacle of copper gilt. Painted on the four sides of the spire bases are the all seeing eyes of Lord Buddha. The Stupa is situated three kilometers west of Kathmandu city. This is located in a hillock full of many small Chaityas and pagoda temples.

Boudhanath is also a famous Buddhist Stupa. This colossal Stupa, one of the biggest in the world, is located eight kilometers east of the capital. It was believed to have been built by Lichhavi King Mana Deva in the fifth century A.D. It is built on an octagonal base inset with prayer wheels. This Stupa is inset on four sides with the all seeing eyes of Lord Buddha. There are various smaller shrines and monasteries around the Stupa.

Chabahil : While going to Boudhanath on the road is Stupa named Chabahil and it is considered to be oldest Stupa built in the 3rd century BC by Charumati, the daughter of the Indian Emperor Ashoka, after she married and settled in the valley.

Gokarna : On the northern side of it, this is a pagoda-style temple of Gokarneshwar Mahadeva.

Temple of Bagh Bhairab : This temple is located in ancient spot known as Kirtipur, eight kilometers south-west of Kathmandu city on the top of a hill, the ancient temple of Bagh Bhairab (tiger God) and other temples and shrines are scattered all over this ancient township.

Shakhu : This place is about twelve kilometers east of Kathmandu. There is Bajra Jogini, very old historic temple is situated.

Chovar : This place is famous for the small temple dedicated to Adinath at the top of the hill. This place is located eight kilometers south-west of Kathmandu. Pharping and Dakshinkali—The temple of Dakshinkali is located at about 18 kilometers south-west of Kathmandu city. This is also a place of pilgrimage for Hindus and many pilgrims visit this temple to pay homage to Goddess Kali.

Bajrabasahi : The temple of Bajrabasahi is in a small green park land about ten kilometers south of Patan city.

Suryavinayak : This is the shrine of Ganesh and is situated in a thick forest. Namabuddha (Dhulikhel) This is situated east of Bhaktapur, about six kilometers from Dhulikhel. It takes 4 hours from Panauti to arrive at the top of Namabuddha hill. There is a stone-slate with illustrates the legend of this place. This place is famous where Prince Mahasatwa attained "Nirvana" and became one of the Bodhisattvas after he gave his own life by feeding his flesh to save a starving tigress and her cubs. There is Stupa known as Dharma Dhatu Chautya.

Changu Narain : This temple of Changu Narain is said to have been built by King Hari Dutta Varma in 323 A.D. There is also a shrine dedicated to goddess of Chinnamasta. This is said to be the oldest pagoda temple in the valley and is situated about 125 meters above the valley. Changu Narain is an ancient temple of Lord Vishnu and has some of the superb stone structures of the ancient time. It is 15 kilometers east of capital city and situated on a hillock. Changu Narain Temple is two-storied pagoda and provides enchanting medium of the glory and grandeur of the Nepali artistic tradition. There are two stone pillars on the left and right sides of the golden entrance of the shrine with Chakra (Quoit) and Shankha (conch-shell), the two emblems of Lord Vishnu.

Besides these sacred temples and shrines, there are many places of religious pilgrimages such as Lumbini Janakpur, Jageshwar, Narayanghat, Devighat, etc.

Lumbini : The birth place of Gautama, the Buddha, is the sacred place for the Buddhists and the sacred Buddhist pilgrimage site. It is situated in the fertile plains about 300 kilometers south-west of Kathmandu valley and south of the first foot-hills of Churia ranges.

Buddha was born in Lumbini Garden in 566 B.C. under a sal grove (shorea robusta) on the full moon day.

Lumbini stands up on an equal position with the holy places dedicated to other world religious. Buddha is not only the Light of Asia but of the whole suffering humanity Lord Buddha proclaimed the Doctrine glorious for the gain of the many for the welfare of the many, in compassion for the world.

Ashoka pillar built by emperor Ashok in 249 BC commemorates the spot as the birth-place of Lord Buddha in Lumbini. Nearby stands the ancient temple of Maya Devi consecrated to honour the Queen. The Ashoka Pillar and the ancient shrine with an image representing the activity of the Buddha are still preserved in Lumbini.

Under the umbrella of Lumbini Development Trust with assistance of the United Nations and efforts of Many nations, a great development effort is underway at Lumbini under the Master Plan. **Janakpur:** Janakpur is located in the Terai region of Nepal. This is a beautiful and historic city dating back to ancient times. Legend has it that Sita, heroine of the Hindu epic Ramayana, was born here and later got married with the equally revered and legendary Rama in the same city.

The city's most famous land mark is the large and artistic marble temple of Janaki, built by queen Vrisha Bhanu of the Indian state of Tikamgarh. Close to Janaki temple is another ancient shrine known as Rama Temple. These two temples are the centre of pilgrimage for the Hindus from both Nepal and India. This place can be reached either by plane or road from Kathmandu. There are a number of other popular pilgrimage destinations in different parts of the country while some are beautiful and intricately designed temples, other places are the centre of unusual fairs and festivals or are lonely bathing spots revered by generations of worshippers.

These pilgrimage places are Dolakha Bhimsen in the eastern part of Dolakha township, Kamala Maisthan in Sindhuli district at the confluence of the Kamala and Gwang rivers, Dhanusha-some twenty kilometers northeast of Janakpur, Jaleshwar Mahadev, in Jaleshwar, the headquarters of Janakpur zone, etc.

In the Himalayan foothills and their valleys are many famous pilgrimage spots and shrines related with the legendary past. Just to name the few-the pilgrimages of Muktinath, Gosainkunda, Ridi, Ruru Chhetra, Deoghat, Valmiki Ashram. Similarly, many other, revered and quite spots of gods described by mythologies—such as

Swargadwari in Pyuthan. Pancha Tirtha in Dailekh Halesi Mahadev in Khotang, Baraha Chhetra in Sunsari, the cave of Gorakhnath in Gorkha, etc.

At the confluence of the Kali or Krishna Gandaki River and Ridi khola is situated on ancient pilgrimage of Ridi where a beautiful black stone image of Rishi Keshava is enshrined in the temple. The Vyas Gufa located at the bank of the Madi River—the tributary of Gandaki near Damauli. Vyas, the writer of great epic Mahabharat was born and lived here. Likewise, about 20 km south of the Kusande Village on the Narayanghat-Butwal highway is Valmiki Ashram, the hermitage of epic Ramayana sage Valmiki.

Then Devighat, a reknowned pilgrimage place 160 kilometers south west from Kathmandu is located at the confluence of Narayani and Kali or Krishna Gandaki rivers.

Swargadwari, is situated in the western part of the district of Punthan (Rapti Zone) is the famous place of Hindu Pilgrimage. This place derives its name from a spot where ancient sages used to do penance.

After these pilgrimage spots, there are Gumbas or Monasteries of Solukhumbu which are famous for various monasteries. These monasteries are located at an altitude of 2,900 metres above sea level and during Mani Rimdu fair, is visited by many pilgrims. There are many Buddhist monasteries in the Helambv region about 72 kilometers north-east of Kathmandu. Kankesy Vihar is situated in Surkhet district of western Nepal is one of the very ancient monastic spot with civilisation stretching back to thousand of years, a culture richly endowed by the union of Hinduism and Buddhism. Nepal holds a unique place for ancient Hindu and Buddhist temples and shrines scattered all over the country.

4 Hindu and Buddhist Pilgrimage Sites in Nepal

The people of Nepal and their way of life act as a major attraction to international visitors and represent an important facet to cultural tourism. The warmth and friendliness of the Nepali people towards visitors are part of their high degree of tolerance towards alien cultures and religions developed through a long course of history of close contact with the people of the two big neighbouring countries, India and China. Nepal has sheltered the indigenous cultural pattern of the central part of the Himalayas even existing between the cross currents of two big neighbours, the seat of ancient civilizations, while maintaining an independent existence. The people of Nepal exerted influence in an unusual capacity for continuous development of heterogeneous ethnic and cultural elements which have been a constant source of attractions to international visitors. Peaceful coexistence of the people of Nepal is confessed by a blend of Hinduism and Buddhism which have served to cause a sense of mutual trust and friendliness among them. Religion is the mainstay in the veins of the people of Nepal. It has given them a distinct cultural identity along with the creation of cultural efflorescence of masterpieces of arts and architectures of their own. These national tracts of the Nepali people can be observed by looking at its numerous temples, shrines, stupas and monasteries which still rank the finest architecture of Asia.

Pashupatinath : One of the holiest of Hindu shrines in

the world. Thousands of devotees visit this pious place not only from the all parts of the country but from abroad specially from India. On the occasion of Shiva Ratri festival, pilgrims in their numbers visit to this temple from far and wide. The temple is situated on the banks of the holy river Bagmati five kilometers north-east of Kathmandu and contains the sacred lingam of Pashupatinath.

Swayambhunath : This place of pilgrimage is famous not only for Buddhists but also for Hindus of either religious faiths. This stupa is situated on a hillock and is two thousand years old. Swayambhunath is an old monument, a typical example of the Stupa architecture. It is located on top of a hillock nearly 4 kms west of Kathmandu city amidst a lovely surrounding. The courtyard of the Stupa contains many chaityas, shrines, sacked pillars and so on. There is also a pagoda temple of Harate, the guardian deity of epidemics. The Stupa represents the essential unity of the Buddha and the universe.

Boudhanath : The Boudhanath Stupa is a vertical hemisphere on four-tiered plinth. It is located about 7 km north west of Kathmandu city and is the largest Buddhist Stupa in the world. The hemisphere represents the word of wisdom which contains the relics of Kashyapa Buddha. It is built on an octagonal base and has about eighty small recesses each containing an image of the Buddha. The Chudami is composed of a steep pyramid. The stupa is inset on four sites with the all-seeing eyes of Lord Buddha. The stupa is also ringed with prayer wheels. Around the Stupa are various smaller shrines and the houses of Buddhist priests. This Stupa is the pilgrimage centre for Buddhists.

Budhanilkantha : A famous place of pilgrimage for Hindu and it is situated eight kilometers north of Kathmandu city. This is represented by the statue or colossal idol of Lord Vishnu, one of the Hindu Trinity, lying on back stretched out in a pool of water in the bed of snakes. This is regarded as the 5th century idol in a big stone carved with fine authenticity. It is well-known place of pilgrimage for Hindus at the base of Shivapuri hill. The stone image of

Budhanilkantha is a 18ft long sleeping idol of Lord Vishnu—God of Protection.

Chabahil: On the road to Boudhanath is the beautiful Chabahil that is believed to be even older than Boudhanath. According to the ancient accounts, it was built in the 3rd century B.C. by Charumati, the daughter of the Indian Emperor Ashoka, after she married and settled in the valley. Here an image of Padmapani Lokeswara is kept which is a beautiful and lovely.

But even before the establishment of Chaitya by Charumati in Chabahil, there was Dhando Chaitya dating back to early Lichharan age. It is believed that this stupa was erected by Dharma Deva, father of King Mana Deva. There is image of Padmapani Bodhisatwa is kept in the monastery situated at the south of the Dhando Chaitya. Chabahil is one of the most important Buddhist pilgrimage sites in Nepal.

Changu Narayan : This temple is dedicated to Brahma, Vishnu and Maheshwor and attracts pilgrims in large number during the Mahashivratri festival. Changu is one of the ancient historical places located at an altitude of 153m. above the level of Kathmandu valley. It is regarded to be one of the stately example of the pagoda style in Nepal. This temple is said to have been built by Vishnu Gupta and was later renovated by Hari Datta Varma in 323 A.D. It is considered to be one of the rare artistic legacies of the Lichhavian era.

This temple is two-storied pagoda and its courtyard is full of images of Gods and Goddess carved artistically in stone. On the left and right sides of the golden entrance to the shrine are placed on stone pillars, Chakra (quoit) and Shankha (conch-shell), the two emblems of Lord Vishnu. The temple enshrines the bronze image of Lord Vishnu mounted on Garuda. Changu is about 12 kilometers east of Kathmandu and about eight kilometers north of Bhaktapur city. The temple provides glorious example of pagoda architecture and grandeur of the Nepali artistic tradition. It is situated at the end of long ridge which runs well into the valley. It has some of the primal stone scriptures and carvings.

Namo Buddha : Namo Buddha is another Buddhist

pilgrimage spot and is known as Namura. Located 30 kms south-east of the Kathmandu valley in Kavre Palanchowk district. This is a famous Stupa also known as the Dharma Dhatu Chaitya which is a venerated place to Mahayana Buddhists all over the world. It is believed that the Buddha paid a visit to Namo Buddha and venerated then Prince Mahasatva by bowing his head. This is where prince Mahasatva attained "Nirvana" and Boddhisattvas scarified himself by feeding his flesh to save a starving tigress and her cubs. This is artistically depicted on a stone slabe nearby as part of the people's reverence of Bodhisatvas. The bas-relief which illustrates the legend of this place. This is located above Panauti and south of Banepa. This stupa is visited by many devotees on a yearly pilgrimage that takes place in early spring. This stupa is surrounded by many stupas, the most famous being the four stupas of Dhyani Buddhas.

Dattatraya Temple : The temple of Dattatraya is as old as the Palace of fifty five windows of Bhaktapur. The temple was built out of the trunk of single tree. This temple was consecrated by King Yakshya Malla in 1427 A.D. It was later on repaired and renovated by King Vishwa Malla in 1458 A.D.

Near this temple is monastery (Math) with exquisitely carved peacock window. The monastery is full of various artistic decorations of latticed windows and engraved columns. Dattatraya is the image of Trinity-Brahma, the creator, Vishnu the preserver and Maheswor, the destroyer into one.

Lumbini : Lumbini, the birth place of Lord Buddhia, is one of the holiest and most sacred place on earth. For the teeming Buddhist millions from all over the world, Nepal, the land sanctified by the birth of Gautam, the Buddha, invokes eternal reverence. Lumbini, the birth place of Gautam Buddha and one of the four major poles of Buddhist pilgrimage is in Nepal and it has its gloious place in the world of Buddhist pilgrims. Lumbini is in the south-west plain of Nepal in the Terai, where the Buddha was born to Maya Devi in 623 B.C. It is sacred place for Buddhists all over the world. It stands on an equal footing with the holy places sacred to the world's other great religions. It is attracting many pilgrims annually and will increasingly attract pilgrim travellers from all parts of the world in general and from Buddhist countries in particular.

Lumbini is situated approximately four hundred and thirty one kilometers south-west of the Kathmandu valley and south of the first foothills of the Churia range in the Nepal Terai. The Emperor Ashoka marked the place with the tall pillar indicating the Buddha was born her. Facing the Ashoka pillar is the temple of Maya Devi, the Buddha's mother, perched on a square platform under a sal tree. Inside, queen Maya Devi is seen supporting herself holding a branch of the sal tree with both of her hands with the new-born Sakyamuni Gautam standing upright on a lotus pedestal. Beside the temple is a royal bath of the Sakyamuni dynasty. This is the pond where Maya Devi gave Gautam Buddha the first purification bath. Lumbini was so important that the world community and the United Nations has now undergoing to development it through massive Lumbini Development project. A major development efforts is going at Lumbini. The Lumbini Museum and Library Complex is located at the northern side of the Cultural Centre. The construction of Pilgrims Accommodation centre has been situated at the Lumbini Village. A deluxe four star Japanese Hokke Hotel is in operation now in Lumbini.

Lumbini is served with 23 km high way from Sidharthanagar. Sidharthanagar is accessible both by air and road from Kathmandu.

Many developments are now going on in Lumbini and many projects are also launched for the maintenance and preservation of Lumbini.

Janakpur : Janakpur, the birth-place of Sita, the consort of Rama of the famous Hindu epic Ramayana, is situated in the eastern Terai region of Nepal. It is a historic city dating back to the ancient times. Janakpur is also known as the land of the famed King Janak, who in himself was a remarkable store of knowledge and wisdom and who also was the father of Sita. So Janakpur was the maternal home of Sita who got married with Rama, the virtuous hero of the Ramayan. This is one of the sacred places for Hindu devotees from India and other parts of the world as well. The temple of Janaki, built by queen Vrisha Bhanu of Indian State of Tikangarh, is made of marble and is full of artistic designs and decorations. Near to the Janaki temple is another ancient shrine equally popular as the temple of Rama. These two temples are thronged by millions of pilgrims during Janakpur's two main festivals, one commemorating Sita's birthday and the other her wedding with Rama. The Janaki temple is elaborately decorated cupolas, ceilings and tiles in the Indo-Persian style. This temple is popularly known as Naulakha Mandir which signifies built at the cost of Rs. 900,000. Many festivals, fairs and festivities are occurred here on Bivaha Panchami and Ram Navami days.

Kapilvastu : Kapilvastu, the capital of the Shakya Kingdom where prince Siddhartha Gautam passed his 29 years, is associated with the Buddha and Buddhist faith. Gautam visited this city many times after attaining enlightenment. This city was devastated by the army of King Virudhaka of Koshala during the lifetimes of Lord Buddha. Two Chinese travellers Fu-Hsien and Huan Tsang visited Kapilvastu in 403 A.D. and in 636 A.D., respectively. Now this site of ancient city of Kapilvastu is identified only by archeologists and historians in'their research. This was testified only in the late 19th century. The excavation conducted by the Archaeology Department of His Majesty's Government of Nepal amply proves that the present town of Tilaurakot was indeed the ancient city of Kapilvastu. The entire region of Tilaurakot has many mounds of ancient stupas, monasteries temples and other structures of monuments as well as ruined pieces of ancient artifacts and settlement.

Niglihawa : It is situated four miles north of Tilaurakot and is identified with the ancient town of Solihawati which is considered to be the birth-place of Kanakamuni Buddha. Emperor Ashoka visited Niglihawa in 245 BC and consecrated the stupa of Kanakamuni Buddha. The emperor also erected a stone pillar and set an inscription on it. The stone pillar is still there lying to the west of a big reservoir locally known as Niglisagar. The Stupas, monasteries and other structures have, however to be traced yet.

Besides these above mentioned Buddhist monument and sites, there are other important Buddhist shrines and monasteries established all over the country. These are some famous Buddhist monasteries such as Thyangboche Monastery in the Everest region, Kyanjin Gompa beyond the Langtang village, Buddhist monastery at Braga in Manang and Kankesy Vihar in Surkhet in Western Nepal. All these Buddhist monuments and sites scattered all over the country reflect an alive and thriving Buddhist tradition down the ages in this Himalayan country. Hidden in the Himalayas, the isolated valleys have long sheltered a Sanctuary for the villagers worshipping nature with faith of Bon's Po of Tibet. Padma Sambhava was the great exponent of Buddhism and his pervasive influence is found in those northern regions of— the country. The himalayan valleys of Nepal are full with a number of Gompa-monasteries. Trail-side rock walls are carved with devotional inscriptions-OM MANE PADME HUM.

There are many other important religious places outside the Kathmandu valley. The importance of most of such religious shrines and pilgrimage sites have their religious and historic values rather than architectural or artistic features. But there are few exceptions such as the marble temple of Janaki at Janakpur, Gorakhanath temple at Gorkha and others. They are all in scenic setting with proximity to beautiful natural surroundings. These religious places mentioned below are known for their pilgrimage and numerous people from far and wide visit these places for paying homage.

Muktinath : The holy shrine of Muktinath on the northern fringe of the Annapurna Himal in Mustang is an important holy place for Hindu and Buddhist pilgrims. This is situated on a high mountain ridge in the vast rainshadow of the Great Himalayas. The temple of Jwala Mai (the Goddess of Flames) known as the chief deity and a female incarnation of Lord

Vishnu, is housed in a small pagoda and is equally revered by Hindu and Buddhist alike. The temple is surrounded on three sides by a stone wall which contains hundred and eight bull heads and made of brass. Sacred water pours from the mouths of these bull heads. The temple of the eternal fire is supposed to signify the three vital elements, the earth, fire and water. To a Hindu, Muktinath is a place of pilgrimage to achieve Mukti (liberation) which according to Hindu belief, liberates him from the chain of re-birth. Saligrams (smooth, round black stones) are found in liberal quantity on the banks and the river-bed of the Kali Gandaki river which is proclaimed to be the emblem of Niranjan or Vishnu, one of the Trinity gods. The Saligrams thus are said to possess mystical powers. All pilgrims visiting Muktinath hardly forget to pick up few pieces of such smooth blackstones. Many ascetics and learned *sadhus* can be seen traversing the rugged trail to Muktinath in quest of spiritual bless as the place, being serene, automatically inspires spirituality in every pilgrim. Devotees gather in this spot during the Janai Poornima and Ram Navami to pay homage to Muktinath. Muktinath is located north of Jomsom and Jomsom has air links with Kathmandu, Pokhara and Bhairahawa. It takes 6 days by Trekking from Pokhara to reach this place.

Gosainkunda : Another famous place of pilgrimage is a cluster of lakes of Gosainkunda, situated at an altitude of 4380 metres above sea level. It is located north-west of Helambu and 132 kilometres north-east of Kathmandu. The Langtang Valley is situated north of Gosainkunda. It is approximately 18 kilometers north-east of Jomsom. Gosainkunda is a religious site in northern Nepal where Hindu pilgrims and nature-loving trekkers make a contant flow. The religious-minded visitors feel spiritual solace and are tempted to bathe in the first of a series of lakes in the month of July as they believe that Lord Shiva is supposed to be present there to bless them.

Gosainkunda is related with the ancient mythology. Legend has it that Lord Shiva after drinking the Kalkuta (the deadly poison) churning the ocean became restless. He came to Himalayan region for solace. He threw his trident (Trishul) into the ground and a fountain spring up to make a kunda (pond) to solace his pain and lastly he was emancipated in this spot.

Swargadwari : This pilgrimage place is situated in the western part of the district of Pevthan in Rapti Zone and is one of the most famous places of Hindus. The holy place derives its name from a sage who devoted his life to meditation in the region. The sage, named Padma Giri, started the practice of Akanda Hom (Eternal Fire) on a holy alter nearby. Many pilgrims from different parts of Nepal and India come to pay homage every year on the occasion of Baisakhi Poornima and Kartik Poornima festivals here. When the great Sage Padma Giri Passed away, he was buried at the same spot where he started the system of Akhanda Hom in it. Then marble slabs were then placed over this holy burial ground and a temple was constructed. Since then, this place is famous by the name of the same sage and many pilgrims visit this pious spot.

Gorkha : Gorkha is the place of the same fame and name. It has two famous temples of Gorakhnath and Kali and is the birth-place of the great unifier of modern Nepal, King Prithvi Narayan Shah. Gorkha also is the ancestral home of the Shah dynasty. Nath-sect has played an important role in the religious life of Nepal. The followers of this sect regard Machhendra Nath, Min Nath, Adinath, Gorkha Nath as patron deities with great reverence. The famous pilgrimage spot of Manakamana is very near from here.

Gorkha most famous landmark can be called the old Royal Palace of King Prithvi Narayan Shah which is situated on the top of a hill. In the eastern part of the temple complex is the famous temple of Gorakhnath. Gorkha is accessible by road from Kathmandu or Pokhara.

The temple of Manakamana is located in the district of Gorkha in Gandaki zone. Manakamana is also worshipped by Bajrayani Buddhists. It is believed that all unfulfilled wishes of the devotees are fulfilled by worshipping the goddess Manakamana. The temple of Manakamana is two-storey pagoda temple. Now the operation of cable-cars to Manakamana one of the most famous pilgrimage sites is undergoing and is 3.1 km route linking Cheres between Kurin and Mangling at Darechowk VDC - 3 of Chitwan District and Manakamana.

Baraha Chhetra : Another equally revered place of Hindu pilgrimage is Barah Chhetra. It is on the banks of the Koshi river, a few kilometres from the main city of Biratnagar. This holy place of pilgrimage lies at the confluence of two rivers—the Saptakoshi and Kokaha. There is also a temple of Baraha, the boar incarnation of Lord Vishnu. It is a historical place as this image of Baraha is regarded as the masterpiece of the 12th century stone sculpture.

Ancient Hindu Puranas state that Baraha Chhetra of Nepal is the actual site where the Baraha form of Lord Vishnu originated. It is believed that it was the Baraha incarnation of Lord Vishnu that saved the earth from a catastrophe.

All these important places of religious pilgrimage are of special interest to the people of religions faith and beliefs. Keeping in view the archaeological, historical and religious value of these pilgrimage places and their interdependent relations with pilgrimage tourism. His Majesty's Government of Nepal has laid special emphasis on the preservation and promotion of such religious sites.

5 Pashupatinath : The Guardian Deity of Nepal

"Among the Mountains, I am the Himalaya." Lord Krishna in Bhagvad Gita about the sanctity of Nepal as one of the holiest places on earth. The Himalaya, or the "abode of snow", is referred to as the early home of Lord Shiva and his consort, Parvati. The Himalaya has a particular importance to the follower of Hinduism since time immemorial. The Mythological period covering the Satya, Treta and Dwapar Yugas, or ages, also contains numerous references regarding the temples, shrines and holy places of the country. Many reflections are expressed in the ancient Hindu and Buddhist texts about the holiness of Nepal as the land of spiritual blessing and tranquility.

The book containing the rules of the language defines Nepal as "Ne Munina Palitam Nepalam", the land protected by sage Ne is Nepal. Many sages and seers preferred the serene environ and quiet natural atmosphere of Nepal as the best place for their meditation. To the Hindus, it is the holy land of Lord Pashupatinath. Many philosopher-saints like Viswamitra, Kapila, Yajnavalka, Balmiki and Raja Janak found endless spiritual inspiration while penancing by the sacred banks of the Koshi, Gandaki and Karnali rivers or in the pristine Sagarmatha (Mt. Everest), Dhaulagiri and Annapurna mountains. Their in-depth observations thinking and analysis of concrete phenomena regarding Hindu religiosity still dominate the intellectual arena. All these great thinkers attained perfection in their spiriually here. The hermitage of all of them was in the tranquit recesses of Nepal.

Nepal houses innumerable holy shrines of Hindu and Buddhist deities. Hinus and Buddhist from all parts of the world come tto pay homage at Nepal's many places of pilgrimage. A large number of devotees of both the religions visit the temple of Pashupatinath, Ram Janaki Temple, Janakpur, Gosainkunda, Boudhanath, Swayambhunath and Lumbini to pay homage each year. Similarly, many religious sites in and out of the Kathmandu Valley have served also as great attractions for international tourists. While some are beautiful and intricately—carved temples built by master builders of ancient times, other places are the centre of religious fairs and festivals. Many such religious sites be near a river or stream with the holy water of which the devotees undergo early morning ablutions.

Pashupatinath : Pashupatinath is the holiest of all the shrines devoted to Lord Shiva, the guardian deity of Nepal, or the preserver of the universe. The temple of Pashupatinath is a three-tired pagoda of gold-gilt and brass of which the gateway are plated with silver. It is situated on the western bank of the Bagmati River, about five kilometers north-east of Kathmandu and a sanctuary of the lingam of Pashupatinath. A countless number of pilgrims pay homage to Lord Pashupatinath on the occasion of the annual festival of Shivaratri (February-March) when thousands of Shiva's devotees pour in to the holy site from as far away as India.

Lord Shiva, one of the Hindu trinity is popular by different names. Pashu signifies living beings or individual soul or Jivatma and pati denotes master or Lord. In essence Pashupati means the master of all living beings of the Universe.

The Nepal Mahatmya of the Skanda Purana tells the legend about the origin of Pashupati. According to this legend Lord Shiva was very attracted by the charm of Sheleshmantaka forest situated in the eastern part of Pashupatinath temple which is now popular as Mrigasthali.

It is believed that Lord Shiva visited the Sheleshmantaka

forest with his wife Parvati in the guise of a deer (mirga). Lord Shiva was missed for a long course of time and caused anxiety to Brahma, Vishnu and Indra the three deities of the heaven. Then God Brahma, Vishnu and Indra came to Sheleshmantaka forest and caught with all mights to the deer in disguise of God Shiva by one of his horns which got broken into three pieces. It is believed that these three pieces of horn were established in three places of Nepal and India as directed by the Lord Shiva himself. Another text mentions that one piece of the broken horn of deer buried under the earth. On this buried place a heavenly cow Kamdhenu used to visit daily and give milk. One day the herdsman noticed this act and amazed by seeing this act. He got this spot dug out and found the cosmic Linga of Pashupatinath. The cowherd began to worship after noticing this godly act and people began to worship the Linga as a guardian deity. The temple of Pashupatinath became a famous place of pilgrimage.

The holy temple of Lord Pashupatinath was beautified and decorated by the different Kings of Nepal. Gopalraj Vansavali, the oldest available chronicle in Nepal mentions that the pagoda temple of Pashupatinath was firstly built by Supusapa Varna of Kirat dynasty, the early ruling dynasty of Nepal.

The existing architectural design of Pashupati Temple said to have been came into existence by the benevolent wishes of the Queen Ganga Devi wife of Shivasimha Malla (1578-1620 A.D.).

The Pasupat Chetra (Pashupati area) covers all about 281 hectares. There are near about 235 temples of different sizes and architectural styles. Besides these religious temples and other edifices there are several guest houses, inns and other types of sheltering places.

Along with many architectural temples and buildings, there are many stone inscriptions and idols from the second and third centuries. Presently the temple and its surroundings are included in the world heritage list of UNESCO. The famous doubled-roofed pagoda temple of gold-gilt brass dedicated to God Pashupatinath is superb architecture. This is the holiest of Hindu God Shiva shrines in Nepal. The doors of the temple are placed with silver. It is situated on the western bank of the Bagmati river about five kilometers north-east of Kathmandu.

The principal temple is situated in the middle of an open courtyard. This temple is nearly a square shaped two storeyed pagoda temple. There are four doors to the main temple and each door has a silver polished tympanum. The main pavilion is beautified with silver and gold sheet carved in superb relief patterns. A narrow space around the temple in the inside part of it the Sanctum Sanctorum provides a good sight of the image. Beautiful religious works of arts, especially the doors of the main temple of Pashupatinath are of silver work of very fine quality. Comparatively, the beauty of this temple is singular and there is no other temples as so attractive in the elegance as this. The wooden struts of this temple are very nicely carved and painted with venous images of gods and goddesses. The pinnacle of the temple is very typical consisting beside of it trident, (trisula), drum (damaru) and axe.

The inner Sanctum, a very illustrative image measuring all about I metre high with four faces, one on each of the four sides while the faith is shapeless on the top.

All the faces indicated above have different names and significance. The face towards east is named Tat purush, the face towards the south is called Aghor, the west face is known as Sadyogat, and north looking face is called Vamdeva. The upper most shapeless face is Pashupati.

Each face has shown having two hands and each right hand has a 16-headed rosary of 12 furrowed rudraksha. In each left hand, there is Kalash (Vase) full of ambrosia (amrit). Some consider that one of the four faces of Pashupati is of Buddha. The Linga of Pashupatinath as it is believed since ancient times has a cosmic effect and is famous for alchemy.

The whole place of Pashupati Nath is a mosaic of other temples and shrines dominated by the big gilled figure of Nandi, the mount of Shiva, this is seated on a stone pedestal opposite the main gate, flanked by a golden trident.

Within the courtyard of Pashupatinath are many shrines dedicated to various Hindu gods and goddesses. These are Ram Mandir, Pancha Deval, temple of Biswanath, Gorakhanath, Manakamana etc. There is the 6th century pagoda of Vatsaleshwori on the back of Bagmati having erotic carvings on its struts. There are famous temples of Basuki Nag and Unmatta Bhairava within the courtyard of Pashupatinath.

The temple of Vasuki was built during the Malla period by King Pratap Malla. The silver gate and the Jalahari contains the image of Vasuki.

On the south of Pashupatinath courtyard is situated the round roofed Kotilingeshwar pagoda temple. There are many Shivalingas around the temple. The sanctum of this temple has the unusual idol of Shivalinga. The temple was constructed by Pratap Malla in 1754 A.D. and he was a famous Malla King.

Another temple Panchamukhe/Hanuman. Together with this, the two storey pagoda temple of Vatsaleshwori is located the east of Pashupati on the bank of Bagmati. Vatsaleshwori is also the name of Parvati, the consort of Lord Shiva. This temple has no image but a Yantrakara mandala. Then the famous Dhando Chaitya near Chavahil cross-road is considered to be of great veneration in Buddhist religion. This Chaitya was built by Dharmadeva, the father of Mandeva. This stupa is as big as Swayambhunath Stupa and a pair of big eyes and a nose like mark is painted on the harmika of this stupa. There is also an old monastery in its south side and it has a very ancient image of Padmapani Bodhisatwa (6th century). This stupa is believed to be constructed during the Lichhavi period.

Pashupati area is also famous for the monastery of Chavihar. This monastery is situated north-facing to the west of Dhando Chaitya. The image of Padamapani Lokeshwor, the guardian deity is placed in the southern side of the monastery.

Panchadeval—five devala or temples were built in 1870 A.D. by the ancestors of the present King. Shivalingas is in the sactum of each of five temples. There are nest houses around these temples. The style of these temples is the royal gumbaja construction.

There is Vishnu temple located on the left bank of the Bagmati and to the north-east of Pashupatinath. The image of Lord Vishnu is in the middle and images of padma and sankha on the either side of the main image. This temple is believed to be constructed in the 7th century by Vishnu Gupta.

Another Gorakhanath temple is situated mingled with a group of temples on the way to Guheshwori temple east of Pashupatinath temple. This is medium sized Sikhar style temple and is believed to be one among the oldest temples of Gorakhanath—the guardian deity of the Nath sect.

The legend endorses that this temple was made by Jayasthiti Malla (1382-1395 A.D.) The Paduka (foot-prints) of Gorakhanath is sanctified in the main sanctuary which is venerated and worshipped by the followers of the Nath sect.

East of Pashupatinath stands at a big courtyard in Slesmantak forest the temple of Vishworup constructed in Rajkiya Gumbaja style. This temple is double-storeyed amidst the small temples in its each corner rounded by nest houses. The sanctum of this temple has a Big image of Shiva and Shakti in Yab Yum posture, with twenty feet in height and with many hands. The Buddhists worship it as Heruk. The small temples in each corner of Vishwarup, have deities in couples in standing fashion: Ram and Sita in the north-east, Laxmi and Narayan in the south-east, Shiva and Parvati in the south-west, and Krishna and Rakdha in the north-west.

This imposing temple of Ramchandra is one the largest temples dedicated to Ram. This temple is situated on a hillock in a place known as Battisputali of Kathmandu City. this temple was built by Sanaksimha Tandon in 1871 A.D. This temple contains the life-size images of Ram and Sita (consort) Laksman, Bharat and Satrughana (his three brothers) in standing position.

Another equally famous temple of Bhuvaneshwori is well-known temples situated in Pahsupati area. This temple is double storey pagoda. The image of this temple contains symbolic yantra. This temple is believed to have been built by a famous Lichchhavi King Shiva Deva. But this temple assumed the present look with renovation made by different Kings at different times.

Equally famous among Hindus as the temple of Pashupatinath is Guheshwori temple. It is located Slesmantak forest on the left bank of the river Bagmati. Guheshwori, Lord Shiva's consort is regarded as the source of energy of all living beings.

This temple stands in the middle of a paved courtyard surrounded by rows of rest houses. This temple has the usual arched construction of tubular metal work covering the main building. Towards the top, it tarnsforms itself into four gilded snakes which hold the crowning piece of the roof. The whole structure of the temple is designed after the tantric yantra or geometric triangle signifying the female principle of procreation. This temple was built in 1654 by King Pratap Malla. There are simply four walls enclosing no image but a Kunda (pool). Right in the mouth of the Kunda, there is a silver Kalasha (Jar) which is worshipped as the goddess Guheswori. The conveyance of the goddess is the lion and is seen on a pillar in the courtyard of the temple.

Pashupatinath is the guardian spirit and the holiest of all Shiva shrines in Nepal.

6 *Far-Famed Stupas of Kathmandu Valley*

The Stupa is derived from Sanskrit word Stupa. The stupa or tope or Buddhist dome-shaped memorial shrine. Tope signifies a Buddhist Stupa or dome for relics. Stupa or relic-mounds-consists of a huge hemispherical dome on a circular foundation. The Stupa is symbolised as the garbh or "womb" representing the creation of the world of nature. Stupa is of essentially Buddhist genre. The stupa represents the essential unity of Buddha and the universe. While writing about the Stupa, Mr. John Sandey, UNESCO/UNDP Expert in Kathmandu explains as "The Stupa and Chaitya are dedicated exclusively to Lord Buddha and are solid hemispherical structures enshrining a relic of the Buddha, whether it be his mortal remains as in the case of the stupa at Swayambhu or some of his belongings, such as his garments or personal effects. The smaller Stupas or Chaitya, usually contain prayers, holy scripts or more especially in the hill areas, the mortal remains of an important holy Lama".

The Stupa is purely Buddhist in concept and execution. The Stupa is a hemispherical mound topped by a square base supporting a series of thirteen circular rings, narrowing towards the top. These are crowned by a parasol. The four sides of the squares base or the harmuka, as it is called, one painted with pairs of mystic "all seeing eyes". The Stupa is often containing a relic. The small stupas are often white-washed with lime stone. The Swayambhu and Boudhanath

Stupas are Nepal's first examples of the Stupa or Chaitya style.

The early history of Nepal is moulded in mythological accounts. No doubt there is early historical account on the Bamsavali—hand written manuscript of 16th century A.D. It throws light on the Kathhmandu valley was a big lake. Then the early history of Kathmandu valley starts with the divine blessings of Manjushree who contributed much by making this valley habitable. The valley was a big lake and named as Nagahrada which is full of serpents. Manjushree was fascinated with the serene beauty of the lake on both sides of which was "Phulchowki" and "Champa Devi" hills. Then Manjushree cut a passage with his divine sword clefting a gorge at the place called "Kotwal Daha" now known as Chovar to let the water out and ultimately joined with Bagmati river. Then he spelt some ritual on the root of a lotus plant and threw it into the lake with the prediction that when the lotus bloom, Swayambhu-self-existing God would appear as burning flame signifying the rays of Swayambhu, the self-existing one. So the origin Swayambhu Stupa is shrouded in such a divine mythology.

Commencement of the early account of Nepal is from a memorable Chinese traveller, Hiuen Tsang who travelled China, Tibet and the Himalayas by the Kuti Pass, passing through little-known country Nepal in the year 637 A.D. His recorded account is as follows :

"The Kingdom of Nepal "Ni-po-lo" is in the midst of snowy mountains. Its soil abounds in flowers and fruits and it has a cold climate. The inhabitants of Nepal are all of a hard nature and they are gifted with considerable skill in the arts. Their houses are wooden, painted and sculptured, they are found of bathing, of drama, of astrology and bloody sacrifice. Irrigation makes the soil of great value. Among them are both true believers and heretics. Buddhism and Brahmanism flourish. Buddhist sanctuaries and the temple of Hindu gods touch each other. Commerce is prosperous and trade is well organised and directed."

The above reliable account of early history of Nepal gives light on various details from a visitor. His account also sheds little on religious tolerance in Nepal. Hinduism and Buddhism are the two major religions of Nepal which exist simultaneously in an amicable and harmonious atmosphere. The blending of the two religions into one entity have inspired and created the distinct culture of its own in Nepal. The symbol of these uniqueness of Nepalese traditional culture can be seen in the every day life of people and in the works of art and architectures even today.

Before touching on the main subject, it is better to know the chronicles of the early history of Nepal which mention the rule of the Gopalas, the Abhirs and the Kiratees in early days. The authentic history of Nepal begins with the Changu Narain Pillar inscription of Lichhavi King Mana Dev I of the 5th century A.D.

The Lichhavis ruled over Nepal from 9th century A.D. and the country achieved a high degree of progress in art and architecture, industry and commerce and religious beliefs and foreign relations.

Important Lichhavis monarch Anshuverma who opened trade route to Tibet. One of his daughter Bhrikuti who was married to Tibetan ruler Tsong-Tsrong Gampo was instrumented in spreading Gospel of the Buddha in Tibet and China. Before the seventh century the sole religion of Tibet was the Bon. This religion Bon a form of nature worship with sacrifice to vaguely defined gods of the earth and sky existed. These Bonpas are of two kinds-using "Red-Hats" as distinct from the "Yellow-Hats" of the later reformation, and having degenerated into Bon practices."

In the middle of the seventh century that Buddhism became a force in Tibet King Tsrong-Tsang Gampo married two wives a princess from China and another from Nepal—daughter of Nepali King Anshuverma as mentioned above. Both were Buddhists and between they converted the King to Buddhism. The King at once begin to preach and build temples. Bon reaction was immediate but the religion Buddhism has come to stay and Tsrong Tsang Gampo is revered as the founder of Tibetan Buddhism. By the sixteenth century, the various schools of Tibetan Buddhism defined.

Yellow Hat sect is known as the Gelungpa. Next comes Kargyut-pa sect-semi-reformed sect founded in the Eleventh Century by Marpa. Another is Nyingmapa or Red Hat order, the unreformed Buddhism of Padma Sambhava.

It is evident here to shed light on the earliest history of Nepal and its relation with Tibet simply because of Buddhism was influenced by the Nepali Prince for she took with her a Buddhist relic and spread the faith throughout Tibet with the religion, native art of Nepal also accompanied which is all of religious origin and function. The result of this influence has rightly commented by Mr. Sylvan Levi, oriental scholar, as "They (the Nepalese architects) have changed the arts of India, built temples and palaces which have served as models to the Tibetans and the Chinese, the classical pagoda hails from Nepal."

One of the oldest Stupa of Kathmandu valley is Swayambhunath Stupa. This is a sacred Buddhist Stupa on a top of a hill overlooking a good view of the Kathmandu city and snowy mountains in the horizon. It is three kilometers west of Kathmandu city and is located on a hillock about 77m above the level of the valley. It is aid to be two thousand years old, making it one of the world's oldest and most glorious Buddhist Stupa. The Stupa is composed of a solid hemisphere of brick and earth on the platform. It rests up a large square platform. It is a large hemisphere representing the Garbha which signifies the womb, the seat of Creation. It is surrounded by a gold gilt squares projection which in turn topped by the Chundamani, a conical canopy of gilt rings. There are four niches having golden images of the Dhyani Buddha on a circular base. There is a square toran with a lofty conical spire separated into thirteen layers of gold plate denoting the thirteen blesses of the Buddhist world. On the four of the torans are painted the eyes of Buddha, on the cube. These eyes represent the all seeing eyes of Buddha. The stupa courtyard is full of innumerable subsidiary Chaityas (miniature stupas) shrines and sacred pillars. The hill itself is a mosaic of small chaityas and pagoda temples with intricate figures of god and goddesses which gives great dignity and beauty. Above the entire superstructure is of metal with four toranas and a stages supporting a series of diminishing stages, the whole is capped by a Chhatravali.

Mr. Duncan Forbes in his book entitled "The Heart of Nepal" describes Swayambhunath Stupa in the following ways:

"Swayambhunath which is contracted to Swayambhunath in colloquial language, means "The self-born Lord" and the Stupa's great sanctity for Buddhists of the Mahayana or Great vehicle, is due to the fact that, when the whole valley was a lake, it was on the spot that the lotus bloomed which contained Swayambhu, the self-born in its petals."

"The Stupa itself, more correctly called a Chaitya since it contains no specific Buddhist relic, is a large hemisphere of Masonry about fifty feet high. This is the garbh or "womb" representing the creation of the world of nature."

The main path to the Stupa from the east leads by a series of steps, watched towards the summit by pairs of creatures peacocks, horses, elephants and lions. These creatures are regarded as the "Vehicles" of the five Buddhas. Gilt Taras guarded, the stupa and a beamy peacock watched over all from the dominance of a huge pillar of stone. At the top of the steps is an enormous Vajra (thunderbolt) known as Dorge in Tibetan rested on pedestal which bears on its base, the twelve animals of the Tibetan calendar. Vajra or "Thunderbolt" is five feet long is considered symbol of sacred power. On each side of the Vajra stands a small temple and they are sanctified to Anantapura (on the left side) and to Pratapur (on the right side). Temple of Harati Ajima—"the Goddess protecting against small pox." Two-tiered temple to the north-west with metal gilted roofs and a decoration of metal as well as wood carvings. It is very famous temple in the Kathmandu valley and it is said to be constructed in seventeenth century. The five Dhyani Buddha together with their wives are enshrined at the base of the Stupa. Around the main Stupa are the shrines of five elements such as Agnipur (Fire), Nagpur (water) Shantipur (sky), Vasupur (earth) and Vayupur (air). There are Shikhara Style temples known as Pratapur, Anantapur, etc. south-east and north-east of the Stupa. Nearby the temple of Harati Ajima is the temple of Saraswati, the Goddess of Learning, who is the consorts of Hindu God Lord Vishnu. On Shree Panchami or Basanta Panchami—numerous devotees visit the temple of Manjushree just behind the Stupa and the Saraswati temple at nearby to pay homage. Buddha Jayanti (full moon day of April/May) is celebrated to commemorate the birth, attainment of enlightenment and the death of Gautama Buddha, the founder of Buddhism more than 2500 years ago. Buddha was born in Lumbini Garden in 623 BC a very ancient place called Rupendehi district and Lumbini Zone of Nepal. This great day is celebrated with prayers and worship in this Stupa by many devotees . Swayambhu Nath Stupa is included in the world heritage sites declared by UNESCO.

Another glorious Stupa of Nepal is **Boudhanath Stupa**. It is situated eight kilometers east of Kathmandu city. This is regarded as one of the world's biggest Stupa. King Mana dev constructed this Stupa in the fifth century. This huge Stupa was repaired during sixth, seventh century and these accounts were written in the Gopal Bamsavali. This is a site of great veneration for Buddhists. The Stupa is located on a circular platform of brickwork on which is raised a solid dome of brickwork, surmounted by a brazen minaret. Its octagonal base in inset with prayer wheels There are niches in each of which are cylinders filled into an iron frame. These cylinders contain Buddhist prayer scripts and the pious devotees is seen the cylinders as they go around the Stupa showing their devotions. The Stupa is known as Buddha or Khasti or Khasa Chaitya. This Stupa is of white garbha of Boudhanath "Lord of wisdom" is raised on a series of rectangular terraces of whole being covered in an outer round wall having prayer wheels and paintings of Five Buddhas. By construction, this stupas is on flat surface and is largest in Nepal. It contains levels of terraces and is painted in pastel and is adorned with prayer wheels. It is designed in the Mandala shape, oriented east-west by north-south. Altogether 108 Buddha idols and 147 insets of prayer wheels cover the base of the huge circular edifice. The big solid dome is based on a widely spread terraces with its gilded brass Chhatra, gajura and Chandura. In the top terrace 108 sculptures are adjusted. Its cubical base and dome indicate water, the centre tower fire, the crescent signifies light and the pinnacle the sky. It is believed to contain the relics of the Kashyapa Buddha one of the former Buddhas. This Stupa is specially attached to the Tibetans because of the legendary affiliation between the construction of the Stupa and the establishment of Buddhism in Tibet. These is circular iron bar with prayer wheels attached to it are said to be sign of the close ties of the Stupa with the Tibetans who had established a Gompa (Gumba) centuries ago which is now a place of pilgrimages every year. A new Gompa has also been built recently near it by Tibetans.

Some sacred relics of Kashyapa Buddha is venerated in the central chamber. Boudhanath Stupa is one of the most celebrated place of Lamaist pilgrimage outside Tibet. Around the Stupa has a number of monasteries of different Tibetan Buddhist sects and a Tibetan people. It is also said that Guru Padmasamvaba had revealed its greatness to the Tibetan King Trisonletsen (742-797 A.D.). The Five Lamaist Gompas situated in and around Boudhanath namely Nyingma-Pa Gompas, the Gelua-Pa Gompa, the Sakya-Pa Gompa, the Katma-Pa Gompa, and Geling-Pa Gompa. This Stupa is encircled by two and three storied houses which accommodate large number of Nepali as well as people from northern areas. There is also one three pinnacle temple of Goddess Ajima, who is said to be the protector of children.

The white mound of this Stupa is about 100 yards in diameter and has contained, four shrines at the cardinal directions. The square monument constituting a base of the dome has four pairs of painted eyes which are said to be the eyes of Lord Buddha. The thirteen tier spire represents Bodhisatwa phenomenon of the Buddhist thinking of the world, towers monument. Many devotees from Tibet, Sikkim and Bhutan pay their pilgrimage here in winter. This place known as Boudha is often known as a mini-Tibet of Nepal.

Boudhanath is one of the largest stupa in Asia. The very

sight of this Stupa emanates an aura of great antiquity while throwing light on this Stupa, Mr. Hassoldt Davis writes in his book, "Nepal, Land of Mystery" as the following :

> "About three miles to the east of Kathmandu rose the largest Buddhist temple in the country, the Bodhinath or Kashachait, one hundred and thirty-five feet high. We saw from a great distance the blue and white enamelled eyes on its spire staring straight at us, daring us to swerve from Buddha's Golden way. Nowhere else in the world are there temple such as this. No where had I ever seen such an awesome religious edifice, so powerful in all its proportions, so vital in the effect produced by those colossal eyes. It is because of them, of course that you feel the temple to be charged with a living faith and not merely housing some quaint oriental religion.
>
> The Bodhinath is old beyond the records of Nepal. The temple stands upon a square and very massive base which is composed of three broad terraces, rising one above and within another. From the top terrace rises a concrete hemisphere ninety feet across. This is encircled by a series of niches each containing a stone relief of Amitabha, the third Divine Buddha."

Due to its great culture and religious value, this Stupa of Boudhanath is declared by UNESO in the World Heritage List. The dome and its base are painted white and coloured with yellow pigment in the shape of petals to mean lotus. It is said that relics of Kasyapa Buddha placed in it. Prayer Flags flutter forming a colourful canopy in the winds. The different colours of the flags signify the elements—yellow the earth, red fire, green water, blue sky, and white infinite mind, the same religious meaning attached with the stupa. The Stupa's base dome, spire, half moon and sun each denote earth, water, fire, air and space. The spire of dises signifies the path of knowledge, the umbrella enlightenment and four pairing eyes awareness in the enlightened mind. The prayer flags appears to provide cosmic message into the wind and indicate the visitor that they are visiting the Buddhist world reflecting custom and costume influenced by Tibet. This Stupa to this day is celebrated place of Lamaist pilgrimage, and is visited by a large numbers of Tibetans. It is, speaking openly, the literal home of Buddhism for in the serene region of Lumbini, according to religious script and to a pillar erected by the Emperor Asoka of India, profound Buddhist, some two thousand years ago Gautama Buddha was born there. Beliefs and practices of Buddhism date back in Nepal to the time of its founder Prince Siddhartha Gautam.

The Swayambhunath and Boudhanath are Nepal's top examples of the stupa. This style of architecture is purely Buddhist in concept and execution. The Swayambhunath is more of a mixed cluster with Tibetan monasteries and Hindu shrines and the precincts of the Bodhanath support people of the Tibetan origin and features of Lamaistic influence.

Along with these two big Stupas—Swayambhunath and Boudhanath there are five Stupas in Patan known for its sacredness and religious history. The ancient name of Patan is Lalitpur, meaning city of beauty. The Patan city is situated three kilometers away from Kathmandu. The whole city is a cluster of fine pagoda temple and stone statues. The ancient city of Patan (Lalitpur) south of Kathmandu city has five Stupas, relic mounds of brickclay at the four corners and one at the centre. These big stupas are believed to be two thousand years old. These Stupas are known as Asokan, Stupas. These Stupas were named after the great Emperor Asoka, (Mauryan King) from India, became Buddhist in his latter part of life and propagator of the Buddhism. It is believed that he paid a pilgrimage to Lumbini in Southern Nepal which is the birth-place of Gautam Buddha. He then visited Kathmandu valley and five Stupas erected at the four corners of the Patan city and one at the centre to commemorate his visit by his wishes later on. So this colossal Stupas contain evidences of ancient Buddhist antiques, arts and architecture. These Stupas are thought to be built in 3rd Century BC. These are made as said above in four corners of the Patan city and one at the centre. These Stupas are made of brick and clay, but now the whole dome is covered with grass. These Stupas have their own architectural style and are quite different from other Stupas in the valley. There are idols of Buddha in various positions around the base or on the top seem to have been adjusted later after the inducement of Mahayana and Vajrayana schools. These stupas built at corner of Patan (Lalitpur), four cardinal points at the city demonstrate monastic character of the city. These Stupas are situated in Pulchowk Lagankhel, Ebahi (way to Shankhamul) and Teta (Way to Sano gaon) and one at the centre (Near the Khumbishwar temple at present). The Buddhists have got great veneration, reverence for these stupas. They are said to protect the city and ordain it with divine sanctity. It is a historical fact that Buddha's disciples travelled out into the near and far Countries to propagate his teachings after his death. So Emperor Asoka's visit looked to be true. But some historians consider this account not correct due to authenticity. However his daughter Charumati seemed to visit the Kathmandu valley as a female monk with the view of spreading Buddhism. She is said to have founded the monastery that is still in existence at Chabahil, six kilometers, northeast of Kathmandu city centre. The monastery even to-day lies there with a cluster of Chaityas, Stupas and religious edifices defaced by the passing of time. The ample proof of this fact and the influence of Budhism in Chabahil and some two thousand years ago five stupas at Patan all for sure proof to honour Buddhism in the Kathmandu valley. There is one rectangular limestone relief showing the birth-scene of Buddha about the ninth century in the Archaeological Garden, Patan found and brought there from Deopatan, a town west of and adjacent to Pashupatinath temple. Charumati Vihar still exists at Chabahil to-day a town north of and close to Devapatan.

A township half way down the Boudhanath road lies Charumati Vihar and "Chabahil Stupa", the courtyard of which present many chaityas of the Lichhavi period (from 5th to 8th century A.D.). So this Stupa of Chabahil is considered to be older than Boudhanath, because it was built in the 3rd century B.C. by Charumati, the daughter of Indian emperor Asoka.

Nepal remain a memorable attraction due to her lovely

panorama of golden pagodas, brown temples and white Stupas and beautiful villages seen in a romantic background. It has been a regular source of attraction to international visitors because of its wealth of important Buddhist and Hindu shrines. It has always been one of the most venerated pilgrimage sites for Buddhists. It has still present antiquity and a Buddhist religious architecture of bygone ages.

7 Popular Shrines of Vinayak in Kathmandu Valley

The Kathmandu Valley is surrounded by hills and green patches of levelled land and these places are covered with temples and shrines of gods and goddesses in their various names. Among various kinds of gods, the shrine of Ganesh-Vinayak, another name for the elephant headed God of wisdom and good fortune is very popular and is venerated by the people of the valley very much. God Ganesh (Vinayak) is revered as the son of God Shiva, the Destroyer but also the Regenerator, one of the triad of Hindu religion. He is considered as benign and elephant-headed in feature and the protector of children. His idol is depicted into the plaster walls or carved into the woodwork of doorways. There are also images of him noticed in different places and villages around the Kathmandu Valley. He is the god of learning and success and so people always put great regard to him by offering worships daily. Anyone starting any occupation or work should first worship Ganesh (Vinayak) in order to prevent any obstacles. On account of this traditional belief and religious prejudice, Ganesh (Vinayak) is first worshipped and propitiated before undertaking any new occupation or start of the work. He is being one of the highly propitiated god of good fortune and wisdom (foresight), there are four famous temples erected at four different parts of the Kathhmandu Valley. They are regarded to be the guardian deity of the valley and the area covered by these Vinayaks is considered to be protected by them. The temples of Vinayak are located in the four corners of the Kathmandu Valley. The temple of Surya Vinayak is located in the east, Karya Vinayak in the north, Jal Vinayak in the south, Ashok Vinayak in the heart of Kathmandu city. Kathmandu Valley's most sacred and famous shrines of Vinayak are situated in different names mentioned above in different places. They are by location—Surya Vinayak in Bhaktapur city, Karya Vinayak in Bungamati, Patan, Jala Vinayak in Chovar, Kathmandu and Ashoka Vinayak in the heart of Kathmandu city near the old Durbar Square, Hanuman Dhoka. Special propitious day to honour Vinayak is Tuesday and many devotees are seen visiting these temples on Tuesday to pay homage to the God of foresight and wisdom. Vinayak (Ganesh) is first propitiated before any work is undertaken.

Hindu religious text and mythology speak and depict Vinayak (Ganesh) as a son of God Shiva and his consort Parvati. There are various legends as to his ascendancy. By an account, Parvati put his son Ganesh to guard the door while she was bathing. By chance God Shiva arrived at the very place where Ganesh stood as a guard and he refused to allow God Shiva to enter. When the God Shiva encountered this episode, he naturally got angry. With many push and talks, Ganesh did not allow God Shiva to enter. After many hustle and bustle, God Shiva was very much angry and cut off the head of Ganesh and smoothly made his way. After knowing this happening, Parvati was very much up set and anxious and began to cry in agony, seeing the death of her son. God Shiva came to know that accidentally he killed his own son. God Shiva was also perplexed and promised to bring back life again intact cutting the head of the first being or living thing he would come across. Saying this, he went to the forest and while going he happened to meet elephant. He, at once, cut off the head of an elephant and transplanted immediately to the body of his son. So God Ganesh (Vinayak) has depicted with an elephant head with only one tusk. This symbolic representation of the image of Ganesh (Vinayak) has a great significance in Hindu religion and he is always worshipped at the beginning of any new ventures or religious rites and worships as he was given a boon by God Shiva as repentance of his mistake of cutting his head.

After going all details about God Ganesh (Vinayak), it is now necessary to know about the temples of him located in the four cardinal points of Kathmandu Valley. The temple of Surya Vinayak is one of the shrines and is situated at south of Bhaktapur city. It is faced in the eastward direction and it is said that the first ray of Sun touches the shrine and so it is known as Surya (meaning sun) Vinayak. It is located at the lovely hill of Surya Vinayak near to the conch-shaped city of Bhaktapur. It lies at a distance of about two kilometers to the south from Bhaktapur. This is one of the four Ganesh (Vinayaks) that are enshrined in different directions of the Kathmandu valley for its protection. The temple is stationed in such a place that the first rays of the sun as it rises over the Kathmandu Valley, fall here. The green forests on its south and west provides an attractive and alluring natural landscape. One can go around the hillock by vehicle even and enjoy the sight of excellent scene and sceneries with lofty snowy Himalayan ranges in the distant horizon. The bird's eye view of the Bhaktapur city can be seen from here is one of the most beautiful. The forest around is rich in flora and fauna.

This temple is said to have been built by King Viswa Deva Varma. The King had a dream in which Ganesh appeared to him which signified lucky omen to have seen him who was regarded as giver of riches and success. The king was very much pleased with the blessing of God Ganesh and fell confident that he would now succeed by reigning. He, therefore, created an image of Ganesh on the spot where he was advised to do so. Hence that day, Ganesh came to be known as Surya Vinayak. Devotees from far and wide come here to pay homage. Tuesday is regarded as an auspicious day to workship Ganesh, so more people throng at this temple on this day. There is popular belief that worshipping this deity brings blessings of happiness and accomplishment.

The temple of Surya Vinayak is in the traditional Nepali style in an idyllic environ. A beautiful statue of the lonely rat, the vehicle of Ganesh stands on a pillar in front of the temple. By its lovely landscape and easy access, it is also a good picnic spot of the people of Kathmandu Valley. Preservation of natural resources are strictly controlled over here in order to upkeep the natural landscapes and cultural and religious atmosphere. Temple of Karya Vinayak is another form of God Ganesh (Vinayak). Karya Vinayak signifies the God with whose blessings one can accomplish what one wants. The temple dedicated to him is located at Bungamati in Patan city in north side. The temple is situated in a lovely place on a small mount above a bend in the river. These are two large villages named as Khokana and Bungumati behind it. These villages are highly populated and full of houses. Bungamati village is famous for the temple of Machchhendra Nath, the birthplace of the god who is regarded as the Protector of Patan. The temple of Karya Vinayak is located in the east of the Bagmati river. In between Khokana and Bungamati villages, the temple of Karya Vinayak, the elephant-headed god, the removal of all sorts of obstacles lies. After viewing the temple, it is worthwhile to visit the village of Bungamati famous as village of wood carvers. The village contains the temple of God Machchhendra Nath, Karunamaya, the kind-hearted who resides in Bungamati for six months and in Patan for the remaining six months. Khokana, another village is popular for oil grinding. It is famous for the production of vegetable oil.

The temple of Karya Vinayak is small and beautiful. This is one storey temple of plated roof. Inside, the image of Karya Vinayak is placed in the main sanctum.

Another equally famous temple of God Vinayak is Jala Vinayak. This temple is located on the right bank of Bagmati river on the way to Daksenkali, south of Kathmandu. This temple, popularly known as Chovar Ganesh or Kwena Ganesh is built in pagoda style. It is one among the four Vinayaks situated at the four corners of Kathmandu presumable for providing city protection. This place is situated five kilometers southwest of Kathmandu, near the Chovar and its famous gorge. Tradition has it that Manjushree cut the gorge at Chovar to drain out Kathmandu Valley which was then a lake. On the side of the river and a paved courtyard, the lofty temple of Jala Vinayak lies amidst lovely surroundings. The altitude of Chovar hill (5,200ft) is a pleasant spot in the Kathmandu Valley.

Just beyond the Chovar gorge, the temple of Jala Vinayak stands. The principal image of the shrine is a big rock. It extends outside the temple on the back, only a tiny portion in front vaguely resembles elephant tusk. The image of this Vinayak is different from other images of God Vinayaks. The temple and its architecture is supposed to belong to the 17th century. There is a small temple of Saraswati in the south-east corner of the temple of Jala Vinayak. The temple of Adinath is noted for it architectural beauty. The beautiful lake Taudaha lies at the lap of Chandragiri mountain. Taudaha legendary lake of "Karkotak" or the God of the serpents dwell in this lake, very near to Chobar hill.

The temple of Jala Vinayak is triple-roofed pagoda temple. It was thought to be built in the 17th century by Bhakti Malla but it was later renovated. Two roofs of the temple tiled while the top-most is gilded. There is also a golden pinnacle which is single and typical. The struts of the temple depict eight Bhairavas and eight mother Goddesses or Asta Matrikas with whom Ganesh is always connected. Some of the struts have figures of Ganesh in company with female figures. The struts have also contained erotic depictions. Above the original stone idol, a bronze figure of Ganesh lies distinctly and beautiful. The door of the temple faces the south and is guarded by two brass lions on two sides. A bronze image of Ganesh vehicle is mounted on a pedestal just outside facing the main image of God Ganesh in a courtyard. Big bells are hanged on both sides of the door. There are rest houses for the devotees to all sides of this temple. The eastern sides outside have cremation sites. There is also a mystery cave known as Chobhar cave. Suspension bridge spans the river and provides a fine view of the gorge on the northside and the temple of Surya Vinayak on the other side. Climbing the steep hill a Chovar village arrives from where snowy peaks are visible in the fair weather.

After Jala Vinayak, the another popular shrine of Vinayak (Ganesh) is Ashok Vinayak. This is also the very ancient shrine of Vinayak. This Vinayak is also known by the name of Maru Ganesh or Kathmandu Ganesh. The temple is located in the west direction just in the heart of the city. The exact location of this temple is in Maru Tol near Hanuman Dhoka Durbar Square, Kathmandu, and it is also named by the Maru Ganesh. The size of the temple of Ashok Vinayak is very small considering about to its popularity in Kathmandu Valley. It is considered to be one of the main shrines dedicated to Vinayak (Ganesh). This Vinayak is equally worshipped both by Hindus and Buddhists. This is single-tiered temple but highly ornate. The whole surface of this shrine is gilded. The roof of the temple was consecrated by the King Surendra Bir Bikram Shah Deva in 1847. The History of Nepal gives an account regarding the antiquity of this shrine. In the reign of Guna Kama Deva, some one consecrated the image of Ganesh in Kantipur (Kathmandu) and named him Asoka Vinayak from the circumstance of there being many Asoka trees around that spot. A hiti or water spout was also built near the place known by the name of Maruhitidhara. This Ganesh is an important place of worship for kings of Kathmandu. The King must pay homage to this Vinayak immediately after crowning by walking to this shrine. Tuesday, a large number of city dwellers are seen worshipping this Ganesh. Although, its records date back to the middle of the nineteenth century, its history and origin are considered to be very old.

Along with these four Vinayaks, another one is very famous and popular in the Kathmandu valley by the name of Chandra Vinayak. Chavihar, popularly known as Chabahil is an ancient place in the north of Pashupatinath temple. Chandra Vinayak a double storey pagoda temple is one among the temples of Vinayaks having great fame and popularity. This Ganesh is also known by the name of Rakta

Vinayak. The idol of Vinayak enshrined in this temple is thought to be one of the ancient images belonging to the 8th-9th centuries. It is a deep rooted belief among the local people that this Vinayak has a unique power of healing sores and pimples of the body. The occasion of Chandra Vinayak Jatra is observed every year on the day of Kartik Sukla Purnima (January) when the image is taken around the locality in a chariot. A large number of devotees assemble here on this occasion. Devotees can be seen here in greater number on Tuesday from different parts of Kathmandu Valley.

The historical tradition of Shaivaism dates back to the Vedic age. Shaivaism has influenced the whole of Asia from the early times. Parvati, the daughter of Himalaya, is the wife of Shiva, Vinayak or Ganesh, the elephant-headed God, is the son of God Shiva and Goddess Parvati is the patron deity to be the decision maker over success or future of all human activities. He is honoured first of all by all Hindus before starting their prayers and worshipping any other gods. He is also worshipped before starting any occupation. Ganesh Chauthi which is held in the month of Magh (January) is in honour of Ganesh, the god of wisdom and success. Devotees celebrate it with fasting and worshipping.

8 *Machendra Nath—The God of Harvest and of Rain*

God Machendra Nath is the patron deity of Kathmandu Valley. He is venerated as the God of Harvest and the God of Rain. There are two famous Machendra Nath out of many images of the Gods of the same name in the valley. Seto (white) Machendra Nath of Kathmandu city and Rato (red) Machendra Nath in Patan city are popular and are venerated equally by the people of the Kathmandu valley. Seto Machendra Nath of Kathmandu city takes second place after the famous Rato Machendra Nath in Patan city of the Kathmandu valley. God Machendra Nath is carried annually the streets of the cities of Kathmandu and Patan in celestial Chariot festivals. Both of deities are identified as the Buddhist God Avalokiteshwor. Hindus worship Machendra Nath in the form of Viranchi Narayana and Buddhists worship as Lokeshwora. God Machendra Nath is an example of religious congeniality. The Red Machendra Nath houses in Bungamati for the first half of the year and Patan city for the late half. The white Machendra Nath popularly known as Jan-Ma-Deo is stationed at Machendra Bahal or Jan-Baha in the heart of Kathmandu city between Indra chowk and Ason Tole. People worship the Red Machendra Nath for good agricultural harvest while the white Machendra Nath are venerated for sound and vigorous health and prosperity.

Rato Machendra Nath is worshipped by Hindus and Buddhists with equal devotion. The temple is situated west of Lagankhel in a place named as Tabahal western part from Durbar Square of Patan. He is also famous by the name of Avalokiteshwor and Adinath. Lokeshwor Machendra Nath is placed here for six months and for other six months the image is carried and placed to the shrine in Bungamati. He is also known as Bungadyo. Red Machendra Nath is also called "Lord Protector of the Fishes". The temple was built in 1408 A.D. on the south direction of the Patan Durbar Square. Two roofs of the temple are made of metal and the roof below tile. Many household utensils and weapons are spread-eagled in the walls of the upper part of the temple. The temple has excellent fine marble filigree in its ceilings. The temple lies in the middle of a wide and green quadrangle just at the outer part of the market place. Many mythical animals of bronze are carved on the four pillars facing the principal gate of the temple. The temple is finely decorated with various bronze images of artistic appeal.

The image of Red Machendra Nath was considered to have been set up in Nepal by the Lichchhavi King Narendra Dev in the 8th century. The temple is Pagoda styled built in 1408 A.D. King Sreenivas Malla, the first King who started the Machendra Nath cart of chariot festival. A fine image of Avalokiteshwor is housed here for six months, and every year after which it is taken round the city of Patan in a colourful, chariot festival beginning in April-May. On the last day after one month of the festival Bhoto Jatra—the sacred vest is displayed at Jawalakhel in the presence of their Majesties the King and Queen, government officials and the general people. The Bhoto Jatra-the climax of the festival when the Jewel bedecked vest of Karkotak Nag or the Snake God is displayed at Jawalakhel at the presence of His Majesty the King and thousands of enthusiastic people. There is a legend behind the celebration of this festival which says that during the rule of King Narendra Dev, a twelve year drought brought famine and disease to the people of the valley. The drought was caused by the great saint Gorakhnath who was a disciple of Lord Machendra Nath. Gorakhnath caused the havoc of draught to punish the people of the valley not giving him worship and offerings and to trouble his Guru Machendra Nath for not meeting him. Gorakhanath did so by imprisoning nine snakes or gods of snakes who used to provide rains to Kathmandu valley. Then the King tried to find out the clue for the emancipation out of the great draught set out for Assam with his advisors where Lord Machendra was in deep meditation. They were later on joined by snake God Karkot Naga on the way. When they reached Assam, Machendra's mother transformed him into a large black bee and hid him in a golden pot carried by one of the King's men. Then some demons stole the vessel. At long last, four terrible Bhairabs the protector Gods came to the rescue. They came to the valley along with Machendra Nath. They all stopped for rest at the place what to day is known as Bungamati. There, Gorakhnath came and paid homage to Machendra Nath after long waiting and released the nine Nagas. Immediately, the dry valley got torrential rain and everything became alright afterwards. Lord Machendra Nath's immense chariot has four Protector Bhairab Gods on the four large wooden wheels. The carved protruding beam in the front represents the Karkot Naga. Lord Machendra Nath sits in a decorated chamber towered by a fifty-foot spire which is covered with green vines. This legend has its own proof that this festival held to ensure the beginning of the monsoon at the most favourable time.

Legend of Red Machendra Nath holds that Bandhudatta a great tantric priest was responsible for bringing the spirit of Machendra Nath from Kamrup (Assam, India) to the valley of Kathmandu by means of trantric power. It is believed that the spirit of the God—'elixir of life' of God Machendra Nath is placed in a Kalasha or holy vessel which is located in the interior of the icon of Machendra Nath. Legend also tells that Gorakhnath visited Kathmandu from Gorkha to pay homage to his Guru (teacher) Machendra Nath. God Machendra Nath is associated with the Gorakhanath sect as well as Lord Minnath is also considered as the cousin of Lord Machendra Nath, the teacher of Gorakhnath. Minnath is also called Chakuwa Dyo is also accompanying Rato Machendra Nath during the entire period of festival. So Minnath is also a Buddhist deity and has many names as Meen Nath, Min Nath, Dharma Raj, Jatadhari Lokeshwara, Padmapani Awalokiteswara etc. Chakawa Dyo is also identified with a great saint Gorakhanath, the top ranking disciple of Rato Machendra Nath. Bandhudatta established the rites of worship. White Machchhendra Nath—The temple of white Machendra Nath is situated at Machendra Bahal in the heart of Indra chowk and Asan tole. The temple is of pagoda style. The main entrance of the temple faces the main ways and is guarded by big images of metal lions. The temple is considered to have made in to the time immemorial.

Legend sheds light that the image of the God Machendra was commissioned by King Gunakama Deva in the 9th century. The temple was repaired and made by the King Yaksha Malla in the 13th century after receiving the image from the farmer who found it while working in his fields. Then afterwards, white Machendra Nath assumed a venerate position in Kathmandu's religious life.

Seto (white) Machendra Nath is commonly remembered with veneration to as 'Jumaleswara' and his present temple in Juna Bahal in divine reference to his first home while reference above 'Jamaleswara' it is better to note the legend not explained in detail above as the image was enshrined firstly by King Gunakama Deva but was carried by an invading King but he left the image abandoning it in the Gandaki river between Kathmandu and Pokhara. The King who abandoned the image without any sanctity, was afflicted with skin diseases and also his sixth generation. Long last, the King came to know the causes of the skin diseases and found out the image back to Kathmandu from the Gandaki river near Pokhara. It was not until the reign of King Yaksha Malla in the 13th century the image enshrined in Jamala, the place where it was firstly received by the fancied and the God was transormed to Matsyeandra Bahal-present site. So the God even now frequently referred to as "Jumaleswara".

The festival of white Machendra Nath, which many have been looked alike as in Patan, is considered to have been introduced by King Gunakama Deva, the Thakuri King (the founder of Kantipur—old name of Kathmandu) in the 10th century. Later on Malla Kings also carried on the annual chariot festival of white Machendra Nath which is running even to the present day. Machendra Nath is equally worshipped by Hindus and Buddhists. The chariot festival of white Machendra Nath is held in his honour for a full week. It is a grand preparation for a large chariot festival for four days—generally occur in the month of March. The God white Machendra Nath is carried from the temple for a brief visit to his native home in a place now known as Jamala formerly a village. Then solemn rituals followed such as the consecrating of the image, ritual bathing and painting before the actual start of the chariot festival. The ritual bathing includes also the changing of god sacred thread (Janai) and this shows the significance aspect of Nepal's social-religious life. The image then is installed in a Khat (carriage). Then the white Machendra Nath is taken in procession to Indra chowk, then up to Bangemuda Square and thence to Jamal. Here the chariot already made stands over the spot where legend says the idol was discovered by the farmer.

The grand chariot of the God is a decorated vehicle on four wooden wheels and is topped by thick branches of pine from which dangle many votive flags. The chariot prepared at Jamal, at the end of Durbar Marg on the days just before to the festival. Then the chariot festival runs for four days. The chariot passes Asan Tole and usually proceeds different places and third night it reaches as for as Hanuman Dhoka and from here to Lagankhel. Then at the end the image is carried back to the temple putting back to the Khat. In such a way the Rath Yatra or the chariot festival of Seto Machendra Nath occurs every year in the month of Chaitra (March-April). A chariot is made ready, is prepared at Tin Dhara Pathsala near the Clock Tower (Ghantaghar). It is an ornate chariot projecting upward curving horizontal beam of great length carved with serpent head—representing Karkotak Naga (the Snake God), over this hung a colourful mask of Hayagiva. At Lagan, the chariot is stopped and where Seto Machendra Nath has to go round the tree at the open space which is supposed to represent his mother as showing respect and honour. The days when the chariot stops in each of the sections of the city, the people pay homage by burning lamps and offerings in the morning or at night.

While Machendra Nath represents Padmapani Avalokiteshwara and is worshipped by Hindus and Buddhists. The God is also called Janmadeo or Machendra Nath. The God is a white coloured image of Lokeshwara or Padmapani Avalokiteshwara. The temple covers the artistic features representing the gods and goddesses of both the Hindu and Buddhist pantheon in the carvings and mouldings. The man sanctum contains the white colour idol so the people like to call it Seto (white) Machendra Nath. The courtyard of the temple contains a wealth of variety of images, paintings, carvings and mouldings. The most important and significant feature is 108 painting of Avalokiteswara in different sizes, shapes and forms. It is actually the best place to know about the different forms of Avalokiteswara. This God ranks second in popularity after Rato Machendra Nath in Patan. Many are of opinion that two idols represent Avalokiteswara who attained the status of Buddha in ages past. The name Machendra Nath actually is derived from Matsa+Indra Nath meaning Lord King of fish of the heaven. Gorakhnath is the teacher of God Machchhendra Nath. Red Machendra Nath of Patan and white Machendra Nath of Kathmandu, both refers as male though people call them sisters. Red Machendra Nath has two homes—Bunga Village and Patan's Tahbahal. Red Machendra Nath is venerated by the farmers of Patan more than others. The God is popularly called Bunga God and its cult is closely mingled to the Newar agricultural cycle. Regarding Red Machendra Nath who used to live in Assam at Kamakhhya Hill near Gauhati until the Saint Gorakhnath came to help Machendra Nath to Kathmandu valley to bestow rain to be off from the drought. Seto Machendra Nath is also widely worshipped by devotees of Shiva and Vishnu as well as Buddhists for the bestower of longevity in children removing the cause of sterility in women—a merciful God of pity known as the "ocean of compassion."

9 *Famous Temples of Bhairava in Nepal*

Bhairava, the terrible spirit or peculiar aspect of Shiva, the third god of the Hindu triad destroyer and reproducer is venerated in Nepal. Their complexion is awesome and fearful. Their eyes are brust upon their sockets and their fierce tongues are sprawling out aghast. This popular form of Shiva is the terrifying Bhairav, who himself has a number of different forms.

Hinduism is regarded as the religion and social institutions of ancient times and its doctrines are to be found on the ancient texts namely the Veda, the Brahmanas, the Upanishads. Hindus worship many male and female deities. Sacrifice and ritual are performed on a ceremonial religion. It has a basic trinity of three Gods Brahma, the creater, Vishnu, the preserver and Shiva, the destroyer. Besides, two of Vishnu's other incarnations—Rama and Krishna, the heroes of classic epics Ramayana and Mahabharat are also worshipped by the Hindus. Other deities like Ganesh, Bhairab etc. are also revered. The cult of Mother Goddess too, occupies a prominent place in Hindu pantheon.

Buddhism, as it appears in Nepal belongs to third "School" which has often been called the third vehicle-Vajrayana i.e. a school strongly influenced by Tantrism. Tantrism has greatly progressed by creating the path of Vajrayana "the Path of the Thunderbolt". The main object used in Vajrayana Buddhist rituals is a small thunderbolt like sceptre that is believed to have the infinite in three dimensions.

Tantrism and its origin is found in the ancient worship of the Shiva-cult, the followers of Lord Shiva, who is considered the destroyer and regenerator of all things. Tantrism is practised both by Hindus and Buddhists in Nepal. Tantrism welcomes all devotees irrespective of caste, creed, sex or wealth. Bhairava who is regarded as manifestation of God Shiva, the Hindu God is equally worshipped by Hindus and Buddhists in Nepal. The Hindu as well as Buddhist exercise worship of God Bhairava handling of the ritualistic "ingredients" including meat and wine. We come to know that another popular form of Shiva is the terrifying Bhairav who himself has a number of different forms. Their worship are performed by image yoga etc. Magic formulas are also utilised to please them. Kathmandu Valley consists of three main cities of cultural heritage, Kathmandu, Patan and Bhadgaon. These cities are full of ancient monuments, relics of architecture and fine arts. Since long, these cities had been maintained its dignified positions as a comprehensive treasure house of the cultural inheritance in the past and as an ancient capital of Nepal. Going around Kathmandu Valley thus helps one to get acquainted with the cultural treasures of Nepal in general since the sixth century to the present.

Kathmandu or Kantipur its ancient name is known as the city of glory. This is situated at an altitude of 1336 m at the confluence of the two rivers—the Bagmati and the Bisnumati in the wide valley. The city of Kathmandu was founded by Raja Guna Kama Deva in 723 A.D.

Durbar Square of Kathmandu with its old temples and palaces epitomizes a grand showpiece of architecture. Durbar Square is centrally located in Kathmandu. The palace square or palace complex is also known as the Hanuman Dhoka Durbar has around it temples and shrines of one kind or another. There is golden gate there which leads to the courtyard of the palace. Just by the side of the golden gate, there is the idol of Hanuman (Monkey God) painted red. A red sheet of cloth covers its body. Pratap Malla, the lover of art and architecture and learned king of Malla dynasty made this principal gate to the palace and put there an image of Monkey to scare away evil spirits in 1672 A.D.

To begin with, it is now better to start with the temple of Degutaleju. This temple was built by Shiva Singh Malla in the late sixteenth century and afterwards renovated by Shah Kings. This temple has a platform and a three-tiered roof. This is nicely decorated and the top of it is capped by a very fine pinnacle. At one end, beneath this temple is the image of "Seto Bhairab"—a huge face known as mask of white Bhairab frighting appearance about ten times life size with long snarling nose normally kept behind the grills. Its height stands about 4 metres high. This image of Bhairab is hidden under the screens and the people are not normally able to see it. During Indra Jatra festival the screened white Bhairab is made public and the people worshipped as a God of rain. Indra Jatra festival occurs in the month of September and a local beer is poured from its mouth. The worshippers are excited to gulp down the local beer coming out of its mouth. The worshippers are very much eager to quench their thrust out of the local beer for their health and prosperity as it has come down from the mouth of the God Bhairab.

The image of God white Bhairab was placed by the King Rana Bahadur Shah in 1796 to make clear of evils and demons from the country. There is also a description of this Bhairab in the treatise named as "Triratna-soundrayagatha written by Sundarananda Bada." It is written in this treatise that King Rana Bahadur Shah had established it to charm the festival of Indra Jatra more glamorous and to drive off evil spirits and ghosts. The image is described as the Sarava symbolizes more stronger than lion and this animal has legs with long nails up and carnivorous. The image of Bhairab is painted with gold.

Bhairab as described above is called the dreadful aspect of God Shiva. This is the apostle of destruction. Usually the image of Bhairab is created with big and fierceful eyes, the standing and fierceful hairs and very long and sharp teeth. The Bhairab God is worshipped very much in devotion. It is an usual practice to establish the image of God Bhairab on the southern side of the temple of Lord Shiva. There are such images of dreadful Bhairabs in the Pashupatinath temple's courtyard and Kumbeshore temple in Patan and Indraswore temple in Panouti. Such dreadful images of Bhairab consist of full body from the leg to the head. But the image of God Bhairab shown in the festival of Indra Jatra has displayed only upper portion consisting of neck and above. Many such images of Bhairab made of earth wood etc. are also put in different places at the time of Indra Jatra festival and can be seen. This is also a regular practice to keep big earthen pots after such images and a small bamboo pipes are joined with the pots and a local beers come out of the fangs of the mouth of God Bhairab. The devotees quench their thrust out the local beers in order to be off from the coming obstacles and illness by the grace of the God Bhairab.

Next to the white image of Sweta Bhairab is the image of Kala Bhairab in a dreadful form. This huge stone idol of Lord Bhairab represents God Shiva in his obstructive manifestations. This idol has its terrifying expression and denotes the sign of death and destruction. This huge image is located close to the temple of Jagannath and northern side of the Degutaleju temple facing north. King Pratap Malla constructed a pond near the place named Bhandar Khal within the courtyard of his palace. In order to fill the pond, the King Pratap Malla made a conduit from BudanilKantha and it is said that he received this huge image of Kal Bhairab in a place named Raniban in a field. By seeing such a big idol of special beauty and grace, King Pratap Malla carried it all along the way with great strength and was set in the present location. This image was animated with Tantrism and put in the courtyard outside the palace complex. So it can be said that this image was constructed long years before after the period of the King Pratap Malla. The image is made of a single stone and is about nine feet in height. There are two big stone lions on either side of this image. This image is depicted upon the body of a Betal (demon) lying flat and the image is seen just on the body of betal by crushing it in upright position, standing in a colossal and dignified manner. Kala Bhairab is decorated with the human skulls underneath the knees. The serpents are set on the ears, wrists and the feets. This image has portrayed with six hands. There are sword and armour in upper two hands. The two hands in the middle have taken hairs and other in the sign of oblation. The lower two hands have shown with a trident and in other with hanging three human skulls. The image has a head with a headgear embellished with human skulls. The eyes of the image are big and dreadful with the eyebrows raised to show the mode of anger. The image of Bhairab being the one of the incarnation of God Shiva is worshipped in Nepal in his destructive aspects. So the image of Bhairab itself shows in a very subversive and ravage depiction of destruction.

The image of God Kala Bhairab is sculptured out of a single stone but the portion on the upper right hand was damaged and repaired by adding another stone. The sun and moon to the left and right sides and the heads of lions in upper part also appear to have been later additions. Such large images made of a single stone are very rare in Nepal.

It is said that criminals during the period of Malla King used to be taken there to speak about their crimes before the image of God Kala Bhairab. Usually the criminals of high blooded crimes are carried there to speak the truth of their wrong doings before the terrifying image and some of the criminals, it is said, had died even by vomiting blood out of nervousness. The people are afraid to be before the image even to-day because of the dreadful and terrifying figure of God Kala Bhairab.

It should be considered that Kala Bhairab is worshipped by the judiciary of the country as the symbol of justice.

God Bhairab is worshipped equally both by Hindu and Buddhists. Buddhists consider God Bhairab as Dharmapalas (Protectors of Doctrine) and so the divinities who help to protect and act as defenders of Buddha's doctrines. They are in general wrathful in appearance to terrify the sinners. Mahakala is believed to be the great wrathful Dharmapala whose image is installed in most of the Buddhist Viharas and temples.

God Bhairavs are worshipped in Nepal as per Tantric rituals. He is settled down in Nepal by offering of blood, meat, eggs and liquors. The popular shrines of God Bhairava in Nepal white Bhairava, Kal Bhairava (as described above) Akash Bhairava, Mahankal, Pachali Bhairava, Bagh Bhairava, Tika Bhairava and Palpa Bhairav etc. So Asta Bhairavas such as Asitanga, Ru Ru, Chanda, Drodha, Pakala, Vishana, Shaker and Unmata have impacts on the entire Nepali culture. God Bhairav being a tantric God is depicted with gigantic image which generally fearful and awesome. Generally the image has very big eyes with raised eyebrows and projected nose showing swelling nostril. The strange appearance has shown with an accurate details of furious presentation.

The temple of Akash Bhairav lies in the main market of Indra Chowk of Kathmandu city. Indra Chowk is the bustling place of markets and the shrine of God Akash Bhairav is stationed here. This shrine shows the unusual pattern of the architecture as the upper sanctuary of the God Akash Bhairab is situated at the top with shops below. This image is displayed ouside the temple for a week during Indra Jatra festival (September). The image is looked like a mask and in some ways, resembles to some extent, Sweta Bhairav, Kal Bhairav and Batuka Bhairav etc. This shrine is three-storeyed located in the same area as the Machhendranath temple in Indra Chowk on the way to Asan when coming from Hanuman Dhoka. This God being Akash Bhairab—the God of Sky is displayed out of the temple for a week day Indra Jatra, the festival of Indra, the god of rain. This Bhairab is believed to be a very powerful God and had connection with long history of Nepal since Kirat period. Thus Bhairab being the God of sky and rain is very much venerated by the people of Nepal.

Mythological period of history mentions the legends regarding the temples, towns and holy places of the country. King Gunakama Deva of the legendary age, initiated God Mahankal Bhairab with the help of his spiritual and tantric guide Shantikar Acharya and installed the image in the main centre of the city now named as Tuhikhel (the parade ground). Many pilgrims visit this shrine of God Bhairab on Saturday for divine blessings. This shrine is also situated on the upper floor of the land with many satals (houses) encircling the main shrine. As the name itself signifies that this Bhairab is regarded as one of the most powerful and dreadful God of terror and destruction. Both Hindus and Buddhists honour this Bhairab equally.

The temple of Pachali Bhairab is also considered to have been built by the King Gunakama Deva with great religious rites in the western part of the Kathmandu city with the image of Ganesh (elephant-headed God) and Astamatrika in and around this shrine. This Bhairab is very much honoured by the people of Kathmandu.

Along with these famous temples of God Bhairab in Kathmandu city area, there is another very reknowned temple of Bhairab in Kirtipur named as Bagh Bhairab in Kathmandu Valley. Kirtipur is a township located six kilometres south-west of Kathmandu city on the top of a hill or plateau shaped ridge. Tribhuvan University lies at the foot of this hill. This ancient township has numerous things to offer ancient shrines, old houses, typical villages with inhabitants typically dressed in old traditional costumes.

This township is built on a plateau shaped hill. This township is said to have been founded by King Siva Deva 111 in the eleventh century. This fortress like township shows typical Newar atmosphere.

The chief attraction of Kirtipur is the temple of Bagh Bhairab, manifestation of God Shiva in the form of a tiger. This temple is rectangular three-storey temple built by the King Siddhi Narshing Malla of Patan in 1655. It was renovated in 1935 A.D. This temple is magnificent with exquisite carvings in woods and shows an extraordinary display of Nepali arts. The temple complex of Bagh Bhairab has a number of smaller shrines, images of gods and goddesses dating back from 4th to 8th century. Its roofs and struts are decorated with weapons.

Bhaktapur or Bhadgaun has also a very famous God Bhairab temple. This temple is of pagoda style and it stands a short distance away from the temple of Nyatapola, the highest pagoda of Nepal. This temple was firstly built by the King Jagat Jyoti Malla on a modest scale. It was later remodelled by the King Bhupatindra Malla, a profound lover of arts and architecture into present three-storeyed temple in 1718 A.D.

This temple is rectangular in shape and looks like a residential complex in nature. The golden pinnacles of the roof top provide the gorgeous outlook due to their series on an unique and excellent ways. The struts of the roof depict the forms of the Matrika and Bhagabati Goddesses. During the festival of Bisket the image of God Bhairab is taken around in a chariot and he is identified with the idol of Kasi Biswanath. There is a very interesting legend with the Bhairab, Biswanath of Kasi (India-Banaras) came one day to see the Bisket festival in the disguise of a human being. A tantric priest recognises him and wanted to capture and to make him prisoner with mantras. But God Biswanath disappeared knowing this trick but the priest cut off his head in despair which is said to be enshrined in the temple.

While writing about the God Bhairab, it is better to know something about the Palpa Bhairab very famous fearful manifestation of God Shiva.

Tansen, one of the most lovely hill resort of Nepal, situated on the southern ridge of the Srinagar hill at 1371 m. above the sea level. Tansen is the administrative headquarters of the Palpa District. Near about 4 kms trek from Tansen is Chandihan Bhanjyang, a well known place of worship. There is the temple of Chandihan Bhairab popularly famous as Palpa Bhairab. Here is also a silver mask of Bhairab is placed in the first storey of the temple. The devotees worship this silver mask. A large golden trident of Shiva can be seen outside the temple. The temple of Palpa Bhairav lies 10 km. west of Tansen and is connected by a fair weather road. Tansen is only 123 kilometre away from Pokhara and 302 kilometres away from Kathmandu. So it is easily accessible.

10 *Sacred Temples of Narayan in Kathmandu Valley*

According to King Gopal chronology the temple of Changu Narayan was built by King Hari Dutta Verma while building the other three Narayans in the Kathmandu Valley. These are Ichangu and Sheish Narayan of Kathmandu and Vishankhu Narayan of Lalitpur (Patan).

Changu Narayan is located on a hill top about 16 kilometres east of Kathmandu city. This is an ancient temple of Hindu God Vishnu which has some of the Valley's earliest stone scriptures and carvings. It is believed to have built in 323 A.D. by King Hari Dutta Varma. The hill in which this temple is situated, known as Dholagiri to the north of Bhaktapur city. The altitude approximately 153 metres above the Kathmandu Valley floor, this place has its distinct historical and architectural significance. Changu Narayan temple's precinct has contained the most authentic and oldest inscription dated 464 A.D. to have been put up by Lichhavi King Manadeva I.

The Lichhavis are said to have penetrated into Nepal from North India in around 250 A.D. The first Lichhavi King of historical importance was Manadeva I. The documented history of Nepal begins with the Changu Narayan temple inscription of King Manadeva I (C464-505A.D.) of the Lichhavi dynasty. This inscription shows the benevolent devotion and reverence to Changu Narayan by the King Manadeva I and erection of Garuda Sthambha clearly provide the establishment of this temple sometime before 464 A.D.

The Changu Narayan temple and its courtyard is full of Nepalese stone sculpture. The idols of Garuda Narayana, Ganesh, Nirsimha and Vishwarupa installed here represent the extraordinary models of stone images of Nepal. There is an image of Garuda on the west side of the temple enhancing the attractiveness of this temple. Similarly, there are images of different deities on the west side of the temple.

There is a single storey temple of Chhinnamastha Devi with gold gilted roof in the south side of Changu Narayan temple. The Ratha Jatra begins on the third moon day of Vaisakh and many devotees assemble and pay homage to the deity.

There is an interesting religious description or mythological account of the shrine of Changu Narain. It is expounded as Lord Rama killed Bali, the King of monkeys without any guilt to protect his close companion Sugriva, the close brother of Bali. But after realising his mistake of killing Bali, Rama later on, repented that he would reciprocate by bestowing his own life for Bali in his next incarnation. This great event happened as the reputation of the holy book describes the hill on which the temple exists to-day as known as Dholagiri in ancient time where Bali passed a pious life as a sage in his re-birth keeping herd of cattle and taming them. On knowing the peculiar happening he was puzzled not finding the miracle of a episode that the cows which supplied much milk to him return back from the forest with her udder fully blank every evening. He tried to find out the reality and concealed himself following his cow. He noticed that his cow was providing her milk to a man on the hill. Seeing such scene of milking her cow by a man on the hill, he got very much angry and striked the man with his sword, in order to kill him. But to his wonder, the noticed the man whom he was furiated to kill, turned into a tree and he saw the cut out tree in his place into two pieces.

Abruptly, Lord Vishnu arrived there with his perfect image with four hands holding the Conch, the Chakra (a round weapon belonged to the Lord) and the Padma etc. on the stump of the tree. Seeing such extraordinary happening, the pious man showed his repentance and begged the God for his forgiveness. At this juncture, the Lord reminded him about the promise in which he had given his vow to Bali in his previous life. In order to justify this event, the image of the God Vishnu on Garuda, His mount, is diverged on the tree stump in the temple.

This temple of God Vishnu on a hill east of Kathmandu city and north of Bhaktapur city is the oldest example of pagoda architecture and a specific legacy of the Lichhavi age. The most richly embellished two-storied pagoda temple stands in a open courtyard full of artistic and impressive figures. As said before, the original temple of Changu Narayan was built by King Manadeva. Later on, the present temple was fully renovated after it was damaged by fire 300 years back. King Bhupatendra Malla installed in front of the temple, his statue and his queen in the state of prayer in 1702 A.D.

The temple epitomizes medieval arts of Nepal by figures in woods and metals. The gateway of the temple is covered by two stone elephants on each side of the path way. The doorway of the temple has contained a large gilded torana. Marry bells and lamp holders are seen hanging from the caves of the temple. The struts of the temple are orgamented with exquisite carved multi-armed deities. The lower roof of the temple is of tile and the upper one of gilded copper with a bright and shinning gilded panacle. There are bells hang in stone frames outside the temple, about five metre high stone pillar with a huge bronze shell and other symbols representing God Vishnu. This Chakra (or wheel) and Shanka (Conch-shell) of God Vishnu mounted on pillars to the left and right side of the golden main entrance to the shrine. The sanctum of the temple sanctifies the famous idol of Baraha, the boar incarnation of Lord Vishnu on bronze depicting Lokeswar mounted on Vishnu who stands on Garuda (the mount-winged bird), interlaced in the Coils of the snakes (nag) and in turn sited on a griffin. The image of the sanctum is worshipped by Hindus as Garuda Narayan by Buddhist as Harihar Lokeshwore. The courtyard of the temple is filled with image of Gods, stone sculptures date back from 5th to 17th centuries.

This temple is the symbol of religious tolerance as the Hindu and Buddhist devotees both worship the deity as Garuda Narayan and Hari Bahan Lokeshwore.

God Vishnu, the Hindu God, the protector and preserver of human being and the universe is the God of Hindu triad. So, God Vishnu occupies a top most place in the Hindu pantheon. Narayan is one of the incarnation of God Vishnu. Narasimgha Narayan—God Vishnu as a wild boar, avatar or incarnation of Vishnu, it is said that descended to the earth to liberate the world from the clutches of demons and of evil. This form of God Vishnu represents a incarnation for the liberation of demons, assuming the shape of man-lion.

The Changu Narayan temple is on way to the historical as well as ancient township of Sankhu, about 16 km. east of Kathmandu. Pilgrimage to this temple can be done by buses and mini-buses from Bhaktapur and the trolley Bus Stop located at Tripureswore. Accessibility is very easy to pay a visit to this ancient temple and pay homage to God Vishnu or Narayan. This temple is located in a lovely surrounding of Changu Village of Bhaktapur about 16 kilometre east of the Kathmandu city. It is only about 4 km. from Bhaktapur. This temple is a representation of religious tolerance. The arts and tradition of Nepal, inspired by Buddhist and Hindu culture are of an astonishing richness in the vicinity of this temple.

Ichangu Narayan : The temple of Ichangu Narayan is situated in the crust of a hill west of Kathmandu Valley. It is believed that this sacred temple of Lord Narayan was very revered by the people from ancient time. King Hari Dutta was very devout of God Vishnu or Narayan. He one day, had a dream of the Lord Narayan and also Maha Laxmi. The King was very much pleased to have such a dream and he visioned that he was instructed by the God Narayana and all necessary arrangements for worship in the Third Century A.D. Afterwards, this temple was devastated by a landslide due to heavy rainfall at the ruling period of Pran Malla, a Surya-Vanshi King. Some times, afterwards the image of God Narayan was recovered by Sivananda Rajopaddhaya while bathing in the Bishnumati river by chance. Then Sivananda Rajopaddhaya considered it as a great achievement and he reconstructed the temple again in the same place realising the almighty's direction to him. He, then made God Narayan as his Ista Devata (Main deity) of his family members. Due to these circumstances, his family member even now works as the priest of this temple and worshipping as their main deity.

Ichangu Narayan temple is located west of Swayambhunath Stupa. The route to this temple goes through road to Swayambhunath (via the Ring Road). After letting the Ring road and taking north-westerly direction on rough way for near about forty minutes, the devout can reach to the temple of Ichangu Narayan Temple on the left hand side. To be precise for the tract to the temple, one can arrive in areas known as Chhagdol and Halchowk. These two places are very lovely as farmland and residential houses encircled them. All parts of Raniban from Balaju to the hill top of Nagarjun can be observed from these places. A shrine of Bhadreswar Mahadev lies in Chhagdol along with stone spout with water flowing at all time. The route from here is covered with Cliff and green shrubs. The beautiful view of Kathmandu city can be seen from the Chhagdol above Sita Paila Village. Then the route aliens at Halchowk and this becomes steep and westerly direction through a pass. There is also a temple of Halchowk Bhairab with gilded roof. The grand view of Kathmandu can be seen. There is another shrine of Aakash Devi (Goddess of sky) a little way off from the Bhairab temple. This area is full of country houses inhabited mostly by Newars and Tamangs.

From Halchowk, the trail goes through farm land. One can see the village life of the inhabitants as this place is called Ichangu Village. This village is popular as fruit garden because of ample production of fruits like peach, plum, oranges etc. After a short interval, a plain site arrives. There are three temples there. The temples are dome shaped made of bricks and stones. Even doors and windows are made of carved stones. The sancturies of the temple have Shivalingas (phallus-denoting symbol of God Shiva). There are Varahas (bulls-mount of God Shiva) in front of the temple. There are five pinnacles in each of the shrines. After going further in the beautiful two tier pagoda temple of Ichangu Narayan stands in lovely surroundings near to residential settlements.

The main entrance of the temple passes through eastern direction and the courtyard of the temple of Ichangu Narayan arrives and here stands a grand stone image of Narayan out of doors of the temple. Many idols of deities and inscriptions are spread around the idol of Narayan. The temple of Ichangu Narayan rests at the middle of the courtyard. The temple is of pagoda style with gilded two tier of roofs full of fine wood carvings. The temple is topped with lovely spine. The door of the temple is on the eastern side and guarded by lions of both sides. There is a big bell dangling in a supporting column just in front of the temple. There are rest or guest houses (darmasala) in the north-western direction. The images of Bhim, Ganesh and Saraswati are seen in the south-east of the temple. Close by in the southern side, a shrine housing the goddess Mahalaxmi stands. This shrine is roof-less.

Ichangu Narayan assumes a gay appearance after the autumn festival of Tihar and lasts for a week likewise, a glamorous festival occurs on the day of Haribodhini Akadashi and many devotees visit here to worship Narayan.

Just to note this temple of Ichangu Narayan in two stage pagoda was built in the region of King Hari Dutta Varma in the third century A.D. Later on, this old temple was destroyed by the land-slide due to heavy rain during the ruling period of Pran Malla. Later on, it was reconstructed as of to-day.

Bishanku Narayan : This is one of the another celebrated God Vishnu temple of the Kathmandu Valley. This temple is also situated in the top of the hill, some about 18 kilometres south-east of Kathmandu. It is remarkedly known as one of the Narayan temples built at four sides of the Valley. It gives a bird's eye view of Kathmandu Valley from the top. It is near the Godavari Botanical Garden of the Phulchowki hill.

The Bishanku Narayan is located at a pass between Kotdada and Sabaridada hills. The temple of Bishankhu Narayan is not so much of architectural representation. The God Bishankhu Narayan is in a cave like plinth not very big but rather small and cosy. After leaving the road, steep climb of stone paved path ways to the temple to be followed, then one can arrive to the entrance. There is a temple of Santoshimata on the right and dharmaṣala (guest houses) on the left. The main entrance to the temple is a large gate. While entering the temple through the main gate, the devotee comes out from the another hallow outlet. This is surprisingly unique to the unforeseen happening of this religious spot. In order to come out, one has to cross through a opening of limestone. By seeing the opening, no body can imagine that he will be come out of this opening as it looks very narrow and small. But any one wishing to pass through this small opening can come out easily not feeling any difficulties or confines of space. The visitor of any size and volume or big and fat can come out easily without any obstruction.

The stone idol of Hanuman (the monkey God) at a the gate guarding the temple with two bells hanging. A stone column with inscription is seen near by the temple. A small courtyard as a platform has been also constructed outside the temple. The temple opens in the morning and in the evening for the devotees. As soon as the visitors enters the door he can see the limestone images of Narayan and Mahadev in their natural formation. Then the trail goes east and passing down the steps, the exist opening arrives. The pathways are uneven and rough of the crevice and the visitor will have to adjust his walking rationally or pertinently. After coming out of a opening, it almost causes anybody to be surprised how he passed through the delicate hole or exit.

The route to Bishankhu Narayan goes through the ancient city of Lalitpur. The areas of Khumaltar and Harisiddhi come across along the way. Then another townships of Thaiba and Badegaon are approached and provide unique settings of urban dwellings with farmland and the houses of the farmers. The houses are seen in artistically decorated windows and doors. There are water spouts hither and dither giving traditional glimpse of Nepalese farm life. A gravelled road leads to the temple of Bishankhu Narayan from Badegaon. The road passes full of natural scene and scenery, landscapes and lovely villages. There are beautiful villages like Godamchaur covered with pine hill and Jenurkcot and Mulpani equally attractive and serene. Godamchaur has a flat land and a market for serving the local rural farmers. The houses are all here coloured with red soil which we see in all parts of the Nepali Villages. After leaving Godamchaur Village and going ahead, a climb comes from where panoramic views of Kathmandu and Lalitpur city as well as mountain peaks on the far distant can be seen.

The temple of Bishankhu Narayan is located at a pass between Kotdada and Sabasidada (two hills). There is no temple here of any architectural design. The shrine of God Bishankhu Narayan is in a cave which is small and narrow having room for two persons. Just right side of the cave shrine of God Narayan, there is a temple of Goddess Santoshimata and rest houses left of it.

A little climb above the shrine of Kotdada named hill magnificent views of mountain peaks can be seen. The attractive landscape fills one's mind with superb ecstasy.

There is no regular bus service to visit to Bishankhu Narayan. It is better to visit there in a private taxi or in a company of a person having his own car. But, there is another way to reach there. There is regular bus service up to Godavari. Godavari is some 19 kilometres southeast of Kathmandu which contains a variety of exotic plant and flower species.

The temple courtyard in covered with many kinds of stone idols of Gods and Goddesses. This places is also a good place to have bird's eye view of Kathmandu valley. Its location actually lies eastern part of Mangal Bazar of Patan. There is an inscription in the lower part of the temple which gives detail that it was ancient temple having old historical accounts. This temple is in a simple and plain style. It is no so much carved and decorated but in the middle part, there are wooden carvings of exquisite beauty. The ancient time's temple has no more now and the image is God Narayan is seen in the midst of crevice. There is an interesting legend of the God Narayan to reside in such a way being free from the evil acts of demon.

It will take an hour to arrive at the plinth of Bishankhu Narayan shrine from Godavari. In such a way, famous pilgrimage to the shrine of Narayan can be made, the earthly abode for veneration God Narayan-the protector is worshipped as the God of creation/protection of life. God Narayan also comes in various forms or incarnations. So there are Narayan temples at four corners of the Kathmandu Valley.

SHIKHAR NARAYAN OR SHESH NARAYAN

Shikhar Narayan or Shesh Narayan is about 14 km. south of Kathmandu on way to Dakshinkali shrine. So there are two famous shrines of Shikhar Narayan or Shesh Narayan in Pharping dedicated to God Vishnu and Dakshinkali venerated to Goddess Kali beyond Chobhar and Chabhar Gorge are famous temples. The temple of Shikhar Narayan represents one of the four Narayan of the Kathmandu Valley. So this temple is also richly endowed with history and art. The holy shrine stands on a hillock beneath a stalactite rock. The Bagmati river flows through Kathmandu below Chobhar and again goes in the mountain range. The Chobhav Gorge in between the hills of Champadevi and the western slopes of the Mahabharat hill. This temple is nearly situated in the south-west of Kathmandu in a beautiful natural surrounding near Pharping on the way to Dakshinkali.

This temple is also like Changu Narayan, another shrine existed since ancient times. It is believed that this temple was also constructed in the time of Lichhave King Hari Dutta Verma in the third century A.D. The architectural pattern of this temple resembles the seventeenth century. Though the temple is near the road, the surrounding here is very attractive and pleasing.

After Taudaha Lake, the road goes little uphill and arrives to this famous shrine in a calm and serene environ. Hindus call the God enshrined in the temple as Shikhar Narayan or Shesh Narayan while Buddhists call it Yanglesho. A Tibetan monastery also seen near this temple which gives real sign of blending of Hinduism and Buddhism in Nepal.

The temple is reached by the cause-way by a flight of steps paved with stone slabs with ponds on either side leads stairs right to the temple. The temple stands under a ledge which has an udder like formation or bulge. The udder like bulge with nipples from which water showers down oozing. The location of this temple is in a forested green area and so it is peaceful and lovely spot. The pond near the temple are full of clean and clear water with fishes. Numerous fishes are seen splashing in the ponds. There are also stone statues in the plinth of the temple and among them some of them denote evidences back to the Lichhavi era (7th century A.D.).

The main sanctum of the temple is enshrined with the idol of Lord Narayan or Vishnu with four hands Trivikrama or Vishnu Vickranta, representation of God Vishnu as the dwarf Vamana (dwarf relief of Vamana, incarnation of God Vishnu, taking one of the three steps which he covered the world). The image of Trivikrama installed in the temple is remarkably attractive. Vamana is considered to be the fifth avatar or incarnation of God Vishnu, asked from Bali, who was terrifying the Gods of heaven after conquering the world, a piece of land. Just behind the temple, there is the cave where the udder of the celestial cow right on top of Shikhar Narayan through which water flows all the year round in drops. It is believed that it is the udder of the celestial cow Kamadhenu, the divine cow which fulfils the desire of all human beings. There is also an old cave where some monk dwells, has also got some resembling sights of heads and hand on its walls.

According to Hindu Mythology, it was Lord Krishna (as one of the God Vishnu incarnate) who had drained the valley of Kathmandu, creating an outlet with his Chakra (divine weapon). The place from where the water of Kathmandu Valley was drained, is known as "Chkra Tirtha". Hindu God

Krishna (one of incarnation of God Vishnu) who cut a chunk of the hill with his Chakra to drain out the water making the land habitable.

As the Hindu mythology, Lord Krishna had to visit this place where now the temple is situated, to find his son Pradyumna, who was kidnapped by Princess Usha, daughter of Demon King Banasur. He had a beautiful palace on Chandrageri hill (to-day known as Thankot Danda) South of Kathmandu and used to live in it. The green hill can be seen from any point of Kathmandu Valley. The Princess was in attraction with God Krishna's son Pradyumna and had seen him in her dream. After that, she had badly fallen in love with him. After identifying the beautiful person exactly as the man seen by the Princess in her dream was identified. The Princess was very adept in magical powers. By using her magical skill, the Princess was able to Kidnap Pradyumna from his sleeping stage together with the bedstead and the beds on it flown to her palace on Chandrageri hill. The beautiful lake was in front of the palace which is Kathmandu Valley at present.

But the Buddhist mythology put stress that it was Manjushri, a saint from China who had drained the gorge at Chovar to make the outlet of water of the Kathmandu Valley to go out. There is also another account in the Tibetan literature which described a famous Indian Tantric Padmasambhava. Padmasambhava was a powerful exorcist who subdued gods, spirits and demons of three worlds from this place by his meditation and thought. After this, he went to Tibet at the invitation of King Trihsong Detsen. While Padmasambhava was in a stupor, at this spot, innumerable venomous snakes made appearance before him and began to disturb him. There are several serpentine frameworks can be seen hanging down from the rocky mountain. There is also a lovely image of Padmasamvabha and a prayer hall. There is also a castle like monastery constructed on a forested slope of the hill. These mythology of both Hindu and Buddhist texts of the hoary pasts indicate that this place is regarded as sacred place of worship and pilgrimage. An account of some interesting mythological backgrounds are essential to have socio-cultural implications attached with this temple.

The two principal religious prevalent in the valley are Hinduism and Buddhism. Both Hinduism and Buddhism have mixed and mangled so much that they have created and united the unique culture of Nepal. Religion is an integral part of Nepali life. Three main religious creeds namely, Hinduism, Buddhism and Tantricism prevail in Nepal. God Shiva as well as Vishnu both have occupied an unique position in the religious belief of the people. Buddhist beliefs and practice date back since the time of its founder, Gautam the Buddha, who was born at Lumbini in west Nepal Terai in about 623 B.C. Buddhism, as it appears in Nepal belongs to Vajrayana, influenced by Tantricism. Every sects and denominations merge into one another to form one unified one.

BUDHANILKANTHA

After describing the famous four sacred temples of God Vishnu at four corners of the Kathmandu Valley, it is important here to present an impressive reclining image of Vishnu Budhanil Kantha which lies at the northern part of the Kathmandu Valley. This image of God Vishnu is a colossal figure reclining on serpents carved from a great block of stone. This place is eight kilometres north of Kathmandu with a pilgrimage site for Hindu devotees. The massive image of Lord Vishnu sleeping on a bed of several headed Shesh Naga (serpent) considered to be the bed of Lord in Baikuntha, (the abode of the God) in heaven. There are also legends about the discovery of the massive image.

God Budhanil Kantha is popularly known by the name of Jalasaya Narayan as the big image of God lies in a pool of water. The image of God is hooded by eleven serpents. The image is depicted with four hands, the upper right and left hand have 'chakra' (disc) and 'gada' (club) while the lower right and left hand possesses 'padmabija' and 'sankha' (conch-shell).

This big and impressive image is considered to have been commissioned or built in this place in the 7th century by a devotee known as Vishnu Gupta. This shrine is situated at the foot of the Seopuri hill containing the tank and surrounding by guest houses all around it. There is also a belief that this huge image of God Narayan came into existence by itself.

All Hindu followers of Vaidic, Saivas and Buddhists come to pay homage with equal faith and reverence. As for example, the Vaidas revered it as God Vishnu, the Saivas venerate it as Siva and the Buddhists worship it as 'Bodhisatwa'. This clearly shows that Nepal has a tradition of religious tolerance. Hinduism and Buddhism are the two major religions of Nepal which exist simultaneously in an amicable and harmonious atmosphere. The reflection of these uniqueness of Nepalese culture can be seen in the shrine of Budhanil Kantha by seeing there.

Many devotees visit this shrine everyday. But, on occasions of "ekadasi" and "dwadesi", large number of people visit here for worship. A great Mela (fair) is observed here in Mangsir (Nov-Dec) and this lasts for a full month. Devotees from India also pay a visit to this shrine and this shrine has always been a great attraction to them.

The colossal image of God Narayana is about 18ft. long and this sleeping image of God Vishnu (Narayan) seems to float in water. It is the famous place of pilgrimage for devotees as God of miracle floating in the bed of snakes.

It is believed that this is the image of 5th century tradition prevents the King of Nepal of visiting this place. But to provide opportunity to pay homage to God Narayan, a small replica of the image of Budhanil Kantha placed at Balaju Water Garden and similar one at Hanuman Dhoka Palace. There are temples of Narayan near present Royal Palace and a water tank near by it and so Royal Palace.

God Budhanil Kantha is also called Nil Kantha Narayan meaning Blue throated one of the name of Lord Vishnu, the creater of the universe. In such a way, famous sacred temples dedicated to God Vishnu guard the Valley of Kathmandu. Shiva, Vishnu as well as Buddha, all have occupied an unique position in the religious belief of the people of Nepal from ancient time.

11 A Conspicuous Religious Pilgrimage Sites in the Hilly Regions of Nepal

Topographically, Nepal can be divided into three regions. The first division is Himalayan region of the north covering almost 15 per cent of the total area of the country. This region includes the highest snowy peaks extending in altitudes from 4877 meters to 8848 meters. The second part is Mountain region which extends 64 per cent of the total area of the country. This region is formed by the Mahabharat range which tops up to 4877 meters.

The people of Nepal are friendly, hospitable and religious minded following different religions and cultural traditions Hinduism and Buddhism are two major religions of Nepali people. Nepali people live together in religious harmony and worshipping both deities of Hinduism and Buddhism and celebrating the festivals of both religions in amity.

The hill regions are populous simply because of the fertile valleys and deltas and main centres of settlement. From the Terai, the southern flat land is ensued by the wide row of central hills. After the Great Nepal Himalayas, mountain or hilly regions of Nepal is made up of anomalous lines of ranges near about fifty miles in depth between the great Himalayas and China Hills edging the Terai. The Mahabharat Lekh, consisted to the range of mountains or hills stretching from the Mahakali to beyond the Kashi Valley.

The Churia Hills, on the other hand, a series of the Shiwalik range of India are covered with timber and savauna grass. The valleys of this hills are known as "Duns" which are noticeable feature of the foothill of Nepal. Southward extends the important and copious steep bending slope famous as the Bhabar. South of the Bhabar and China Hill as the Terai, the low fertile alluvial plain. This Hilly areas begin from 1,200 meters above the sea level and covers the 15 per cent area of the country, covering an area of 22,850 square kilometres. The width of this belt varies from 20 to 30 kms. The Central Hills have a very lovely climate and so a settlement of different variety of ethnic groups.

The Gorkha township is the headquarters of the district of the same name. Gorkha is the birthplace of King Prithvi Narayana Shah, the Great, the founder of modern Nepal. This is also the ancestral home of the Shahi Kings of Nepal. There are two attractive temples of Gorakhnath and Kali inside the old palace known as Gorkha Durbar. Only Hindus are allowed inside the temple of Gorakhnath, from which the township got its name.

The Gorkha township is situated on a hill overlooking the snowy peaks of the Himalayas. The famous holy place of Manakamana is very near to it. This famous place of Gorkha is located at an altitude of 1135 meters above sea level and is 156 kms away from the Kathmandu Valley.

Accessibility of Gorkha is easy. There is road connection from Kathmandu, Pokhara, Narayanghat (Chitvan), Birgunj and Bhairawa. It is nearly 6 or 7 hours from Kathmandu by driving. There are hotels and lodges for stay and also restaurants for food.

Side by side with historical importance, this township of Gorkha is equally famous for religious temples and shrines. There are historical places such as the Gorkha Durbar on a fortified hill and this is the landmark of this place. The most ravered another place is Gorakhnath cave. It is believed that Gorkha derives its name from the sage Gorakhnath. Sage Gorakhnath is regarded as a very well known hermit who was known all over India and other parts of South Asian regions. He is depicted as a sage of godly powers and can show his mystic powers of creation and dissolution. He was the founder of Gorakhnath sect which was famous all the times and also at the present. He was firstly usher in this world or initiated the acquisition of mystic powers from Gorkha. There are even now places in Gorakha where this learned sage has undertaken penance or atonement. There is Gorakhnath cave which is considered to be the place where Gorakhnath stayed and practised his penance. There are many legend which are full of evidences and accounts of the learned sage who used to give advice to the Kings of Gorkha for carrying out the diplomacy and administration of the state.

After Gorakhnath cave, there is another place of religious importance known as Hanuman Bhanjyang which is situated on the eastern side of the Gorkha hill. There is an image of Monkey God Hanuman in stone. People visit there for worship.

Equally another religious place of Siddhi Ganesh is situated in a lovely place. The idol of God Ganesh is installed in a standing posture. The idol of God Ganesh has not been so far put in a temple in a standing position and here in Gorkha, this has been ordained in a temple.

After the religious places, two historical sites such as Upallo Kot and the Tallo Durbar (Lower Palace) with Malla arts and architectures can be described. Then comes a rare dome shaped temple of Ramessor, Krishna temple, Ganesh temple, Bhimsen temple, Baldeva, Mahadev temple, Haliya Thok and Rani Pokhari Gorkha, being a historical place of great importance, contains valuable historical and religious places of Nepali culture. Gorkha is the main centre of Gorakhanath sect and so popular all around the world. It is also known as over all the world as the place of "Gorkha soldiers" who is regarded as valiant warriors.

Manakamana Temple : This sacred temple of Manakamana or wish fulfilling deity is about four hours trek uphill from Abu Khaereri on the Kathmandu-Pokhara Highway. The temple is situated in a hillock which provides a panoramic view of the Himalayan range, the mountains Prithvi highway, the lovely valley of Daraundi and the excellent view of the Gorkha Durbar. The glittering peaks of Himalayan snowy mountains as Manaslu (8163 m) Himachal (7895 m) and Ganesh Himal (7429 m) can be seen at close angle.

The temple of Manakamana is situated in a hill having a altitude of 1,302 m. The deity enshrined within the temple is one of the manifestations of the Hindu Goddess Bhagwati who is credited or reckoned to have the assurance of fulfilling each and every devotees for their wishes. This is one of the very famous and popular pilgrimage sites in Nepal.

The temple is associated with many legends. It is considered to be built before 17th century and was worshipped as most reverent. The origin of the temple is recorded after the death of King Ram Shah of Gorkha in 1636 A.D.

This temple of Manakamana lies 125 km to the west of Kathmandu valley. It is a steep climb of four hours walk to reach to the hill top from Abu Khaireni on the Kathmandu—Gorkha highway. But now a cable car is operated to Manakamana, the most famous pilgrimage sites of Nepal. The cable carways runs from Darechok VDC Charesh (between Kurintar and Mugluntar), Chitwan district and the Manakamana temple in Gorkha district. This is a two-way cable car for the pilgrims. This cable car route looking Cheres of Chitwan and Manakamana of Gorkha is 3.1. kilometre.

Various services facilities for foodings and accommodation at the Manakaman temple and its vicinity and Cheres area have been available and are managed by all local people. The package tours are also available for the pilgrims and they can come back in the same day enjoying lovely sights. The pilgrims can stay at Manakaman if they like to worship the goddess for more days.

Package tours are available and the pilgrims can return in the same day.

Ridi or Ruruchhetra—This religious place is famous for the Nepali people since long years before. The route to reach the holy place of Ridi is through Tansen. Tansen is a lovely Himalayan town situated on the slopes of a hill called Shreenagar Dada. It lies at an altitude of 1,371 m above the sea level. Tansen is only 123 kilometres away from Pokhara and 302 kilometres away from Kathmandu.

This famous pilgrimage spot of Ridi or Ruruchhetra can be reached by Batase Dada route. This route gives very excellent views. Ridi is situated at the back of the Kali Gandaki river. The exact location of this holy place lies at the confluence of two rivers—the Kali Gandaki and the Ridi Khola mid-west Nepal. There is a temple of Ridi Rishi Keshab dedicated to God Vishnu which was recorded as built by King Mukunda Sen in the 15th century. The King Mukunda Sen is considered to have passed his last period of his life as saint or being a sage in Ridi. The image enshrined in the temple is said to have been received by King Mukunda Sen after being a saint in the river Kali Gandaki at the time of his bathing.

Along with this temple, there are cave temples in Ridi containing excellent images made by stalactite and stalagmite popularly known as Bhriguteswor and Galfal. These are worshipped by the pilgrims as deities. Equally conspicuous, a Sugandha Vihar, a Buddhist monastery of near about 18th century lies in the centre of Ridi Bazar.

A big Mela (fair) occurs in Ridi on Maghe Sankranti in January. Large number of pilgrims from the surrounding hills visit here and worship the Ridi Rishi Keshab with deep veneration.

There are very popular religious sites after walking three hours up the Ridi Khola stream known as Deule Archale. There is a natural cave Siddheswar Gufa which is visited by the pilgrims.

Ridi as believed to be a sacred place a second only to the Lord Pashupatinath temple in Kathmandu. This temple of Rikheswar Narayan temple has its holy cremation places or ghats as in Bagmati of the Pashupatinath. Pilgrims in large numbers from all parts of Nepal as well as India assemble in this holy place on Makar Sankranti for a religious bath in the confluence of two rivers—The Kali Gandaki and the Ridi Khola.

Ridi is connected with the Tansen, township by a 30 km long drive road (motorable road) which usually takes 2 hours drive. In order to reach to this holy place from Tansen takes 5/6 hours as it is 10 km hilly tracts.

Tansen can easily be arrived by bus from Siddharthanagar (52 kms) and Butwal (39 kms). This township is also connected by bus service with Kathmandu. Side by side with road connection, Pokhara and Siddharthanagar are linked by daily flight from Kathmandu. Tansen is the administrative headquarter of the Palpa District. Ridi is connected with the township of Tansen where accommodation and fooding facilities are of no problems. Every kind of accommodation is available.

12 Nepal : The Land of Mother Goddesses

Dasain is the grandest of all of Nepal's festival. It is the national festival of Nepal. The festival lasts for fifteen days. It starts on the new moon day (September/October) on the bright half of the Aswin month of the Bikram Calendar. Dasain is generally popular by different names as Durga Puja, Vijaya Dasami, Mohani, Nava Ratri etc. The kind of celebration differs merely in different parts of the country but the principal character is the same. Legend of this festival has it that Lord Rama, obtained a victory over Ravna, demon King of Lanka who was the embodiment of all evils. Lord Rama, the epic hero of Hindu epic Ramayana is worshipped as the incarnation of Lord Vishnu, the second god of the Hindu tread, the preserver and as the protector of human virtues. His victory over Ravana is thus considered as victory over vices and sins and as such Dasain is celebrated as the day of victory. On this day, images of Devi, Durga Bhawani, Bhagawati, Lakshmi and Saraswati are worshipped. Its highest importance is reflected in worshipping the Shakti Goddess. Shakti Goddess in Hindu religion is most significant for having the spirit of triumph over evil and for saving human beings from miseries and sufferings. So the most important Astamatrika Devis (eight forms of goddesses) are worshipped in eight consecutive days. The eight Matrikas are Mother Goddesses. They are Brahmi, Maha-Laxmi, Kumari,

Vaisnavi, Barahi, Indrani, Chamunda and Mahalaxmi. The holy text entitled "Devi Mahatma" narrates that all forms of Goddesses were unravelled from the singly lone body of Uma, the consort of Lord Shiva. Thus the festival Dasain not only signifies the multi-purposes of Hindu religious tradition. The first nine nights of the festival are known by the name of Navaratri (nine nights) since each night is assigned to the worship of a mother Goddess. Festive mood pervades not only in the cities of the Kathmandu Valley but also in the far off towns and villages. This festival also marks the end of rainy season and the beginning of winter—the pleasant season of the year.

Dasain, is indeed the festival meant to worship Durga in her various forms and manifestations. Durga, the Mother Goddess is called Shakti when symbolizes dynamic divine energy. So Shakti occupies a very special reverence in Hindu Pantheon as the destroyer of evils. Kumari is the virgin form of Durga. The tradition of Kumari, the vestal virgin is considered as the living incarnation of Durga or Shakti which is unique to Nepal. Durga is also known by another name of Kali. Durga or Kali has many manifestations both peaceful and terrible. Shakti has many names such as Kali, Durga, Ghawani, Mai, Bhagbati, Durga or Kali is propitiated by offering of blood (animal sacrifices). The terrible Kali is black Goddess who is specially blood thirsty and always asks for sacrifices. There are many Kali shrines but the important ones are Dakshinkali, Bhadrakali, Raktakali, Naradevi, Maitidevi, Shobha Bagbati, Bindhyabashni, Maisthan etc. There are equally famous temples dedicated to Durga or Bhagbati all over Nepal and just to name some of them are Taleju, Kumari, Living Goddess, Guheshwori, Vatsala, Nala Bhagvati, Chandeshwori, Bhairavi, Kamala Maisthan, Palanechowk Bhagwati, Dantikali, Kalinchowk Bhagawati, Manakamana Mai, Gorkha Kali, Lamjung Kalika etc. All these temples of Durga Bhavani are worshipped and many people throng there for offerings and animal sacrifices during Dasain festival. Bada Dasain or Durga Puja commemorates the victory of Goddess Durga over the buffalo-headed demon

Mahisasoor. So this festival is celebrated all over Nepal. Feasts are held and this is a happiest occasion of all and is celebrated with open hearts amidst joy and festivities.

The first day of this festival is known as Ghatasthapana—the placing of the sacred vessel. Barley seeds are planted in every household and nurtured for nine days. For the next nine days, devotees visit to different Durga Bhavani temples for early morning worships. The next major events happen on the seventh days of festival known as Phulpati Day (offering of flowers)—The sacred flowers and leaves are brought from the holy shrine of Goddess Kali, the goddess of valour from the township of King Prithvi Narayan Shah's Gorkha Durbar. King Prithvi Narayan Shah the great who unified Nepal during the 18th century was born there. All government officers in national dress with all rank and file assemble and turn into a colourful procession to Jamal to bring the Phulpati. The grand procession marches towards Hanuman Dhoka Durbar carrying a holy vessel containing flowers brought from Gorkha, the ancestral home of Shah Dynasty. There is also a large military parade in the royal Military Pavilion, Tundikhel in the presence of the King. A valley of gun fires buzz in honour of the Durga Bhavani. The eighth day of the festival is popular as Mahastami and is celebrated by a fast by all orthodox Hindus. Animal sacrifices are offered at temples of Durga Bhavani. A great worship occurs at Taleju Bhavani temple inside Hanuman Dhoka and many people visit the place of worship. The temple of Taleju Bhavani is located at the northern end of Hanuman Dhoka palace. The temple is two-tired and constructed in 1576 A.D. and houses Tantric/Shakti Goddess Taleju. There are many small shrines around it. There are struts in the temple depleting Kali, Bhavani and the Matrika Goddesses. Similarly Mulchowk of Patan Durbar Square has the shrine of Taleju in the southern wing. The courtyard of this temple was built in 1966 (B.S.) by Srinivas Malla.

This three-tiered temple is octagonal and in the traditional style. The temple struts have the Bhairabs and the figures of Matrikas. The doorway has torana and flanked by two seventeenth century repousse figures of Ganga and Jamuna. Degu Tale, temple in Patan, three-tired brick temple built by King Siddhi Narsingha Malla but rebuilt by King Shrinivas Malla in 1662 after burnt down by fire. It also contains Taleju Bhavani Shakti Deity. Bhaktapur has also Shikhara-style temple of Durga at Layaku of Shakta religion. Another equally famous temple is Batsala Devi, of Shakta region. The temple was built by Bhupatendra Malla in the late seventeenth century and the image of an eighteen armed Mahishamardevi enshrined the sanctum door. This temple is also made of stone and a central a landmark of the Durbar square.

Maha Astami or Kalratri is celebrated in the eighth day by visiting temples of Durga Bhawani and making sacrifices of goats and buffaloes etc. A great Puja ceremony takes place at Taleju Bhavani, inside Hanuman Dhoka and many people visit the place of worship.

On the ninth day, Nawami as it is called all Durga temples are red with blood bath of many sacrifices of animals. Even vehicles and mechanical instruments are worshipped and given sacrifices so as to keep off accidents during the coming year. All institutions, weapons and implements of all professions are worshipped for the blessings of Durga Goddess. There is an elaborate animal sacrifices in the Taleju Temple in Hanuman Dhoka. The peak of Dasain festival is celebrated on the tenth day known as Vijaya Dashmi or Day of Victory. All the Hindus are supposed to visit their elders, superiors, relatives on this day, beginning with their own parents. The chief purpose of this visit is to receive Tika (a red dot on forehead) and a Jamara (roots of barley shown on the first day) by the senior relatives. Red Tika consists of vermillion powder, rice and curd substance which are used in Hindu worship daily. This ceremony of receiving Tika goes on until the end of the festival. There is also a special ceremony of "Khadga Yatra" performed in the courtyard of Hanuman Dhoka on this day. The Buddhists perform Khadga Yatra by tantric way in the various localities of Kathmandu. Mal Siri song has originated from the prayers of Goddess

Durga. The coming of the Durga Puja (Dasain) festival is announced by this song. It last all through the festival days.

Many Durga Bhagabati temples in and around Kathmandu Valley are worshipped and offering of flowers, fruits and animal sacrifices are usually made. People visit in large numbers in these temples to make prayers. Some of these Durga temples are mentioned here.

Adjacent to Lord Pashupatinath Temple, the temple of Goddess Sati, Lord Shiva's consort, named as Guheswori Temple stands in the middle of courtyard. This single-storey temple is said to have made after the tantric Yantra, denoting the female principle of procreation. It is said that Lord Shiva carried his wife Sati (Parvati) on his shoulder after she had been to fire unable to bear the insult heaped on her husband by his father Dakshya Prajapati. Her private organ had fallen on this spot and so it is called as Guheswori. The Goddess in a form of a Kalasha. Devotees regard the Kalash as a holy orifice of Parvati, Shiva's consort and offer wine, eggs etc. on Dasan time.

Shobha Bhagabati temple is located on the bank of the Bisnumati river west of Kathmandu and it contains the ancient sculpture of Bhagabati during the rule of Queen Navasagar, wife of King Vicram Keshar. Later on Lichhavi age, King Shankar Deve renovated it in 507 A.D. Many people visit this temple in Vijaya Dasami festival for worship. Bhadrakali is situated on way to central secretariat Singha Durbar and this Goddess represents terror. This temple is also called Lumashi Devi temple. Side by side, the Goddess is regarded as the trinity of Mahankal Lumhir and Shankata. Equally famous temples such as Raktakali, Naradevi, Maitidevi, Naxal Bhagabati are well known and lot of devotees pay their visit at Dasain for prayers and offerings. Outside near the city of Kathmandu, there is Dakshinkali Temple which tops the list of places of pilgrimage in relation to Hindu Goddess especially in Dasain festival. It is said that image of Dakshinkali was carried in accordance to the vedic tantricism during the reign of King Jaya Prakash Malla with the advice and assistance of tantric Lambakarna Bhatta. Devotees visit this holy place and goats are sacrificed in large numbers during Durga Puja Festival. It is situated 28 kms away at the southern part of the valley, after Chobar Gorge.

There are many shrines in and around Kathmandu valley dedicated to the cult of female deities Yoginis. The principal shrines of these mystical Goddess are stationed on the hill sides at the ancient townships of Sankhu, Pharping and Bijayeshwori near Shobha Bagawati. These are considered sites consecrated to the Ashta Matrikas, the divine Mother Goddesses, the terrible and horrible form of Tantric Goddesses : Bajra Yogini temple is situated in the uphill from Sankhu, an ancient village, 23 kilometres north-east of Kathmandu Valley. This temple is constructed on a hillock over a single huge stone in 1276 B.C.. The goddess represents Buddhist Pantheon. She is the Mother Goddess holding a Tantric weapon called Bajra. She is also called Khadga Yogini because she holds Khadga (a magic sword). Hindu and Buddhists, both consider her as the manifestation of the Goddess Kali. Vajra Barahi is also known as one of the four Yoginis. Guheswari, Vajrayogini, Khadgayogini and Vajra Barahi of Kathmandu Valley. Vajra Barahi is one of the popularly known Mother Goddess among Astamatrika. Vajra Barahi temple is situated in woodland about 8 kilometres south-east from Patan city. It is two-tired Pagoda temple built by the King Shri Nivas Malla of Patan in 17th century. Barahi, is regarded as purely of Savia Mohter Goddess cult. She stands on the heads of a pair of water buffalos with four arms, lower arms in Vindu Mudra and upper right arm holding a citrus, seed of lotus and left arm holding a fish. She has a face of a boar. Her consort is Vairava and her vehicle is water buffalo. Bajra Jogini was originally a Goddess of the Buddhists only but is now worshipped by Hindus as well. Her temple is on the Manicure mountain near Shankhu. Not far from her temple is that of Khadga Yogini where fire is always kept burning and near which is the image of a human head.

The ancient Gana Nritya or Astramatrika mask dance is performed from Ghatasthapana to Vijaya Dasami in Patan every year. There is also a public performance of the Nava Durga dance. The festival of Pachali Bhairav is also celebrated and people pay homage to Goddess Ajima. The performance of ritual dances, 12 dancers representing Ganesh, eight Mother Goddesses or Asta Matrkas are staged. The main figure of dance is Badrakali. The performance of the dance begins in Vijaya Dasami or tenth day of Bada Dasami festival. Different localities of Kathmandu city such as Wotu, Bhimsenthan, Tebahal, Gana Bahal and Sankata as well as Mana Majju.

Vijaya Dasami or Dasain is a national festival of Nepal and so it is celebrated all over the kingdom of Nepal with equal enthusiasm and reverence. No doubt, there are local colouring for the rites for celebrating it but the remain form of celebration is the same. In the Central region of Nepal, Kamala Maisthan, religious place in the district of Sindhuli, is visited by many pilgrims and sacrifice goats and pigeons. Equally famous is Palanchowk Bhagawati, historic temple situated 7 kms north of the Paanchakhanl and built during the reign of the Lichhavi King Man Deva. This temple is enshrined with the image of black stone Bhagwati. Many people visit to worship this spot. Nuwakot Bhairabi also is reputed for pilgrimage an many devotees from Dhading, Rasuwa, Sindhuplanchowk and Kathmandu assemble here for play and worship. Another famous temple of Tripurasoondari is located in Trisuli Bazaar and fairs and festival held here during Durga Puja.

The western region of Nepal is also reputed for having many popular religious places of Mother Goddesses. As for example Pokhara, lovely valley with lakes and mountains is 200 kms distance from Kathmandu. Bindabasini temple is located on the top of a lovely hill and contains the ancient shrine of Goddess Durga of Saligram formation. The next one is Bairabi temple on a small island in the middle of Phewa Lake. The temple is visited by a lot of pilgrims during Durga Puja festival. The township of Gorkha is located on a top of a hill. This town is the headquarters of the district by the same. This town is the brithplace of the King Prithvi Narayan

Shah, the great. The historic Gorkha palace has a holy shrine of Goddess Kali, the goddess of divine energy. On a lovely ridge southeast of the township of Gorkha lies the holy temple of Manakamana, the goddess of fulfilment. Every Nepali is very ambitious to make a pilgrim trip to Manakamana Goddess. Manakamana (fulfils all wishes of devotees) is visited by thousands of people every year to pay homage. The next town Lamjung is also popular for old historic buildings and temples built at the time of Chobesi Raja. The temple of Kalika is very popular and many pilgrims from far and near places visit here for worship and sacrifices. The western region, especially Sallyan is noted for the temple of Khairrabang Bhagwati which is located on a hill, near about 6 kilometres from the district headquarters Khalanga Bazaar. Then Doti has Saileswori temple dedicated to Goddess Bhagawati.

Besides, there are many other sacred temples of Mother Goddesses in the eastern region of the country. There are many local fairs and festivals which are observed by Hindus and Buddhists regard—Dantakali temple, Bijayapur, Pathibhara Bhagawati, Taplejung, Mai Pokhari, Ilam and Sinhadevi Temple, Panchthar etc.

Dantakali temple is situated at a hillock named Bijayapur on the northeast of Dharan Bazaar. Legend has is that Lord Shiva, one of the Hindu triad was carrying the dead body of the wife Sati Devi to the Himalayas. At that moment, Danta or teeth of Sati Devi fell on this place where now the temple stands. So many devotees visit this temple during Durga Puja and pay homage to Sati Devi who is regarded as one of the manifestations of Mother Goddess. Next to Dantakali temple, there is Pathibahara Bhagabati at Taplejung of Mechi zone as it houses the ancient image of Goddess Bhagabati. Many people pay homage and worhip the Mother Goddess. Mai Pokhari, Ilam is known for its religious significance. Some 123 kms north of Ilam Bazaar lies Mai Pokhari. Antu Danda is situated at an altitude of 1677 meters in the Ilam district and is famous for its extraordinary views of Everest (8848m), highest peak in the world and

Kanchenjunga. This place is scenically and religiously worth-seeing place of interest. Side by side mountains and Himalayan regions and valleys. Terai regions in the south have also many sacred places consecrated to Mother Goddesses such as Bindyabaseni temple north-west of the town of Birgunj. The consecration of the image of Bindyabaseni was made during the reign of King Rana Bahadur Shah. Deity Bajai temple is located near about 2 km southeast of Birendranagar, and goats and chickens are offered. In such a way, every villages and towns of the Terai are full of temples of Mother Goddesses where the people worship daily and make sacrifices of goats and chickens. Music and dance known as Jhijhiya in the areas covered by Gandaki and Kosi rivers in the Terai, the girls in group go house to house dancing and singing with flares burning on top of water. Jar on their heads during nine nights of festival of Dasami in praise of Mother Goddess. So Nepal is the land of the Mother Goddesses where folklore and ritual dances can be appreciated everywhere in the country and all the year round, religious feasts and festivals bring life and colour around all temples of Mother Goddesses.

The importance of Shakti sect is noticed everywhere in Nepal. Kali, Tara Sodashi, Bhairabi are Shakti Goddesses drawing equal respect of the Buddhists as well and Saraswati, Biswarepeni, Adisakti, Sarada, Bageswari, Brahamani and Brammabadheni are the Mother Goddesses and cherished by the Jains and Shaivas. Nepal is the only country in the world and has a tradition of religious tolerance which is truly amazing. So the people worship Mother Goddesses considering her as subtlest force to eradicate evils and to arrive at truth and brotherhood.

13 Nepal : Land of the Living Goddess

Kumari, a Sanskrit word literally means Virgin girl. When the word Vestal combined with Kumari signifies a girl of spotless chastity or a girl dedicated to celebacy. In the case of Raj Kumari the—Living Goddess of Kathmandu, on the other hand, stands significantly among "Mother Goddess". Raj Kumari—the Living Goddess of Kathmandu traditionally identified with either Goddess Taleju or the Goddess Durga, Hindu Pantheon, wife of Lord Shiva the third God of the Hindu triad, destroyer and reproducer, as Goddess of divine energy.

The origin of the Raj Kumari, the Living Goddess of Kathmandu is hazed in legends. Nonetheless, the Taleju Bhawani, a deity whose retincarnation instigated the Raj Kumari worship has been considered an essential rite of the Nepali people since early times. Historical account has it that Tulaja (Taleju) Bhavani was brought from Ayodhya, Kingdom of Lord Rama, the hero of the Hindu epic Ramayana to Bhaktapur, one of the ancient town of Kathmandu Valley by the King Harisimhadeva in 1323 A.D., getting installed at a number of places but it was not until many years after that a temple was built to her. Tuleju Bhavani was adopted as the tutelary divinity by the Malla kings of Nepal. So the Taleju temple is a intrinsic feature of all the three palaces in the Kathmandu Valley as Taleju Goddess was their family deity. All these Taleju temples of Kathmandu, Patan and Bhaktapur Durbar squares stand by their own specialities, but the one at

Kathmandu ranks over the others by its impressive tallest size. King Mahendra Malla of Kathmandu used to visit Bhaktapur every morning to worship Tulaja Devi appeared to him in a dream and told him to construct a temple for her in Kathmandu itself, so that he would not have to trouble by paying visits every morning from Kathmandu to Bhaktapur. Having divine ordain from the Tulaja Bhavani, King Mahendra Malla constructed the temple for her north of Hanuman Dhoka palace in 1563 A.D. This two tiered temple is regarded, one of the best example of pagoda style temple. This is the tallest of all the temples on the Hanuman Dhoka complex. This pagoda enshrines the historic image of Goddess Tulaja Bhavani, one of the incarnations of the female deity of the Hindus. Tulaja Bhavani was venerated by the medieval Malla Kings as their Guardian Deity and the temple was for many years, the private altar of the Malla kings. It is said that Malla kings could even have audience with the Goddess Tulaja Bhavani in person (in human form), when invoked. Legend has it that Tulaja Bhavani when prayed used to give divine instructions appearing in person to Malla kings from time to time. One night when Jaya Prakash Malla, the last Malla King of Malla dynasty (1428-1482 A.D.) was having audience in the gracious presence of the Goddess Tulaja in one of his rooms in Hanuman Dhoka Palace and asked him to play dice with her. The King Jaya Prakash Malla while playing with the Goddess excited and developed erotic thoughts about her. The Goddess at once came to know the amorous intention of the king and at once vanished. Later, the Goddess Tulaja Bhavani appeared in ethereal dream in which she warned him to be cautious about his reign and she would never appear before him in person. The Goddess advised him that she would incarnate herself now onwards in the form of a vestal virgin girl of the Newar Buddhist caste. Overcome the King realised his mistakes, hastened to carry the divine advice. He at once, called a gathering of his courtiers and priests and they advised him that those who melted gold and made ornaments could be considered a candidate for would be Kumari. So the would be Kumari was chosen from the Shakya community professionally engaged in making ornaments. Ever since, then the Kumari, vestal virgin of Kathmandu are selected for Shakya community of Newars who are by and large Buddhists. After this, King Jaya Prakash Malla hastened to build a temple for the Kumari who was yet to be selected. He built the temple and its courtyard in 1757 A.D. Although the tale of Tulaja Bhavani originated in the 10th Century under King Guna Kamadeva and later on King Harisimhadev and the Kumari sacrament predated the Malla dynasty, but the course of things were given their present form during the reign of King Jaya Prakash Malla in the mid-18th century. He also directed with instituting the drawing of the chariots of the Kumari and began the custom of seeking her blessing during Indra Jatra, the festival in veneration of God of rain. Kumari, hence considered Raj Kumari, Vestal virgin Goddess to be an, incarnation of the Goddess Taleju or Tulaja Bhawani, King Jaya Prakash Malla fulfilled all the predictions given by the Goddess. Goddess Taleju or Tulaja Bhawani's prediction became true since it was during the festival of Indra Jatra in 1768 that King Prithvi Narayan Shah Dev the "Father of Modern Nepal" marched with victory on the Kathmandu and thus ending Malla dynasty rule in Nepal.

The temple or the abode of Living Goddess, Raj Kumari is situated in the proximity of Hanuman Dhoka Palace Square. The temple or the residence of Raj Kumari is the house like edifice at the far end of the open courtyard known as Basantapur. The building is regarded as of high standard of craftsmanship owing to its profusely carved wooden balconies and window screens. The pleasing wood carving of the windows is of high quality. This building or abode of living Goddess is three-storeyed and it has quadrangle courtyard (Chowk or Bahal) richly set off with fine decor. The big windows on the first floor hold peacock portrait which represents life-like posture with a touch of reality and high quality of craftsmanship. The second floor windows are equally singular in outlook with two clumps of triple windows at either end painted black. The third storey of the building is especially attractive with its bay windows with circular makeup in the middle in which Raj Kumari appears from time to time escorted by her guardian prestress to watch and to present herself before her devotees. The roof of the building is supported by carved struts having images of various deities is crowned by the triple spire pinnacle. The inside courtyard or Kumari Chowk or Bahal as it is popularly known is also very attractive due to red and black colour decoration. There are square pillars not so much carved seen there supporting the structure of the building providing balance in tune of simplicity and intricacy. There is "torana" above the doors and windows. This building looks like a Buddhist monastic building as it also contains a Buddhist shrine on western site opposite the entrance door. There is a room in the second floor having eighteenth century wall painting used as Kumari shrine.

The Raj Kumari, vestal Virgin of Kathmandu is a Hindu Goddess but she is selected from a Buddhist caste. The remarkable feature of Nepal is the religious homogeneity that exists specifically between the Hindu and Buddhist communities. The concept of worshipping the Shakti Goddess was more popular in earlier days in the Kathmandu Valley. The worship of Goddess Kumari was in vogue ages before, so the cult of Kumari seems to be extremely old. Kumari is the Virgin form of Durga and the Parvati, the benevolent consort of God Shiva also appears in the intimidating form of Kali or Durga. The Parvati is the Shiva's Shakti and the Kumari is considered as the Virgin form of Durga. The tradition of Kumari, the living incarnation of Parvati or Durga or Shakti is unique to Nepal, a Buddhist cult accepted by the Hindus. Worship is offered by both Hindu and Buddhist. There is school of Shaktism, a branch of Tantricism (Hindu religious teaching and ritual instructions including the use of incantations, diagrams etc.) takes the Kumari as the Shakti or consort of Kumara. Actually for all Hindus of the Kathmandu Valley, the Kumari is a representative of the Goddess Durga. Though Kumari is selected from among the Sakya (Buddhist community) and yet it is a custom to regard as an incarnation of Taleju Bhagavati (a Hindu Goddess) and naturally even the religious rites of Taleju (Tulaja Bhawani) is performed according to Saiva sect of Vedic religion. This Co-existence of Hindu and Buddhist divinities shows the unique feature of Nepali culture. Every Newar town in the Kathmandu valley has a Kumari. As for example, Patan city has its own Living Goddess who resides in Gabahal with strict austerities as Kathmandu but with less prestige. Bhaktapur city has also its own Kumari but she has no austerities to follow and also no closed life. Bhaktapur Kumari makes a public appearance every year in Dasain or Durga Puja occasion. The people of Bunga, Chabahil, Kilgal and Thamel have their own Kumaries but they live normal lives but assume the Goddess roles only during a few festivals or special local events. The Kumari was fostered in order to provide Lord Matsyendranath, God of Rain and Harvest, a guardian and spiritual companion in Bungamati, a little known Newar village in southern Patan city. The institution of Kumari, the Living Goddess is so imbuded in the life and blood of Nepali people that every household having small child (female) who have not lost teeth and blood, performs "kumari Puja" literally meaning "Living Goddess" worship to them on the ninth day of Dasain or Durga Puja, the great and grand festival of Nepal. So the Nepal's rulers historically followed the dictum of religious homogeneity in order to promote the religious welfare of the people. The Thakur kings who founded Kantipur (Kathmandu city). Licchhavi kings, Medieval Malla kings and present Shah Dynasty survived the religious tradition in pretty much the same manner as in their inception. The people of Hindu or Buddhist religions observe traditional customs and rites that both religions demand.

Goddess Raj (Royal) Kumari or vestal virgin of Kathmandu is the most important and she is above all other Kumaries of Kathmandu valley. The girl chosen to represent the Goddess comes from Shakya, a Buddhist caste, though she personifies Taleju or Tulaja Bhavani a form of the Hindu Goddess Durga. The committee composed of high class priests make the selection according to physical characteristics. There may be more candidates, more than one at the time of selection. The small female child must have perfect health scratchless skin, black hair and eyes and she should be devoid of the slightest blemish. In order to be a divine Goddess, she must possess thirty-two perfections. If the child fulfils as criteria, she has to undergo tests. She is placed in a dark room with the bleeding cut off heads of buffaloes, various masked men like demons to frighten the child. If the little girl shows no sign of fear, she is chosen. After the selection, the Goddess Raj Kumari lives her life and entire time only few yards west of the old Royal Palace—Hanuman Dhoka. This building consisting of three floors with a central courtyard has a roof tiled in typical Nepali style with windows richly carved in wood. The building is a focal point in Kathmandu and where the Raj Kumari may make public appearance from a fine window on the third floor. A pre-menstructed girl who symbolizes the fully mother Goddess Tulaja (Taleju) Bhavani has a high place in the Nepali Pantheon. In such a way, after traditionally selected among the members of Newar Buddhist family of goldsmiths belonging to the specified clan of "Banra" or "Shakya" she lives within the confines of the Kumari Ghar at Durbar Square being the object of elaborate prayers every morning and visits of devotees for worship. She serves in this divine image until her first loss of blood either from a tooth loss, cut, nosebleed or menstruation. When this sign notices at which time it becomes necessary to choose a new one and the ex-Raj Kumari returns to normal life.

The Raj Kumari has an important place for socio-religious significance. During the day, the Raj Kumari is dressed and made up in such a way as to personify the Living Goddess—a peaceful, exquisitely beautiful child with no expressions of emotion. Her black hair is dressed up in a high top knot, showing a wide forehead in the middle of which a third eye distinctly put. Here eyes are touched with lamp black (mixed with oil) mixture which is applied in a line from the corner of each eye to her hair line. She dresses a long and red colour one piece gown, richly decorated with precious jewellery at them. The utmost care is taken to ensure that she always happy and healthy. Raj Kumari dressed in special attire and decked with a gold tiara. Raj Kumari in her divine dress and make-up gives the appearance of ethereal grace and charm of deity. Kumari means Vestal virgin and for the Living Goddess of Kathmandu, Newari tongue calls Devamaju (Goddess Mother) and for all others Raj Kumari because the King of Nepal pays homage to Kumari, the vestal virgin Goddess and the Goddess gives him her blessings.

Though Kumari worship and her annual festival existed among the Nepali in the ancient times also, but the annual lovely chariot festival in the present form was inaugurated by King Jaya Prakash Malla in the mid-eighteenth century. Indra Jatra vis-a-vis Chariot festival of Raj Kumari, Living Goddess both are celebrated with great fanfare and pious homage. The Living Goddess will makes her ceremonial public appearance on the occasion of the Indra Jatra festival. Indra Jatra is the most spectacular festival in honour of the King of the Gods, Indra. Lord Indra's chariot is carried in the shoulders and taken to different parts of the city for giving opportunity for all the people to pay homage to the deity. Indra Jatra festival has also attached with a legend which says that Indra had come down from heaven to Kathmandu to collect the flower Parijat 'Nyctanthes arbotretis' for his mother's Teej (festival of women) rites. The Great God Indra temple to steal from a garden in Kathmandu. But he was captured red-handed and kept as a prisoner. Indra's mother come to know about it and she hurriedly came to Kathmandu and requested the people of Kathmandu to let her sons free. Indra's mother promised the people of Kathmandu that she will bestow the dew and mist regularly in exchange of their benevolent acts, when she revealed her identity to the people, the people came to know about the reality and protested in his honour. The God Indra was pleased and went back to heaven with his mother. The week-long festival begins on the twelfth of Bhadra or early Aswin in September by creating Yashin or Lingo, a tall wooden pole brought from Nala area near Bhaktapur is installed representing the standard of Indra, the King of Gods, in Hanuman Dhoka Palace square. Wooden statues of Indra and large wooden masks of Bhairab are put on display in the old city areas. Many groups of ritual dances like the Devinach, Majipat Lakhe, Bhairab and Bhakku and Mahakali nach come into life and began dancing around the courtyard of Hanuman Dhoka putting masks and costumes to celebrate the Indra's visit. On the third day of the festival of India Jatra, the Living Goddess Raj Kumari is taken out in procession in a lavishly decorated chariot. Then the blessings of the Gods and Goddesses have invoked for the growth of crop. Indra—Rain God is very important for Nepali farmers because they have to depend for sufficient rain for good crop. Drought and famine can harm them. So the most important part of the festival of Indra Jatra is the chariot festival of Kumari, the Living Goddess. Living Goddess, Raj Kumari is taken out in a procession in a ornate chariot from her abode with the other two smaller chariots seated by Ganesh (Her brother, a symbol of wisdom and learning) and Bhairab (her father, the God of war and protection). The three chariots are dragged around the Kathmandu city amidst huge number of worshippers line up in the streets who pay respect to the Living Goddess and other gods by throwing vermilion powders, flowers and coins. The Raj Kumari image can be quite exciting during the chariot festival because she is decorated with the exotic jewels, tied up hair and third eye make up. In front, between and behind these moving chariots, the army regiments with their silver bands march in row with group of devotees with torches, incenses and masked dancers dancing gallantly. During the festival occasion, Mahakali, Mahalaxmi and Dashah Avatar (ten kinds of incarnation of God Vishnu) are staged on the plinth of Narayan Temple just opposite the Kumari abode. Bairab and Lakhe dances are the most spectacular of all dances. The dance of Bhairab with his followers Bhakku is also equally interesting.

Nepali people not only worship idols but also practice a custom of regarding a vestal virgin Raj Kumari (the symbol of purity) as a Goddess. The famous bahal of Kumari stands on the south of Hanuman Dhoka where a female child selected by an esoteric process is reverently housed as Raj Kumari or Living Goddess. The King and the people all pay homage to Living Goddess with all devotion.

14 *Temples of Goddess Kali or Shakti in Nepal*

Large number of temples and shrines are dedicated to the Goddess Kali or Shakti, the female aspect of Shiva, one of the God of Hindu triad. The harmonious balance between opposites evolved from the ages gone by into a system of worshipping male and female forces. This particular system of worship further crystallized in the form of Shiva-Lingum in perfect union with Shakti-Yonis, giving rise to the Shiva-Shakti cult. In the Shakti sect, female or sexual energy is worshipped as the Goddess Durga, Kali etc. and Shiva is considered to be the guardian and protector of Nepal. One finds a temple of God Shiva and close by a symbol or temple of Shakti. Shiva's power can not be fulfilled without the aid of Shakti. Tantrism is based on the worship of the Shiva cult who is the destroyer and regenerator of all things. The regeneration of the entire world depends on the procreational union of male and female. Absolute consciousness as Shiva is manifested in the male principle, and power as Shakti is manifested in the female principles. The creative process is possible only through the union of these two principles.

In the beginning of the fourteenth country B.C. Nepal came under the influence of a new religious movement that culminated in the belief of uncommon spiritual powers comprising of magic charms, dealings with the dead as means of divination and use of large number of abstract symbols.

The new religion is named after its holy texts, the Tantra or it is commonly known as Tantrism.

Tantrism can be called an amalgam of Hinduism, particularly of Shiva worship and Buddhism bringing about a kind of blending of the two religions. The reconciliation is to be noticed even today in Nepal where Buddhists visit Hindu temples and vice versa.

Tantrism is defined as the extension or elaboration of the knowledge for the perfection of the wisdom or intuition. So the Vajrayana Buddhist believe in the idea of the full identity of Nirvaṇa and Samsara which ascribe the absolute and the phenomenal modes of existence. Tantrism lays stress on its systematic emphasis on the identity of the absolute (Paramarth) and the phenomenal (Vyavahara) world filtered through the experience of sadhana.

Tantrism symbolizes the images of Lord Shiva representing his five aspects Vamadeva, Tatpurvas, Aghora, Sadyata and Isana, giving different colours, different directional controls etc. In the same way the five Dhyni Buddhas also have attributed different colours and directions. Tantrism is generally associated with the images of Lord Shiva, Ganesh, Bhairava, Visparupa, Navatmaka, Heruka, Mahasamvara, Vajravarahi etc. (male aspects) and Kali, Chinnamasta, Brahmani, Maheswari, Vaishnavi etc. and fifty four Yoginis on all their frenzied female grandeur. It maintains that it is possible to utilize the supernatural powers of these terrible gods and goddesses if one is acquainted with the magic practices. A person well-versed with special Tantric knowledge skill and training is then able to do or compel deities to appear by invocation at will and to associate himself to their powers.

Tantrism is said to be based on three mystic words of hidden meaning such as Bija (mystic symbols), Mantra (magic spells) and Mudra (significant gestures). It is connected with the notion on the oneness of everything, deep thought on the profound connections between microcosm and macrocosm. The deep meditation of images and the absorption into them, is the most important element for tantric practices. It casts spell on the female element and on the pleasures of the senses. Female goddess like Tara and Vidya are symbolized as keeping control over knowledge or spells (Vidyadhani) and having a power of moving freely in the air, their bodies are as swift as quicksilver (Urdhvatandava).

Buddhists who follow Tantrism has given it a new name-Vajrayana (Diamond Vehicle) after the symbol Vajra (Thunderbolt) which represents magical dagger. The word is also related to connote the emptiness or nothingness (Sunyata) which Vajrayanists regard as the absolute. It is also used to signify the phallus—'Thunderbolt' or Mani (Jewel) and the female organ is 'Padma'—i.e. lotus. In this way, Vajrayana regards a way to salvation by means of the sacred enjoyment of love. It considers love-making an indirect sanctification and a way to salvation.

Tantrism welcomes all devotees irrespective of caste, creed, sex or wealth. Bhairava who is regarded as manifestation of God Shiva, the Hindu God is equally worshipped by Hindus and Buddhists in Nepal. It unites Shakti, Shiva and Bhaisnava and Known as Vajrayana in Buddhist terminology and its influence is pervaded all the religious practices relating to various sects in Nepal.

Buddhas and Bodhisatvas permit female counterparts which serve as their Saktis or strong powers. Example for it is not far to seek—Mahasamrava is represented with 17 to 74 heads and is depicted in sexual union with his Sakti—an imagination of greatest force that is focused to blast the whole universe. Likewise, Vajravarahi is depicted as holding human skulls full of blood in the hands. All these teachings and rituals do not confirm to practice of Buddhist frame-work, however, they mean ancient popular religion, the profound faith and belief in great Mother Goddess and in the sacredness of the act of procreation.

Tantirc images which we usually see in the Buddhist framework depict the unique symbol of the female sex embracing the male. The symbols usually refer to male and male stands for Buddhist principles. The male figure represents the expression of compassion. The female image represents Prajna or spiritual mystery—the knowledge and the symbol of Absolute, Shunya, the void.

The centre of pilgrimage is known as Pitha (seat) in the tantric tradition. There are four kinds of Pithas as written in Buddhist texts viz., Atmapitha (the temple of the self) Para-Pitha (the temple of supreme), Yoga-Pitha (the temple of meditation and asceticism) and Guhya-Pitha (the secret esoteric Temple). These Tantric texts also speak of various kinds of Vajrasatvas and their copulation with the Yoginis with Prajnaparamita and others.

The Tantras indulge in six Sandhya language. Madya is used to refer to the nectarine essence ozzing out of he brain where the soul resides, Matsya means the suppression of vital airs, Mamsa is the vow silence, Mudra means the counting of figures during religious worship—a process for the enhancement of the concentration of the worshipper. Maithuna is meditation on acts of creation and destruction. According to Sandha usage, Bodhicitta means 'Semen, Vigour or strength. Bodhi-citta results from the union of Prajna and Upaya which are considered as the male and the female deities in sexual union. It signifies on parallelism between metaphysical conceptions and physical events. Sexual polarity symbolism are shown both from a psychological and a mythological angle to make clear the creative or emanative function of the intellectual intuition more static and dynamic. This type of thought is common to all ancient cosmic thinkers.

The mainspring of Tantric philosophy revolves round the notion that the whole universe with the totality of its phenomena forms one single whole in which even the minute element has a powerful effect to the largest, thus forming the eternal foundation solid and string.

While elaborating the essences of Tantricism, it is easier to understand the elements of religion in Nepal. There are Tantric strains both in Hinduism and Buddhims in Nepal. One of the objective of Tantrism usually refers Sakti. The most famous temple of Sati, dedicated to God Shiva's consort, Goddess Parvati is situated about a quarter kilometer beyond God Pashupatinath temple known as Guheshwori temple on the opposite bank of the Bagmati river. This temple is dedicated to Shiva's Shakti in her manifestation as Kali or Durga. The whole structure of this temple is designed after the tantric Yantra or geometric triangle signifying the female principle of procreation. The Hindu mythology predicts that a decomposed body of Satidevi, Shiva's consort was carried by God Shiva after taking her body from her father's house Dakshaya Prajapati as she sacrificed herself in the sacrificial fire by jumping in it to avenge the insult caused by him insulting to her husband Siva and her sacred part was dropped in the place where now stands as Guheshwori. Guheshwori, the word itself signifies the secret Goddess or the Great Mother. The superstructure of this temple is modelled after Tantric Yantra or symbolic design suitable to Guheshwori who herself is represented inside the temple by the simple female sign of the geometric triangle representing sacred organ. This temple is single-storey shrine with latticed windows. It has a golden gate with torana having Vhanduva, Jhadar Kinkijal and Nagas. The main sanctum of the temple have imges of Guheshwori kunda and Bhairab, Asthamatrika, Shiva Bhagwati, Vasuki and Guhyakali. The Goddess in the form of a Kalasha (jar) is in a sunken spot in the courtyard.

The unusual structure of the temple is remarkable and it is situated in a courtyard lined by rest houses. The temple has the simple arched construction of tubular metal works. Towards the top it transforms itself into four gilded snakes which maintain the crowning piece of the roof. Its construction is quite peculiar feature. This temple has prehistoric mythology which refers that this temple was constructed during the reign of King Shanker Dev of the Lichhavi period with the help of great Tantric Narisingha Thakur by name. King Pratap Malla got the temple repaired with the advice of a noted Tantric Lamba Karna Bhatta in the year 1654 A.D. Later on King Rana Bahadur Shah presented various musical instruments to be used, during the prayer and worship of the Goddess in the temples. As already told the temple of Guheshwori houses no idol of any Goddess. Devotees worship in a holy orifice which has been regarded as the place of worship since time immemorial.

After Guheshwori, there are many Kali shrines in Nepal, but the important ones are Dakshinkali, Bhadrakali, Raktakali, Naradevi, Maitidevi, Shobha Bhagbati, Bindhyabashini, Maisthan etc. Goddess Kali or Durga has many forms both awesome and peaceful. Kali or Durga is considered as Sakti having divine energy in Hinduism. Durga, Bhawani Mai, Bhagbati are various names. Kali or Durga is worshipped by offerings of blood—animal sacrifices.

Dakshinkali is the black goddess—black refers the most terrifying aspect of Shakti. The temple of Dakshinkali is located about twenty-two km. from Kathmandu city. The famous shrine of Dakshinkali is situated at the southern most of the Kathmandu valley. She is regarded as the most powerful and benevolent Goddess. She is one of the very important places of pilgrimage of Goddess which dates back to time immemorial. This sacred place lies at the southern edge of the valley, by passing Chobar gorge and the Bagmati. Devotees visit each Tuesday and Saturday to make sacrificial offerings of chicken and goats to Kali. Actually it is two kilometers from Pharping.

The temple of Dakshinkali is also designed after Tantra-Yantra—the geometric trinangle signifying the female principle of procreation. It has an open arched metal roofs which contain four figures of gilded snakes supporting the crowning part. The temple courtyard is paved and the entrance to the temple guarded by row of metallic lions—vehicles of the goddess. There is a small idol of Bhairab on the left side of the courtyard under a canopy. The side walls are full of images of Ganesh and other goddess. The idol of Dakshinkali is placed in front of the main entrance on the left side. She is beautifully decorated with a tiara and various ornaments. The goddess is represented with eight arms standing on her legs and raising her body upon to Shiva, justifying victory. There is a place for priests of the shrine on the right side, and they receive visitor's offerings and sacrificing of animals. Just above the Dakshinkali image is beautiful metallic tympanum (toran), containing Makara (alligator), sea monsters and serpent maids. A large peacock is imprinted on the left side of the image on squared marble slabs as decoration. The temple walls are painted with sketches of human skeletons signifying of various spirits and super human beings all around the goddess.

The temple of Bhadrakali is centrally situated in between Singha Durbar and Shahid gate. The goddess is also popular as Lumhri, the trinity of Mahakali Lumhri and Shankata. The word Bhadra refers "good" and Kali means the wife of Shiva in her terrible form of the female power. She is regarded as a destroyer of demons. This temple is known as Lunmashi Devi temple in Newari Language "Lunmashi" means loaf of gold. There is legend attached with this temple. This area was once farmland in ancient time. A farmer heard a girl crying in a pitiful way one day while he was on the works in his farm. He tried his best for finding the girl near by and tried to control her from the grief offering her the loaf of bread which he had brought from his own home. But to his surprise, the girl at once vanished leaving the loaf where it was but the loaf turned into gold. Having notice such a occurrence, the temple was build on this holy spot and now is a pilgrimage spot.

Shova Bhagawati—The shrine of Shova Bhagawati is situated on the bank of the Vishnumati River, just west of Kathmandu on the way to Swayambhunath stupa. She is also considered a goddess to fulfill all the wishes of her devotees. The temple is small but is favourite goddess of the Kathmandu valley. Close to the Shova Bhagavati temple there are two temples of Bijeswori and Indrayani—other important manifestations of the mother goddess. Similarly, such places Raktakali, Naradevi, Maitidevi and many others are scattered all over the Kathmandu valley each having their own legendary history. These all goddesses are regarded as Shakti which represent divine energy. Shakti is considered as the Mother Goddess which is embodied in the consort of God Shiva, Parvati who appears in the different names and forms of Kali or Durga.

Sankhu : There are various shrines of Yoginis in

Kathmandu valley. Yogini means mystical goddesses and the cult related to it. Sankhu is located on hillsides twelve kilometres east of Kathmandu. By passing a small ancient Newari town, up a long flight of stone steps is Bajra Yogini temple.

The Bajra Yogini temple constructed on a tall hillock over a single huge stone in 1276 B.C. consisting of nine Dhunge Dharas (Stone water spouts), nine pokharis (ponds) and nine Guphas (caves). The lengend of the goddess Bajra Yogini is depicted as a supreme power holding a tantric weapon called Bajra. She is also called Khadga Yoginis because she holds Khadga (a magic weapon). She is female deity.

The shrine of Mother Goddess (Bajra Yogini) is about 2 meters tall with two separate temples and two similar figures with different colours for the same idols referring different meaning as red figure symbolises anger and temper whereas the yellow indicates peace, calm and serenity. The devotees are forbidden to touch the red figures since it is believed that it will cause to destruction. So the devotees only worship the yellow figures.

The Licchhavi Kings, Manadeva and AmsuVarma are also associated with the history of Bajra Yogini. In late Malla inscriptions, she is referred to Ugra Tara. The present three tiered structure of the temple is erected by King Pratap Malla. Later on renovated by the King Mahendra Malla. Afterwards it was repeated by Queen Rajya Laxmi Devi Shah wife of King Rana Bahadur Shah in 19th century. In the eleventh century, a Buddha image was installed at Gu Bihar known as Buddha Sakyamuni and is worshipped as an supreme image in the shrine of Bajra Yogini today. This clearly indicates the Hinduism and Buddhism assimilation of the Goddess Kali as one supreme female Tantric deity and reverence to her.

In the same manner, there is famous temples at Pharping and Bijayaswori near Sobha Bhagwati. These yoginis are also represented as Ashta Matrika—the divine mother goddesses the terrible forms of Tantric gods. There are many depiction of Ashta Matrika images are carved on the struts of temple and even sculptured in stone.

Nepal has a remarkable tradition of synthesis and mutual toleration among different faiths. The people venerate Hinduism. Buddhism and Vaishnavism are the three main faiths. Closely liked to Hinduism is Buddhism. It has attached deep into the Nepali life. From the tenth century A.D. onwards, a mystic and esoteric religion developed. At this time, the earlier Buddhism entered into powerful Tantric Vajrayana sect. The female or Shakti element and sex were freely introduced in both Hinduism and Buddhism and attitude of acceptance and assimilation has been the stimulus for the Nepali culture. So the goddess Parvati is the Shiva's Shakti. Kumari is the Virgin form of Durga, another name for Shakti. The tradition of Kumari, the living incarnation of Parvati or Durga or Shakti is unique to Nepal, a Buddhist cult accepted by the Hindus. Worshippers visit equally both by Hindus and Buddhists to many Kali shrines and pay homage to her and sacrifice live pigeons, hens, goats, flowers, incense, sandal paste in order to please their beloved and benevolent mother goddesses.

15 *Reputed Temples of Yogini in Kathmandu Valley*

Yogini is believed as female form of the gods as Shakti with most energetic powers in Hinduism. No creation can happen without the inclusion of the female energy. The most powerful female principle, Shakti or by different name Yogini is embodied as the consort of God Shiva, one of the Trinity of Hindu religion. The duality concept of God Shiva is prevailed in the duality idea of Shiva—Shakti but female principle denotes the significant inception of Hindu Cosmogony and as so rank at the source of worship.

God Shiva has popular with many names and his consort is also known by different names. Shakti is also provinced and regarded the Mother Goddess who has mentioned by different names as Parvati, Gouri, Devi, Durga, Chandi, Kali, Sati and Yogini.

Female Goddess is represented by two features of the female power, one benignant and another destructive. So female Goddess has shown differently in her two aspects, Her destructive representation is shown with a horrible and fearful, appearance.

Nepal has been a melting pot of diverse linguistic and ethnic groups. The temperate highlands are the natural home of the Mongoloid tribes while the lower tropical and sub-tropical zone are the habitats of the caste-stratified Cakasoids.

Nepal is the only Kingdom in the world. Religion is an

integral part of Nepali life. There main religious creeds namely, Hinduism, Buddhism and Trantricism prevail in Nepal. The Nepali people observe various forms of Hinduism such as Shaiva, Bhaisnava, Buddha Sakta, Nath in both tantric and non-tantric forms. Shiva as well as Vishnu both have occupied an unique position in the religious belief of the people.

Hinduism is based on the Vedas, Upnishads and the Puranas, its religious texts. It has a basic trinity of three Gods, Brahma, the Creater, Vishnu the Preserver and Shiva, the Destroyer. Besides, two of Vishnu's other incarnations—Rama and Krishna, the heroes of Classical epics Ramayana and Mahabharat are also worshipped by the Hindus. Other deities like Ganesh, Bhairab etc. are also revered. The cult of Mother Goddesses too, occupies a prominent place in Hindu pantheon. Nepal has a tradition of religious tolerance. Hinduism and Buddhism are the two major religions of Nepal, which exist simultaneously in an amicable and harmonious atmosphere.

Buddhist beliefs and practices date lack to Nepal since the time of its founder, Gautam the Buddha, who was born at Lumbini in west Nepal Terai in about 623 B.C. He was a prince who relinquished royal in search of enlightenment. He preached the Eight-fold path for the liberation of human soul from worldly bondage and the endless wheel of existence. The Eight-fold path included right understanding, Right Resolve, Right speech, right action right living, right effort, right mindfulness and right meditation.

In about 100 A.D., Buddhism split into schools of Hinayana and Mahayana. Hinayana does not practice idolatry while Mahayana worships the idols of Buddha. The Nepali Buddhists are the followers of Mahayana School. One of the main beliefs of this doctrine is that man can liberate himself by "Bodhi" meaning essence. Very few other Nepali Buddhists have adopted the Hinayana School of thought, choosing rather to follow Mahayana Teaching.

The Mahayana canon contains a larger proportion of the esoteric wisdom than any other religion and has always adhered more closely to the "Heart" as distinct from the "Eye" doctrine, the eternal life rather than the changing form of the Message.

Tantrism had greatly influenced Nepali Buddhism by creating the path of Vajrayana "The Path of the Thunderbolt." The main object used in Vajrayana Buddhist ritual is a small thunderbolt like septre that is said to represent the infinite in three dimensions.

Buddhism, as it appears in Nepal belongs to a third "School" which as already told, has often been called the third vehicle—Vajraya or Lamaism i.e. a school strongly influenced by Tantrism.

Lamaism, as the Buddhism of Tibet is to be described is a mixture of the best and worst of Buddhism and much that lies between. At its best, it is a noble part of the Mahayana.

Lama means the "superior one." It is a term which should be referred for the heads of monasteries and the highest dignitaries but by courtesy is given to all of the fully ordained rank.

By the sixteenth century, the various schools of Tibetan Buddhism mere reasonably well defined. The established Church as it were, is the Gelungpa or Yellow Hat' sect. Next popular by the name of Kargyit-pat sect founded in the Eleventh century by Marpa. This may be called the semi-reformed sect and its members shut themselves in caves on the hills or caves eating minimum of food and water given by their disciples.

Another is Nyerigmapa or Red Hat Order, the unreformed Buddhism of Padma Sambhava, which was first introduced to Talent in the middle of the 7th Century A.D. Padma Sambhava was also known as Guru Rimpoche.

Tantrism's origin is found in the ancient worship of the Shiva-cult, the followers of Lord Shiva who is the destroyer and regenerator of all things. The regenerators of the entire world depends on the procreational union of male and female. Absolute consciousness, as Shiva is shown as the male principle, and pioneer as Shakti is manifested as the female principle.

Tantrism is practised both by Hindus and Buddhists in Nepal. Tantra is so much important in the religious beliefs that Nepal has preserved rich divinities for the study of high ideas in the forms, of Yoginis. Tantricism maintains that it is possible to make use of the powers of these Goddesses. Yoginis of devotee are initiated into certain magic practices by following strict texts relating to them. The devotee is then able to conjure up deities at will and to acquire himself to their powers. So the central Sadhaka of tantricism, Buddhist and Hindu alike, is the exercise of sexual contact under tantric "Labotatory" conditions. Like the Hindu Gods, Buddha and Buddhisatvas are allowed female which act as their Shaktis or female powers Hinduism and Buddhism both refer Shakti, the female principle and performance of esoteric rites as well as sacrifices.

Yogini, a word meaning a female Goddess usually attached to Vajrayana Buddhism, Many versions of the Yogini gained importance in Nepal, exist since ancient times. Goddess Yogini's temples are situated in the four different parts of the country. They are Khadga Yogini is located in the direction of east, Bajra Yogini in the south, Bidyadhari Yogini in the west and Nairatma Yogini in the north. Yogini is a Tantric deity in female form and the Buddhist religion and cult practices Yoga meditation, esoteric rites and fervent religious activity and handling of the ritualistic "ingredients" attached to symbolic occultism, magic and image-worshipping.

Tantricism as defined in this treatise as the extension or elaboration of the knowledge for the perfection of the wisdom or intuition. So the Vajrayana Buddhists believe in the idea of the full identity of Nirvana and Samsara which ascribes the absolute and the phenomenal modes of existence. Tantrism lays stress on its systematic emphasis on the identity of the absolute (Paramartha) and the phenomenal (Vyavahara) would filtered through the experience of Sadhava.

In tantric Buddhist tradition, the devotee takes refuge in Triple gems which is called as the outer refuge. The shelter of the inner refuge is said to be Gurus, Istadevas and Dakinis. Dakinis are generally representatives of Sangha in the inner refuge. They are peaceful as well as fierce or furious. They are represented with bone ornaments, some are shown in dancing as well as some in almost nude. These Dakinis are said to be a traveller in empty space and so sky-goers. They usually guide the devotee by clearing different obstructors and helping to realise the path of enlightenment. They are skilful to grant eight super-powers-Astasiddhi to all devoted devotees. These Dakinis are animal faces like Sambavaktra (lion-faced), Vajra-vahahi (Boar-faced), Sardula Mukha (tiger-faced) and many others. Vajrajigine is said to be Sarva-Buddha Dakini who grants Buddhahood to the devotees. So all Dakinis are said to be the assignee of wisdom or Prajnapeeranuta.

An important pilgrimage of worship is also the sacred spot of Yoginis circumfused in the four different parts of the Kathmandu Valley. They represent as Khadga Yogini in the east, Bajra Yogini in the south; Bidyadhari in the west and Nairatma in the north parts of the Valley. These Goddesses plays a big role in the Yoga meditation in the Buddhist religious cult and are called female tantric deity.

The temple of Khadga Yogini is situated in Pharping Hill. Pharping was a township sense long times before. It is considered to be a place where Padmasambhava, the founder of Lamaistic school of Buddhism in Tibet, a great scholar from Nalanda University of India mediated in this hill of Pharping. So there are many Buddhist monasteries noticed even to-day around here. Pharping is located between the beautiful hills of Champa Devi and the western slope of Mahabharat mountain.

Pharping is the present name but it was known by its ancient name PHAN-PEE-GU and SHIKHARAPURE NAGARI. It is situated on 1500 m. altitude above sea level on the lap of green hill Chandagiri between the holy places—Ashura Cave Sheshanarayan. It is about 20 kms south of Kathmandu city. The pilgrims walk through monasteries and green and lovely hill and also to the famous shrine of

Sheshanarayan, temple of Narayan built in and around 239 A.D. After this Narayan temple, the pilgrims arrive at Chovar gorge. There is also a temple of Jalabeenayaka, the elephant headed God.

Pharping is surrounded by a lovely natural beauty of green hill, streams, jungle, temples and monasteries. The most famous temple of Kali Goddess known as Dakchukali is situated on the southern part of it separated by two streams.

The temple of Khadga Yogini temple is located in a hill of medium height on a single huge stone. It is believed to have been built in 1276 B.C. There are some about nine stone water sports, nine ponds and nine caves around the temple. The temple of Mother Goddess Khadga Yogini is, about 2 meters tall consisting of two in numbers and the images within these temples consisted of same images but with different colours indicating two different meanings. The real image symbolizes anger and heat while the yellow image signifies peace, calm and security. The worshippers are forbidden to touch the red image since it is said that this will lead to destruction. So the worshippers worship only the yellow image. Both the Hindus and Buddhists worship the goddess. Bajra Yogini represents the wrathful Goddess to keep away the civil sports and so she is worshipped by offering Bali (animal sacrifices, and blood-shed because she is a Tantric Goddess. She is ferocious by nature and holds or throw her weight an two corpses on her feet—an act of conveying arrogant and high-handed feelings.

As per legend, Bajra Yogini is the mother Goddess holding a tantric reform called Bajra (thunder bolt). She is also called Khadga Yogini as she also holds Khadga (a magic sword). Bajrayan Buddhism has presented Yoginis and among them Khadga Yogini and Bajra Yogini who has in hand a sword and a Bajra (a thunderbolt) respectfully.

Shaktipithas (pilgrimages) are many in Nepal and also Shakta festivals are celebrated in many places in traditional ways. The Buddhist shrines of the Yoginis are all looked after by the Bajracharyas. Bajracharyas are the High Priest of the Buddhist shrines including Yoginis. They always in charge of Bahal or Bahil from ancient times and they are assigned the right of exclusive care for them. The hymn or invocation of all Bajrayan texts are in Sanskrit language, the classical language of south Asia. All temples of Yoginis are under the control of the Bajracharya.

There are innumerable shrines in Kathmandu Valley assigned to the cult of female deities Yoginis. The principal shrines of these secret goddesses are located on hill sides at the ancient township of Pharping which has already been described above and next on at the old town of Sankhu and another one at Bijayeshori near Shabha Bhagawati.

After the Khadga Yogini shrine of Pharping, there is another shrine of Yogini at Sankhu, a legendary township 23 kilometres north-east of Kathmandu centre. It derives its name from Sankhapura which means conch shaped town. This township used to be one of a very popular trade route to Tibet from 7th to 19th century A.D. There are numbers of ancient houses, raised pavilious and forts of by gone age, a stone paved path way for half an hour walk, the temple of Bajra Yogini arrives. It is in the middle of a hill surrounded by green forest. Many caves on rocks exist for mediators.

The temple of Dakshinkali is located about 22 kms from Kathmandu city. The road going to the temple is covered with many lovely rural views and interesting panorama. The first place arrives a small Newar township known as Kirtipur through a motorable road. It has a beautiful Ashoka stupa and the temples of Baghhairab and Uma Maheshwara. Further from here along the way to Dakshin Kali is a gate having yellow signboard having the words "Ishwari Marg" i.e. road to Goddess. From the gate, the pilgrim goes up the stairs to reach Chovar village. Here is a famous temple dedicated to Adinath, constructed during the early Lichhavi period.

The Chovar has gorge, legend has it that the kathmandu. Valley was formerly a lake until a saint named Manjushri cut through the hill here with his divine sword, letting the water drain out. After desending the hill near the gorge pilgrim arrives the famous temple of Jal Vinayak or Ganesh the elephant-headed deity. Then Taudaha like is noticed and after Sheshnarayan temple approaches. Then this direction leads to the town of Shankhu. From the northern part of Sankhu town, there are narrow road which carries the pilgrims to the magnificent temple of Bajra Yogini. A motorable road leads upto the foot of the hill below the temple area from where it is a steep climb of 15 minutes to reach the temple. Many stone water sports, Buddhist Chaityas and temples are scattered on the trail. The forest has Buddhist Gumbihar temple complex which is very interesting to visit. A small temple of Chhetrapala Bhairab approaches. There after comes flight of stone stairs leading to the temples of Bajra Yogini. Firstly pilgrims arrive at a large stone lions located at the western side of the temple complex.

Bajra Yogini temple of Shankhu is of three tiered pagoda built around 17th century. This temple is full of artistic and traditional architectural marvel. Innumerable bells be outside the temple. The front entrance of the temple is guarded by a pair of lions. The King of Sankhu, named as Sankhadev is considered to be the builder of this temple. The walls and struts of the temple are full of carved images of gods and goddesses. There is an dreadful image of Bajra Yogini with Khadga (dagger) in hand and flanked by Simheni and Byaghrini (Lion and Tiger faced female Goddesses). The steeple of the temple crowns it with its shining golden colour. A tall stone column stands in front of the temple having a magnificent brass lion atop facing the temple.

There is two tiered temple of Buddha very near to Bajra Yogini temple. This Buddha temple is built in pagoda temple which is one of the few examples in the country. This shows the example of religious amity and tolerance in Nepal.

Bajra Yogini is the most important goddess for the resident of Sankha as well as for the people of Nepal. The goddess is very popular for the pilgrims. This venerated temple is very venerated as she has got a very powerful attraction due to her wish fulfilling graces to her devotees.

The temple of Bajra Yogini is visited and worshipped by both Hindus and Buddhists. The main priest of the temple is a Buddhist but the large number of visitors to this temple are Hindus. This shows an example of the religious harmony and tolerance between two religions—Hinduism and Buddhism.

While writing about Yoginis, it will be better to write about the Goddess Dakshinkali. The temple of Dakshinkali is situated about two kilometres from Pharping. Pilgrims congregate at this temple to sacrifice the animals every Tuesday and Saturday and worship the goddess Kali. Actually speaking, Dakshinkali is an image of Chamunda standing on a *betal* (a corpse). Her loved companions are Astamatrikays, Kumara and Ganesh who always accompany the goddess.

A little above the temple of Goddess Dakshinkali, lies the shrine of Brahmi who happens to be the mother of Dakshinkali.

The image of Goddess Dakshinkali, the most powerful female deity is kept on the left side of the main entrance. Her idol is very much decorated with a glittering tiara and many other ornaments. The Goddess is shown having eight-armed on standing posture and her body seems to be lifted up a little onto an image of Lord Shiva, pointing victory over time.

A beautiful metallic tympanum is above the Goddess Dakshin Kali, depicting Makara (alligator), sea-monsters and serpent minds. On the left side of the image is a piece of square slab with a large peacock figure engraved in it for decoration. The temple walls in some places are painted with human skeletons which signify the ideas of various evil spirits and demons, which are always around the Goddess.

It is recorded that King Pratap Malla constructed a beautiful temple for Goddess Dakshinkali. This shrine, along with the Bajra Yogini temple are situated in the south cardinal point of Kathmandu Valley. Dakshin means South.

Chmapadevi is a hill having 2278 m. height and is situated on the western side of the hill surrounding Kathmandu Valley. The track to the hill starts from Pikhel on the way to Dakshin Kali. Dakshinkali and Pharping is situated two kilometres apart.

Kathmandu valley is very famous for the cult of female deities and many shrines are scattered all over the valley dedicated to the cult of female Goddess. The worship of mother Goddess is recorded since long in the history of the country. Many ethnic groups since long showed a remarkable affinity for the maintenance of social and ritual organisations showing respect and love for females as chiefs of the communities.

The Kirats of East Nepal one of the ancient ethnic group of Nepal also worship mother Goddess as their chief deity. There are visual evidences of organised rites and festivities followed by these communities to pay homage to their guardian deity a number of her manifestations. There are many ethnic groups in Terai as well worship the Mother Goddess in different forms and names. The unique character of Nepali culture is unity and oneness in diversity. There are many castes and creeds but no rigidity. There is religious tolerance everywhere. Everything is based on compromise and understanding. This unity of tolerance is evidenced by the shrines of Goddess Yogini. Existence of Hindu and Buddhist temples side by side here exemplifies the religious harmony and tolerance in Nepal. Another singular features of the Yogini temples, the main priest who conducts the daily rituals and prayers to the Goddesses, also worship the Buddhist shrines existing nearby. While worshipping the sacramental rituals in Bajra Yogini temple, the main priest, though he represents Buddhism and named Bajracharya he follows purely Hindu rules and traditions. The same person in Buddhist temples, performs the rituals in accordance with the rule of Buddhist texts.

The shrines of Yoginis are seen in existence in many places of Kathmandu valley specially in the complex having Buddhist stupas and Chaityas. Many scholar and experts on Vajrayana maintain that there are four Principal Yoginis in Kathmandu Valley and these deities are situated in the cardinal points of the valley guarding it from equal catastrophes. To be in preuse form—the temple of Khadga Yogini in Pharping in the east, Bajra Yogini in the township of Sankhu in the south, Bidyadhari in Swayambhu in the west, and Nairatma in Balaju in the north. It is also remarked that there is a shrine of Yogini at Bijayiswari near Shovabhagawati. Kathmandu valley has always been a renowned centre for Buddhism and Buddhist rituals and rites since time immemortial. Besides these famous temples of Yoginis, there are many Vihars (monasteries), Vahis (small monasteries) and various places of Buddhist learning, a thorough research and search will have to be made in order to know more about the theology attached with them.

16 Lumbini : A Great Pilgrimage Site

Lumbini is situated in the south-western Terai of Nepal. This holy place is regarded as the most venerated site to the millions of Budhists all over the world. Lumbini is the most sacred place where Lord Buddha—the apostle of peace and compassion was born in 623 B.C.. This place is full of many kinds of artistic, historical and cultural treasures as all these evidenced even up till now by laying many ancient ruins of by-gone ages all around. Many international Buddhist visitors from all over the world pay visit this pilgrimage site where ancient monuments epitomize the birth-place of the Buddha.

This place is the sacred place for the Buddhist and the sacred Buddhist pilgrimage site. This sacred place was at the eastern edge of Sakyan Kingdom of Kapilvastu on the bank of Telar river in ancient time. It was famous for the natural beauty and calm environment due to shady grove of Sal trees and many kinds of flowering plants. Maya Devi, the queen of Sakya King Suddhodava of Kapilvastu, gave birth to a baby while visiting to her maternal home Devadaha via. Lumbini. By chance, Maya Devi gave birth of a baby by holding a branch of a tree with the pangs of labour on the Vaisakha full moon day 623 years before the birth of Christ. Such kind of description is given about the divine birth where Queen Maya Devi gave birth to Prince Siddhartha so, Lumbini is the birth-place of Lord Gautam Buddha, the prince of peace.

Maurya Emperor Ashoka visited this sacred place in a Pilgrimage and erected a stone pillar in 249 B.C. with inscription citing "The Buddha, the sage of the Sakyas, was born here." Slowly Maya Devi temple was also constructed by passing time and the favours Maya Devi sculpture was carved and installed in 2nd-4th century. The old monastery the artistic stone image of Maya Devi, the mother of Gautam Buddha are important relics that are worth visiting at Lumbini Garden.

Lumbini Garden, the nativity of Lord Buddha was visited by a famous Chinese traveller Fd-Hien. He described in his travel account the tree of nativity, bathing tank well and other religious places such as Kapilvastu and Devadaha in the beginning of 5th century.

Similarly, another famous Chinese traveller Huein-Tsang visited Lumbini in 7th Century A.D. He also had given many kinds of descriptions about Lumbini and its surroundings. In such a way, many devotees of Buddhism visited this sacred place and has an unbroken tradition of pilgrimage to Lumbini

Regarding the importance of sacred place Lumbini, His Majesty's Government of Nepal has considered the integrated regional development along the North-south axis as a necessity for smooth and balanced economic growth of the country. So the development of the Gandaki/Lumbini zone in which Lumbini, the birth-place of Buddha lies, has been given top priority. In order to cover up the technical assistance and financing, HMG requested United Nations Development Programme (UNDP) for assistance. Then, a joint venture had been undertaken under the axis of HMG/UNDP and a development scheme in the Gandaki/Lumbini region in two Western sector had been considered. Further HMG/ UNDP was lunched a comprehensive programme in the development of the Lumbini sacred garden, birth-place of Lord Buddha into a pilgrimage and touristic centre.

During Mr. U. Thant, the former secretary general of United Nations visit to Lumbini in 1967 suggested to His Majesty's Government of Nepal that Lumbini be developed as place of pilgrimage and tourist centre. According to his suggestion. His Majesty's Government of Nepal requested technical assitance from the United Nations in developing Lumbini in 1967. Since, then various measures have been taken as a result of Missions sent by the United Nations UNESCO and UNDP. All amply know the outstanding potentiality of Lumbini and its proper development is sure to attract a great number of tourists and pilgrims. The Master Plan was finalised and approved by the UN and HMG which was done by Kenzo Tange as a consultant. The Master Plan was approved in 1978. Lumbini Development Trust Act came into existence and Lumbini Development Trust was formed. Lumbini is now being developed under the Master Plan of Lumbini Development Trust, a non-governmental organisation dedicated to the restoration of Lumbini and its development as a pilgrimage site.

Lumbini has the Ashokan Pillar signifying the first evidence relating to the birth of Lord Buddha. Then the image of Maya Devi showing the bas-relief image of Maya Devi is enshrined in a tiny pagoda style temple which the image depicts the scene of Buddha's birth and Maya Devi holding by her right hand to a branch of Sal tree.

After these two religious structures, Puskarni—the sacred pool which is believed to be the sacred pool where Maya Devi bathed before giving birth to the Lord Buddha and where the infant was sanctified with the first purification bath.

The most important and venerated site in Lumbini is Sanctum—Sanctorum of the Birth place which evoked holy sentiment to the entire Buddhist world, situated deep in this place.

The comes the Buddhist temple is constructed inside the surrounding complex of Lumbini as a modern Buddhist shrines in Nepal. This temple has a big prayer hall with a large idol of Buddha. Medieval style murals are depicted around the walls of the temple.

There are many places related with ancient Sakya Republic such as Kapilvastu, Aroarakot, Chatradei, Gotihawa, Niglihawa and Sagavhawa. All these places related with the life of Buddha and have contained many remains of ancient monuments and archaeological finds.

The Lumbini is easily reached and it is connected with the town of Bhairahawa. The town of Bhairahawa is linked with Pokhara and Kathmandu by air as well as by road. Bhairahawa and Lumbini are buked with all weather road and regular bus service.

Bhairahawa has many moderate hotels for the visitors. There are hotels and guest houses for the pilgrims at Lumbini Complex.

Lumbini village, Monastic enclave and the Sacred Garden as suggested in the Master Plan prepared by Mr. Kenzo Tange are now going to be constructed and many kinds of constructions are underway.

A newly operated four-star class hotel—Lumbini Garden Hotel—is situated opposite to the entrance gate of Lumbini Sacred Garden where "The Light of Asia", Gautam Buddha, was born in 623 BC. Lying at a distance of 18-km from Gautam Buddha Airport and 28-km from Sunauli (Nepal-India border), the hotel can be reached by walking for five minutes from the Lumbini Garden.

The construction of a new stupa in Lumbini has recently been completed. The stupa is said to be the biggest one in the world.

The stupa was constructed by Nipponzan Myohoju, a Buddhist Sangh founded by Fujii Gurii of Japan. The Sangh has already constructed 73 such stupas in the world. The pagoda was designed by Dr. Minoru Ohoka of Japan. The project of constructing the pagoda took 7 years for its completion.

The stupa is 41.5 meters high and its diameter is 59 meters. Buddhist followers are already started their procession to Lumbini from Kathmandu on foot. It is said to last for 25 days to reach Lumbini to take part in an inaugural ceremony of the stupa.

17 *Prominent Religious Pilgrimage Places in the Terai Regions of Nepal*

Nature has enriched Nepal with all kinds of attractions. Nepal's physical picture and character is regarded as extra-ordinary and spectacular. Nearly, rectangular in shape, Nepal covers an area of 147, 811 sq. km (5,4000 sq. miles). Topographically, Nepal presents a contrasting look. She is situated in the Southern slopes of the mid-Himalayas, the formidable peaks of eternal snows. The nearest sea coast is about 1, 127 km. for its border.

Nepal gives a unique variety of geographical regions dotting from the tropical lowlands to the artic plateau. Terai Region is the lowland which covers open flat country side and forest clad mountains. It is a fertile plain stretching from east to west in the southern part of the country. Its altitude maximum 305 m and occupies 17 per cent of the total area of the country. The length of the Terai is about 880 kms. The climate of the Terai is tropical. Terai region can be called a region of the religious pilgrimage sites where many religious places, temples, stupas, art treasuries and monuments are scattered all over. There are national cultural religious centres as Janakpur the birthplace of Sita, the heroine of Hindu epic Ramayana and consort of God Rama the son of the King Janak of Audhaya and Lumbini—world known nativity of Gautama Buddha "The Light of Asia" and other equally famous religious places Varahakshetra, Devghat, Balmiki Ashram, etc.

Janakpur is situated in the eastern Terai. It is a famous religious pilgrimage spot which is regarded to be the birthplace of Sita of the Hindu epic Ramayana. The Rama and Sita temples are the centre of pilgrimage here. Janakpur is located about 375 kilometres to the southeast of Kathmandu city in the Terai region of Nepal. This city is known as a city of temples and ponds.

Janakpur was believed to be the capital of ancient Mithila (Videha State) in the ancient times. It was known as Mithila in the legendary times and as Videha in the historical time. This Videha State was very big as it used to cover wide area of Nepal's Terai region and a major part of India's northern Bihar State. It was demarcated by the rivers Kosi, Ganges and Gadaki and the fringes of the Himalayan foothills.

Mithila was very prosperous country in the legendary times and its name and fame was reputed far and wide. Mithila was famous simply because it was made famous by the king Janak who was very wise and always ruled over for the benefit of his subjects. He was the father of Sita and was adept in the affairs of the state as well as versed in philosophical ideas. He had installed a high council of religious matters with all the wise men of his country. All biggest and wise philosophical discussions and principles were consulted in his great council. So Janakpur is said to have named after the name of wise and good King Janak.

So far as the historical times are concerned Janakpur is known as Videha (Ancient Mithila) was able to restore its rich tradition and culture. The Malla dynasty was ruled over in the valley of Kathmandu from 11th to 18th century, the influence of Mithila language had gained a great footing in the Malla Court. Not only that in the sphere of administration, state affairs, social and religious institutions, the glorious influences of Mithila was visible. Due to the glorious and high tradition, Janakpur and its nearby areas, are still to-day retained Maithili culture which is considered to emulate glory and honour.

The city of Janakpur's landmark is the large and famous artistic temple of marble of Janaki, consort of Rama, Sita, built by queen Vrisha Bhanu of the Indian State of Tikamgarh. The Janaki temple is popularly emphasized as Naulakha temple because nine lakh (900,000 rupees) were considered to have been spent on its construction. This temple is also known by other names as Sismahal, Sita Palace etc. The style and architectural style of this temple is modeled after Mugal and Rajputana arts. It is estimated that about five hundred domes are in this temple with the gold pinnacle. This temple is thought to have built in 1911 A.D.

Another religious place is Bibaha Mandap which was made as the place of remembrance of the spot where the marriage ceremony of Rama and Sita occurred. This Mandap lies on the northern side of the Janaki temple. This Mandap is about 65 feet in height and contains 20 pillars with having 96 images of variety of gods and goddesses. There are railing all around the temple with a pot of lamps and many bells giving gentle sounds even with a slight touch of the air. This Mandap is in Pagoda style and the episode of the marriage of Rama and Sita is solomonized here by various designs. A beautiful park is built and many images of divinities are installed around the park.

Equally famous another temple is popular by the name of the temple of Rama. Many believe that this temple was constructed about 1839 B.S. This temple is also in Pagoda style and the roof of this temple was made by Rana Prime Minister Chandra Shum Shera in 1984 B.S. with polish of gold. There is an old Batabriksha (Balyan tree) in this temple and many old images around it. There is another temple of family deity of King Janak as Raj Devi on the northern side of it.

There is another temple dedicated to the King Janak.

During Janakpur's two main festivals commemorating Sita's birth and her marriage with Rama two temples Janaka temple and Rama temple become a centre of pilgrimage for the Hindus from both Nepal and India. There are many sacred ponds here. The pilgrims, apart from paying their homage to Lord Rama and Goddess Sita to the various temples in Janakpur, visit Dhanusha, about 15 km. north of Janakpur. Dhanusha marks the spot where the epic hero Lord Rama had broken Lord Shiva bow to show his strength and be able contestor to win Sita on marriage. King Janak, the father of Sita had asked for test for the princes and kings for able suitors for taking Sita in marriage to lift the great bow of Lord Shiva and also string it too, Lord Rama was only one to lift the mighty bow and broke it while stringing.

This sacred place is connected by road from Kathmandu. There are also air services to Janakpur from Kathmandu. There are good accommodation facilities to stay to the needs of pilgrims in Janakpur. Nepal's railways also links this famous city with other Indian cities via the Indian border town of Jayanagar in Bihar state of India.

Another pilgrimage spot in Lumbini the birthplace of Sidhartha Gautam Buddha, the founder of Buddhism. Lumbini is a sacred place for Buddhists all over the world. This sacred place is situated in the plain south of the foothill of the Churea range. The Buddhists pay homage to this pilgrimage site for inspiration of compassion and devout by visiting here. There is a pillar made by the great Emperor Ashoka to show the place where Buddha was born. Emperor Ashoka, the great Maurya ruler paid a pilgrimage to this holy land in 245 B.C. The Emperor had erected the famous Ashoka Pillar and constructed many stupas in and around Lumbini. But this sacred place was unattentive for about seven centuries when the reknown Chinese monk, Fa-Hsien visited Lumbini in 403 A.D. He remarked the importance of Lumbini and Kapilvastu as the place of birth of Buddha. This place is now amply proved that Siddhartha Gautam was born here in 623 B.C. Dr. Feuher, the great scholar and researcher discovered this site and proved that this Lumbini Garden was the place where Lord Buddha was born. After this discovery, many developments and activities started making this sacred place popular and significant. Now the people from all over the world know the birth place of Gautam Buddha, the apostle of world peace.

Lumbini Garden and its calm and peaceful environs are

situated in Rupendehi district. Rupendehi district placed in western terai, covers pockets of villages and two cities of Butwal and Bhairahwa.

The noticeable religious place in Lumbini is the temple of Maya Devi, comprising a stone relief engraving the birth scene of Lord Buddha. The bas—relief evinces Maya Devi supporting herself by holding on to a branch of a sal tree and the newborn infant Buddha standing upright on a lotus pedestal. Two nymphs are shown in the act of putting water and flowers from the heaven. This shrine has been worshipped by both Hindus and Buddhists since the beginning of the Christian era.

To the south of the Maya Devi temple is the famous sacred pool of "Puskarani"—Known as "Siddhartha Kupa" where Queen Maya Devi, the mother of Lord Buddha was given his first purification bath and queen Maya Devi bathed just before giving birth to Buddha.

The Ashokan Pillar is another most remarkable monument in Lumbini. This monolith made of stone in three feet in diameter, twenty feet high and its eight feet is under the ground.

There are two Buddhist monasteries have been built in the surrounding complex of Lumbini. The architectural style of these monasteries are modern. The prayer hall of the Tibetan-style monastery contains a large image of Buddha while ancient murals decorate the walls of both monasteries.

There are ancient ruined walls a restored rectangular pond. Many kinds of archaeological finds and large number of historical artifacts have been also found in the surrounding area.

Under the Lumbini Development Trust with assistance of the United Nations and efforts of various nations, a major development activities is underway at Lumbini towards the implementation of the Master Plan designed by the world renowned Japanese architect Prof. Kenzo Tange. The Master Plan of Lumbini Development Trust, a non-governmental Organisation is now going to develop Lumbini as a pilgrimage place. Kapilvastu, near Lumbini is also considered to be developed as this place also dedicated to Lord Buddha where he spent his years in the beginning of his life and his renunciation. Lumbini, being the birth of Lord Buddha, the compassion of peace has been included to the list of World Heritage Sites by the World Heritage Committee of United Nations, Educational, Scientific and Cultural Organisation. Lumbini where the Lord Buddha was born is a great pilgrimage sites for all the Buddhist people from all over the world. The nearest town to Lumbini (22 km.) is Bhairahwa or the Indian border, Sunauli (29 km.). There are regular air flights to Bhairahwa from Kathmandu and Pokhara. Lumbini is about 300 km. from Kathmandu. There are accommodation facilities at Bhairahwa and Butwal Lumbini complex has now hotels and guest houses for the pilgrims. This holy place is accessible by air from Kathmandu to Bhairahwa from where one can proceed by car or bus. Buses to Bhairahawa depart Kathmandu everyday.

Balmiki Ashram was a hermitage site is said to be made a place of penance by the great Hindu sage Balmiki . This site is located in a forest on the bank of the Tribeni river at the south-western part of the Royal Chitwan National Park. It can be reached by boat.

This sacred place is considered to be a place where Sita, the consort of Rama, the great epic hero of Ramayana came here to live with her two sons Laba and Kusha after separating from Lord Rama. Many kinds of statues and artifacts were excavated in the area during an archaeological excavation in the late 1960's.

Nepal is very rich in number of rivers. They are some big and some other small. So this country is very rich in water resources. Snowfed rivers are the life blood for Nepal. The Gandaki river system in Central Nepal consists of the Kaligandaki, Budhigandaki, Marsyandi, Trisuli, Seti, Madi and Daraundi rivers. The Kaligandaki is the longest river and the Trisuli, the main tributary of this system. The Kaligandaki originates in Mustang and converges with the Trisuli at Deoghat in Chitwan. The river is then called Narayani and goes on to meet the Ganges in India.

Balmiki is the author of the Ramayana. He was a great saint and learned person. He was a poet and had also played an active role in the story of Ramayana. After Sita banished from Ayodhya, she came to take shelter at his ashram. While staying in the ashram of Balmiki with her two sons Laba and Kusha Sita devoted her time doing penance. Her two sons were later on taught by Balmiki. So this place of Balmiki Ashram is situated in Nepal as Nepal has been regarded a veritable reknowned place of Hindu culture and civilization. Nepal situated amidst the snowy ranges of the Himalayas and so serenely blessed by gods and goddesses since time immemorial. Nepal is known as favourite spots of Gods and many saints and sages used to come to the lap of Himalayas for meditation and solace. Balmiki Ashram is one of the holy place blessed by the learned sage Balmiki for practicing meditation. So pilgrims visit this sacred place to worship the holy land where the sacred river and its bank of Tribeni is very pious.

Barah Chhetra—is considered to be one of the four greatest Hindu pilgrimages. It is located in Eastern Development Region and its district Seensari's north-western section. This is very lovely place at the confluence of the mighty Saptakoshi and Kora rivers. This is situated at near the city of Biratnagar in the Kosi zone of Nepal and 'Seven Kosis' lies the north-west part of it. This place has been described in Barah Purana, Brahma Purana, Skandha Purana and its Himabat Khanda as a very venerated place of worship.

This place is dedicated to Varaha and is considered as the third of the ten incarnations of Lord Vishnu, the second god of the Hindu triad. This pilgrimage is described in all the Puranas that Lord Vishnu took the incarnation of the Varaha or boar to save the world from a dilution or immersion. This Barah Chhetra is the actual place where the Varaha form of Lord Vishnu originated. The Hindu holy text Vedas also acknowledge this tale.

This sacred place is full of various temples such as temples of Guru Varaha, and Nageshwor along with Surva Varaha Koka Varaha and Indra Varaha. There is also dharmasala (guest houses) stationed here.

The temple Varaha is a single-storey stone structure and stands on the left side of the main entrance while the right part of this main temple of Varaha is hold by an old dharmasala. This temple was very old and there are inscriptions available so far indicate that in 1783 A.D. this temple was restored by a priest of Chatara Matha (monastery). The door which carries the pilgrims into the inner courtyard is full of artistic decorations. There is a golden tympanum engraved on the ground and just above it, there is a spire or finial with the carved image of Garuda on it. There are figures of crocodiles, lions and other gods and goddesses all around it. Among these assemblage of images there is a imposing image of Bhimsen with his armour Gada. The tympanum is covered on its both sides with the stone idols of guards. It is famous pilgrimage site from the times immemorial.

Dev Ghat: This pilgrimage of Nepal is located nearly eight kilometres north of Bharatpur of Narayani zone. It is on the confluence of the Kali and Trisuli river and hence is known as Narayani river.

The Hindu religious text of the Hemavatkhand of Skanda Purana enlightened the significance of Dev Ghata. This religious spot is also reputed by the name of Harihara Chhetra and has a collection of temples and images dedicated to Vishnu, Shiva and Chakreshwori Madadev. This place is attracting many pilgrims everyday. This being one of the most venerated place of worship, devotees visit her for performing marriage ceremony of their family members and for many kinds of religious ceremonies.

Actually speaking Devghat also popular as Narayanghat is now a small township near Narayani river (Seven Gandaki rivers) in Chitwan Valley. It lies south-east of Kathmandu Valley about 128 kilometres by car. Pilgrims from all parts of Nepal and India visit here in large numbers to acknowledge the occasion of Magh Sankranti. The Kaligandaki river here joins the Trisuli and becomes the Narayani. Dev Ghat is very famous religious place to Hindus. A number of temples, guest houses and meditation centres are stationed there.

Chitwan is a district of Nepal and the main attraction of Chitwan is Royal Chitwan National Park, famous world heritage site. This place of Dev Ghat is dedicated to God Vishnu, the second god of the Hindu triad. He is regarded specially the well wishes of man in his many avatars or incarnations. Here the images of Hari (God Vishnu) and Hara (God Shiva) and their temples and a cave which is believed as the ascetic site of great sage Basistha. Side by side with these religious places there is Jhotriglinga temple built by Galaswara Baba and Iswaranandha is equally remarkable.

There are many Dharmasalas (guest houses) built here to cater for visiting pilgrims. This sacred place is spread over five thousand four hundred thirty four hectors extending from Tanahu, Chitwan and Nawalparasi districts. So Dev Ghat is easily accessible by road. There is no problem for stay as well as foodings. There are daily flights and bus services from Kathmandu. Many pilgrims pay their visit here on the day of the Makar Sankranti (winter solstice) festival in January.

Simrongarh is famous religious place of Nepal in the Terai region of Nepal. It is situated in Bara District of Narayani zone of Nepal. It is near Indian border. This area was the capital of the King of Karnakat dynasty and King Nanya Dev had developed this place by all kinds of facilities and prospects. Simrongarh had been prospered when it was the Capital of Mithila in ancient times. This place was known to many western visitors and Christian fathers. Many of them had visited this place for making their visit to Nepal or specially Kathamandu Valley. Among them, Hadson, the British resident of India visited this place and he highly spoke about the artistic arts and security walls of this religious place.

There are areas as Laxmipur, Kotwali, Bhagabanpur, Devapur Teta, Hariharpur, Kuchidiha, Kachorpa, Amitgunj, Golaganj and Srinagar Bonriya etc. nine villages in Simrongarh. Many kinds of ancient images and artistic artifacts are found scattered in various places and can be seen to-day. There are many ponds there and it is considered that these are made for security of the country by the King of Karnatak dynasty.

Here lies the famous temple of Kaṇkali Mai and this temple of goddess is very prominent temple of Simrongarh and many people excluding pilgrims used to visit for worship. There is a Ascetic near this temple belonging to Baba Mansaram; a great ascetic. This Samadhi is located within the temple as a mound of clay and a pair of slippers are kept near to it. This slippers are changed in every year in the day of Ram Nawami. A fire place is also near to it and it is burnt and it is believed that any one who put ashes of it in his forehead is sure to receive his all wishes fulfilled. Near this temple, there are many images of different gods and goddesses broken into pieces and it is considered that these are all broken at 1326 A.D. by the attack of Gayasyuddhin Tuglak, Mohammedan Emperor of India. These images are all engraved in black stone in Pali style and design. Also, a wide pond is near the temple called Esava pond.

The temple known as Raniwas or Ram Janaki temple is also revered by the people of this place. Rana Prime Minister Jung Bahadur Rana usually was very much interested in big game shooting in the Terai jungle and visited this place while he was in his hunting safari. Later on, his queen showed an interest to construct one temple here and his son Jit Jung built the temple of Ram Janaki Temple in 1935 B.S. in Sikhara Style. This holy place sanctuaries with the images of Rama, Sita and Laxman in the altar of lotus engraved in bronze and the tympanum is equally artistic with flowers, umbrellas and Nagas in bronze.

The most extraordinary thing to be witnessed here is the Black Rice (Rice having black colour) which is there on the security wall lying south east section of the temple of Kankali Mai. This black rice has many mysteries which is to be analysed and searched.

Equally there lies one chest shaped stone full of artistic designs buried in the bank of a Canal. This stone chest many consider as an object of great cultural and religious importance.

Nepal being the only Hindu Kingdom in the world, there are many holy shrines here. The people of Nepal will be found visiting to various religious pilgrimage sites they worship different gods and goddesses who represent various incarnations of three Hindu triad in their different manifestations scattered all over the country. They worship their different Gods and Goddesses in order to show their reverence simply because of that they would not like their holy shrines should be desecrated.

18 *Popular Hindu Pilgrimage Sites in the Himalaya*

The enduring products of God—the combination of natural beauty along with the artistic creations of man lends to Nepal a charm and individuality which is distinct and unique. So Nepal provides a visitor with an opportunity to enrich thought of history and culture by exploring a land with rich religion and culture. Nepal, really speaking a cultural centre where the existence of spiritual and cultural treasures bless each and every visitor by paying a visit a land with a rich religion and heritage. Nepal has a culture nourished by the fusion of Hinduism and Buddhism since a civilisation stretching back to thousands of years. Religion is an integral part of Nepal life. Main religious creeds namely Hinduism, Buddhism and Bhaisnava, Sakta, Nath in both tantric and non-tantric forms prevalent in Nepal. Nepal has a tradition of religions tolerance. Hinduism and Buddhism are the two religious of Nepal which exist simultaneously in an amicable and harmonious way. Among the wealth of varied attractions are the temples, stupas, monasteries, pilgrimage sites, religious edifices and the historical monuments which are found in all parts of the country.

The Great Himalayan peaks drag its majestic length along its northern fringe topped by 8848 m. Mount Everest, the highest peak in the world with other peaks of over 8579 m and about two hundred 4899 peaks. When a visitor travels to the ancient pilgrimage sites of Nepal, lying in the lap of

Himalayas, seeing shrines and sculptures, standing as they have for centuries. Nepal has quiet religious centre that is world apart. The existence of spiritual and cultural sites in the serene atmosphere in the remote Himalayan regions. Due to its serene and lovely atmosphere Nepal is regarded as the best place for meditation and penance by the sages and saints of all ages. They came for meditation and penance in the calm and quite places in the Himalayas. That is why, the faith and images of Gods and Goddesses are to be seen everywhere. Here are many pilgrimage sites in the lap of Himalayas, producing secret messages laying away for ages in the unique beauty of vast mountains deep beneath valley of wonders. A symbol of peace and calm that mark beauty and allure at all these pilgrimage sites. Religion has played an important role in moulding the outlook, altitude and ways of life of the people. It has given them a distinct cultural identity. So many scholars and researchers have defined Nepal as the land of thousand Gods and Goddesses and a world of temples and pilgrimage sites....... the land of Himalayan mountains. So the writer of the book Mr. Paul Brunton has described in his book "Hermit in the Himalayas" as the following :

"Whether the temples are useless collections of mere stones or whether gods are figments of primitive man's imagination, to live in the Himalayas for a while is in itself a memorable blessing".

Being the chosen place for the sages and saints for their devotional attainment, the Himalayan abode of Nepal is reknown in an ancient Hindu scripture "As the sun dries the morning dew, so are the sins of man dissipated at the sight of the Himalaya."

One of the popular Hindu pilgrimage sites in the Himala is Muktinath. It is located in the district of Mustang-north-western Himalayan region. The temple of Muktinath is situated at an altitude of 3,749 metres. This is famous for the temple dedicated to Lord Vishnu or Muktinath or Lord of Liberation. This holy place is accessible from Pokhara either following the 10-14 day trekking trail or air service up to

Jomsom and a short distant trek from there. Jomsom and Muktinath make splendid one week trek from Pokhara. The trekking route provides a vast panorama of glittering Annapurna massif as well as the glimpse of the world's deepest gorge flanked by the Annapurna and Dhaulagiri ranges.

Muktinath or the Lord of Liberation is mentioned in Hindu Puranas and Buddhist Sutras. This holy spot is held sacred by both Hindus and Buddhists. The main temple is a pagoda shaped and is situated on a high mountain range. Actually, is located about 18 kilometres north-east of Jomsom. The principal duty is Jwala Mai (Goddess of Flame) is housed in a pagoda temple. There is also a Buddhist monastery near to the temple. There are 108 water spouts set into a wall around the temple. The holy water comes out of 108 water spouts. The Jwala Mai temple has a spring and an eternal flame burning on the ground in front of a stone alter. Hindus regard this temple as the seat of other form of Lord Vishnu, the Preserver of the Hindu world. Lord Vishnu is represented by a black Saligram (ammonite fossil) in the holy shrine of Lord Muktinath. A bath in the 108 water spouts is a must for the pilgrims to wash away all their sins. The area around Muktinath is known as Muktichetra—place of Liberation and is filled with Saligram.

There is a Buddhist monastery close to the temple. Buddhists revere this holy site as a sacred place of "Fire burning on Earth, Stone and Water" which signifies three of the Five Elements of the Buddhist world. This shrine is honoured by the Buddhists in a belief that this holy place blessed due to the visit by Padmasambhava, one of the most revered incarnations of Lord Buddha, and rocks there having the foot imprints of him. Padmasambhava was a great Buddhist saint who travelled from India to Tibet to preach the Tibetans the Mahayani doctrine (The Great wheel) Buddhism.

The way to Muktinath is through the Muktinath trek—Pokhara—Jomsom—Muktinath. Dazzling Himalayan peaks like Annapurna III, Annapurna IV, Dhaulagiri I and III and

Tukuche Peak can be seen on the route which tower above the holy and famous shrine of Muktinath. The pilgrimage route passes from Pokhara to Ghorepani Pass. The trail continues onwards to Jomsom. From Tatopani (hot water spring) till Muktinath, the pilgrims walk through the great Kali Gandaki Basin. The Kali Gandaki Basin is one of the biggest and deepest gorges of the world.

The Holy Muktinath pilgrimage site highlights the peaceful co-existence of all religions in Nepal. There is also Helicopter services on request. There are rest houses, lodges and restaurants at nearby. The best months to visit of Muktinath are Jeshtha (May-June) and Magha (Jan-Feb). A mela (fair) is also observed here on that occasions.

Another sacred pilgrimage spot is Gosainkund which is situated at an altitude of 4,380 m to the north of Kathmandu in the Himalayan region. This is holy lake and the most important place of pilgrimage. The holy lake is to the north-east of Helambu. The best approach to Gosainkund is through Dhunche. Encircled by high mountains on the north and the south and by higher landscape on the east and west, this lake is grand and picturesque. On the east and west of this Kund, there are nine famous lakes such as Saraswati Kunda, Bhairav Kunda, Soorya Kunda, Ganesh Kunda etc. Regarding this holy Kunda (lake) is considered to have been created by Lord Shiva. When Lord Shiva swallowed dangerous poison and it caused a burning pain in his throat. In order to cool himself from the burn of the dangerous poison, he thrust his trident into a mountain to receive cold water to quench. This lake is believed to be a place to receive Lord Shiva's thrust. There is a large rock at the middle of the lake which is regarded as Shiva's idol and exactly gives an impression of a big person lying in the lake.

This holy Kunda lies in the region of Ganesh Himal. Pilgrims congregate in big numbers on the occasions of Dasahara and Sravana Purnima (August fullmoon day). Lodges and small hotels are available for the pilgrims.

The route goes through Dhunche (1,866 m) which is connected by road from Kathmandu. Then the Syabru Village,

Ghora Tabela (3,048 m), Kyanggin Gompa, Lama Hotel Sing Gompa high above the Trisuli and after passing these places Gosainkunda arrives. The topography automatically changes and becomes alpine. The famous holy lake of Gosainkunda is in a harsh granite surroundings with the forest lying far below. Here every year, the pious devotees of Lord Shiva travel to this holy place of worship, the divinely image of God emerged deep in the water of ice-cold Kund. This is another very famous pilgrimage places of Hindu shrines which stations in the alpine region of the Himalaya like Amarnath in Kashmir, and the mouth of cow, the source of the sacred Ganges at Badrinath in Kumaun. Gosainthan is equally revered by all Hindus. Equally famous pilgrimage place is Swarga Dwari. This holy place is located 26 kilometres west of Khalanga bazaar, administrative headquaters of Pyuthan district, Swarga Dwari signifies the meaning of 'the gate to Heaven' and is one of the most important place of pilgrimage in Nepal. This sacred place was selected by the saints and sages for the place of meditation since the ages. It was the famed spot where the Bal Tapaswi (child sage Padma Giri) also practiced meditation. This great child sage made famous this place as Swarga Dwari. This child sage is known as Swarga Dwari Mahaprabhu who made this place known as a sacred pilgrimage site. Many saints and ascetics practice meditation even to-day in this place living in caves where Swarga Dwari attained perfection of sagehood.

Swarga Dwari is located 450 kilometres in western Nepal in Pyuthan District at Khaal about 2121 metres high altitude. It is believed that this place was actually one which was known since the Hindu epic Mahabharata times. Pandavas made their way to heaven by practicing religious penance from here to heaven and so it is known as "gate to heaven". This place is located on the top of Mandavi river and there are dense forest and meadows all around it. At the top of a ridge, there are temple of Swarga Dwari, rest houses for the pilgrims, police and health post. All the temples are decorated artistically and full of fluttering flags. There are image of

Swarga Dwari Mahaprabhu, big fire place for making religious rites and Shiva Panchayan, Devi Panchayan, Vishnu Panchayan, Surya Panchayan, Ganesh Panchayan etc. and their images and worshipping places are there. Noteworthy of all the places is the place of meditation of Swarga Dwari Mahaprabhu and the way the great sage used to go for bath in the Mandavi river. There are meadows for grazing the hundreds of cows kept by this sacred place.

The very surrounding of the place is attractive due to its very composition of religious environment by seeing the yellow colour clad ascetics and the Patasalas (teaching schools) for all of them and the people gathered for religious attainments. Here specially in the months of Baisak Purnima and Kartik dark moon day a mela (religious fairs) are occurred which provide religious, cultural and historical importance attached to it. Geographically and physically this place is also attractive as the mountains of Gulmi and Arghakanchi in the east, the natural vistas of the district of Dang and Rolpa in the west, the snow-clad Himalayan sights of the Rolpa and Baglung in the north and the unique views of Dang and Arghakanchi in the south. There is possibility of viewing the night sights of the Uttar Pradesh, India in the fair weather in night by seeing the lights glowing in the area from the top. The sights of the Himalayas, lowland hills and even Terai in the south are visible from this sacred place.

Swarga Dwari Mahapraphu established his place of meditation by seeing and receiving blessing by the almighty in the form of white flame. So the great sage made to construct a fire place (Yajna Sala) in 1952 B.S. and started to perform World Peace performance in 1953 B.S. and perineal religious rites in 1954 B.S. This great sage left his physical body in 1947 and this religious place is established in accordance with his wishes.

This sacred pilgrimage site is visited all the year round by the pilgrims from all parts of Nepal and even from India. But many pilgrims are seen in large numbers specially in the month of Falgun to Kartik. The followers of all religions are equally received and honoured here irrespective of their creeds and sects. There is arrangement of free foodings and lodging for all the pilgrims visiting here.

In order to reach Swarga Dwari there is difficulty in transportation. The pilgrims can reach Swarga Dwari by trekking about 12 hours from Dang. There are bus services from Bhalubang to Piuthan. The road is not good for bus service and so this bus service is not so comfortable. In spite of not getting good transportation, many pilgrims pay visit to this sacred place for receiving blessing and solace in their life.

Ashram of Khaptad Baba, a learned religious sage is situated in the Khaptad National Park. The Khaptad National Park is nestled at the foothills of the Himalayas. This is a place of wilderness in far west Nepal. It has diverse collection of flora and fauna. This area is proclaimed as national park and is full of forested slopes and grasslands. It is full of oak, bamboo, coniferous trees and rich in medicinal herbs.

The altitude of this place is varied and so it ranges from 2000 to 3000 metres. There is a flat land at the highest point and is known as the Khaptad Lek at 3,430 m. The Khaptad National Park is very attractive hilly terrain. The Park area covers 225 sq. km. of Bajhang, Bajura, Dote and Acham districts of far west Nepal. The headquarters of this park is at Khaptad, 32 km. from Silgarhi Dote and 30 km. from Champur Bazaar (Bajhang). This area is not only popular for nature viewing but also a famous place for a spiritual penance. This is really a place of quite atmosphere.

This place not only rich in its natural grandeur but also in religious significance. Here are religious sites such as Tribeni, Sahashra Linga and Ashram of Khaptad Baba, a very learned spiritual saint. This place is thought to be realised as spiritual centre. Apart from religious environs, there are Patans (meadows), Khaptad lake known as Khecher Daha, Maisthan are very lovely and beautiful. All these meadows are full of green grasses and variety of flowers which provide a glamorous views at the time of spring season. This sacred place is described as Khacheradigya in Skanda Purana which signifies a place on earth kissing the sky. In total, there are four religious places here as Sailinga temple containing Uma and Shankar idols of ancient times, Tribeni—the confluence of three rivers, Khaptad Lake big lake and Siddhagram temple near the bank of this lake.

This calm and quite place is covered with rhododendron bushes and their attractive flowers bloom in every season. The river of Nigla which flow like a zig zag way and looks as if made by an artist which is known all over the world as spectacular creation of nature. All kinds of fruits are seen in the trees. The main Ashram of Khaptad Baba is the centre part of this area. In every sense this area looks like a place of meditation and spiritual penance. The very surrounding of this area creates solace and peace to the mind. This is a place of peace. It is the site of the Ashram of Khaptad Baba, a great saint which looks like an earthly paradise as the eternal magic of the surroundings allure, enthral, enchant. The visiting to this place of reverence emanates an aura of consolation to the mind and heart. This calm and quite area casts the since grandeurs of the plain valley with serene lake, rolling green country side and the friendliest people everywhere. Khaptad scenic beauty, its flora and fauna, ethnic culture and lovely settlements—the place of a visit to this spiritual and religious centre, pilgrims will find it the most rewarding of all pilgrimage experience.

19 Other Sacred Sites of Pilgrimage

Gosainthan—North of the Kathmandu Valley, situated at an evenation of 4380 meters above sea level for the sacred Gosainkund Lake encircled by snowy mountains is one of the most revered pilgrimage spots in Nepal. This sacred spot lies to the north-west of Helambu beyond a pass at 4602 meters. The best route to Gosainkund is through Dunche 132 kilometres north east of Kathmandu. This place is also related with the mythology of God Shiva. Surrounded by high mountains on the north and the south and by higher landscape on the east and west, the kund (lake) is picturesque and grand. On the east and west of this Kund there are other nine famous lakes such as Saraswati Kunda, Bhairav Kunda, Soorya Kunda and Ganesh Kunda etc.

This sacred place is sum up by the ancient mythology that this famous lake has been associated with God Shiva. Legend sheds light that Lord Shiva after making use of the poison that flowed into it after inspissating or squashing the ocean, became restless due to the swallowing of venomous object. In order to settle the effect of restlessness due to taking or swallowing up of deadly poison, he came to the Himalayan region for solace. Lord Shiva became so much agitated due to the after effect that he bored his Trisul (trident) his weapon into the ground and a fountain arised out to form a Kunda (lake) where Lord Shiva lies to relieve his agony. This spot is now a big lake with a big stone in the middle. By observing from a far distance a vision comes outright of a huge person lying in the lake.

Gosainkund (altitude 4,380) is situated in the region of Ganesh Himal, on the Langtang trail. It is believed that this sacred place has altogether 108 Kundas (lakes). Here every years the religious devotees of God Shiva come to worship the divinely carved representation of their God, submerged in the water of ice-cold lake. Pilgrims attempt to visit this sacred place on the occasions of Dasahara and Sravana Purnema (August fullmoon day) in large numbers, gasping due to heights and shivering from the intense cold.

This holy lake has a link with a pleasant 2-day walk up hill from Dvnche (1,950 m) which is approached through 118-km mountain road from Kathmandu via Trisuli Bazaar. There are pilgrim hotels and other occomadation shelters along with other facilities needed to the pilgrims. This is the great pilgrimage place which lies in the ice-bound fastness of the Himalaya.

Muktikshetra or Muktinath—Muktinath is famous sacred place among the Hindus all over the world. This place lies in the remote Himalayan district of Mustang at an altitude of 3,800 m. In the crest of Himalayan wilderness, 'pilgrims visit this sacred place dedicated to God Vishnu for worship and dedication. Hindu pilgrims visit this place from all over the world to make veneration to God Muktinath praying for Mukti (freedom from evil).

Muktinath is situated at an altitude of 3,800 m about 110 km north fo Pokhara. The man shrine is a pagoda temple dedicated to God Vishnu to be on side images of Bhu Devi and Sri Devi. South of the temple of Muktinath, is the shrine of Jwala Mai and the principal sanctum has the image of Jwala Mai (goddess of eternal flame) natural gas oozing out of the ground. Behind the temple of God Muktinath, holy water spouts numbering 108 situate in the courtyard of the temple and a monastery close by. God Muktinath is equally worshipped both by Hindus and Buddhists in equal veneration and pay homage with equal degree of faith and belief.

Muktinath has got descriptions in the great Hindu religious texts Purana and Mahabharat and was very famous as a sacred place in the ages past as it is of to-day.

This place is very greatly honoured by all Hindus as it is believed that even God Bramha used to perform his religious sites (yajna) here.

The location of this religious place is in north-central Nepal. It can be reached by walking about a week from Pokhara, the tourist resort and lake district of Nepal. There is an air service from Kathmanu to Jomson. Jomson is the headquarters of Mustang district, and Muktinath is located north of Jomson. Jomson has got air links with Pokhara as well as Bhairahawa. One can reach easily to the shrines making about six-hour trek. It will take 10 to 14 days by trekking all the way to this holy place.

Saligram (a kind of holy stone of black shining colour) found in the Kali Gandaki river back on the way to Muktinath. All Hindus worship Saligram as an emblem of Lord Vishnu.

The best months to make pilgrimage to Muktinath, Jeshtha (May-June) and Magha (Jan-Feb) are considered appropriate as many pilgrims pay visit and a mela (religious fair and festivities) are observed. There are rest houses for pilgrims. Many lodges and restaurants are also for the services of the pilgrims.

Ruru Chhetra—This is also an ancient pilgrimage place. It is knwon as Ridi and is considered as a very sacred place. The main temple contains a beautiful black stone idol of Ridi Rishi Keshab or the Rishi Keshava Narayan. There are many other temples of Radha Krishna, Gayatri, Ruru Kanya etc. with its auspicious cremation ghats.

Ridi is located at the confluence of two rivers—the Kali Gandaki and the Ridi Khola in mid-west Nepal. Hindu pilgrims from all over Nepal as well as from India assemble here on Makar Sankranti festival in January (winter solstice) for a ritual bath in the river. Ridi Rishi Keshava can easily reached from the hill resort of Tansen. A 50 km dirt road links Ridi with the town of Tansen.

Tansen, an ideal township, situated at an altitude of 1,371 meters above the sea level on the floor of beautiful Shreenagar hill of western Nepal. Tansen looks like Kathmandu with typical Newari building, the cobbled streets, pagoda style temples, shrines and stupas. The majestic Himalayan panorama of Dhaulagiri, Annapurna are seen in their attractive scenes from the top of the Shree Nagar hill.

Tansen is connected with all the major towns and cities of the country. Regular bus services are plying from all important places like Kathmandu Pokhara, Bhairahawa. Tansen is also well linked by air as the nearest airports of Tansen are Pokhara and Bhairahawa. Regular air services are covered both places Pokhara and Bhairahawa.

Ridi-Rishikeshab is located some about 700 meter of the sea level on the banks of the sacred Kali Gandaki river. As this place lies in a tropical river valley and so it is better to pay visit from October to March. Tansen offers comfortble hotel as well as guest houses facilities. Tansen is also the starting point for making pilgrimages for places of religious interest in Palpa and in the surrounding districts of western Nepal. Such places like Bhairabsthan, 9 km west of Tansen, Rani Ghat, two hours trek to the north of Tansen, Ramdi-located along the Sunauli-Pokhara Highway, 30 kms north of Tansen and Lumbini, 76 km south of Tansen can be reached comfortably.

Rafting from Ridi (one of the ideal points of the Kali Gandaki river) can be arranged upto Narayanghat, Chitwan via Ramghat-Ramdi-Trisuli river and Narayani.

Manakamana—The temple of the Hindu Goddess Bhagawati is located 125 km to the west of Kathmandu. Goddess Manakamana is said to have power to fulfill wishes of devotees. So many devotees make a pilgrimage to this most popular sacred site. This holy temple is situated in a steep hill top which takes three-hour walking to the site from Abu Khaireni on the Kathmandu—Gorkha highway.

The temple of Manakamana is a two storied pagoda style temple. This temple is placed at the top of hill, surrounded by tall trees. The famous temple of Goddess Manakamana

Mai of Gorkha is one of the reknown pilgrimage sites of Nepal. In order to reach here, it takes some about three to four hours walking from Abu Khaireni of Prithavi Rajmarg highway after crossing small bridge in Marsangdi river. Historical account describes that this famous temple was established at the time of King Ram Shah of Gorkha as the temple of powerful Goddess of power. Later on it was renovated by the great political leader of that time named Lakhan Thapa. This temple architectuarally resembles the style and model of Malla rulers of Kathmandu valley, the duty as of the priest of this temple is up till now carried by the Magor family of Thakan Thapa dynasty.

The holy spot of Manakamana is very near to Gorkha, which is the headquarter of the district of the same name, the birth place of King Pritivi Narayan Shah, the great, the founder of modern Napal. Every Napal has a ambition to visit this holy place in his life time to be belessed by the Goddess.

Manakamana is located in a hill top. The route to the temple passes through steep three-hour trek to this hill top from Abu Khaireni on the Kathmandu—Gorkha highway. But now cable car route covering 3.1 kilometre linking Cheres of Chitwan and Manakamana Mai of Gorkha becomes easy to visit for worship.

Manakamana is now linked with a well-equipped cable car service. The devotees willing to worship and pay homage to Goddess Manakamana can easily use the cable car services. The calbe car route which is 3.1 km linking Cheres (between Kuren and Mungling). Cheres is 104 km from Kathmandu on the highway to Pokhara. There are accommodation facilities at Manakamana and the devotees can stay comfortably. Along with the cable car, there is now consideration for the adequate infrastucture for all the pilgrims who visit to the beautiful village on the hilltop that houses Manakaman mai, the Goddess fulfilling all the worshipers' wishes.

Devaghat—This is famous pilgrimage site situated about 160 kilometers south-west from Kathmandu. It is located at the confluence of Narayani and Kali Gandaki rivers, the tributaries of river Ganga. These rivers are considered very holy.

Devaghat is celeberated for its ancient cave where it is believed that the epic famed Sita, the consort of God Rama of Great Hindu Epic Ramayana left her physical body by entering into the earth from this place at the end of her life. Many legend have accounts that the gods and goddess and also demons used to visit this sacred place for meditation. There are temples of Ganesh, Vishnu and Shiva. These are popular as the Pashupatinath. Due to serene atmospheres, saints and benevolent piovs persons live here for meditation and salvation.

Specially, on the day of the Makar Sankranti (winter solstice) festival in January, pilgrims assemble here to bathe in the confluence of Narayani and Kali Gandaki rivers. Hindu devotees regard these rivers are the tributaries of river Ganga which is considered to be the source of it in the heaven.

The name of this sacred place is popular as Harihara Chhetra. It has contained a number of temples and shrines having idols of Vishnu on them. There God Shiva and Chakreshwori Mahadev are popular among devotees and many pilgrims visit for devotion every day. Usually the people come here for organising marriage ceremonies and many kinds of religious functions. Pilgrims from all parts of Nepal and India visit here in large numbers to observe Maghe Sankranti (festival in January). Devaghat is regarded as a very famous place among the aged people who consider this serene and calm place as a suitable site for doing religious rites and attaining salvation.

Its location is 6 km to the north of Bharatpur. Bharatpur is knwon as the gateway to the Royal Chitwan National Park. Many hotels are available at Bharatpur. Daily bus services are plying from Kathmandu and also daily flights by air to Bharatpur. Buses for Narayanghat are always available at the central Bus Park, Kathmandu.

Balmiki Ashram—This spot is about 22 km south of Kusande village on the Narayanghat—Butwal highway. This holy placed is knwon as the hermitage of famed sage Balmiki.

Mythological account narrates that Sita, wife of God Rama, epic hero of great Hindu epic Ramayana passed her exiled life in this place and she gave birth to two sons named Lava and Kusha. Balmiki provided education to these two sons of Sita—Lava and Kusha.

This place is near to Triveni Ghat and a great religious fair is held on the occasion of full moon day in the month of Magh (January/February).

The exact location of this sacred place is situated in a forest on the bank of Tribeni river precisely at the south-western corner of the Royal Chitwan National Park. This religious site can be reached by boat. It is situated nearly about 22 km south of Kusande village on the Narayanghat—Butwal highway. This is the sacred place of hermitage of famous and pious Ramayan famed sage Valmiki.

Vyas Gufa—This sacred site is situated at the side of the Madi River, the branch of Gandaki near Damauli. It is said that the sage Vyas, (the learned sage) had written the great epic Mahabharat at this place. The religious text Skanda Purana acquainted that the great poet and sage of Hindu epic Mahabharat was born and passed his days here. Along with this sacred site, there is another place near it a cave or abode of Parashar, the father of sage Vyas. There is another equally famous cave and this cave is believed to be the place where Sukhadeva, son of Vyas conducted meditation in solitude. To glorify this place, a life-size statue of sage Vyas is immortalized in one of the temples situated at the bank of the Madi river.

There are two parts in the cave. The upper part of the cave is believed to be spot for meditation and lower part as for knowledge, as the sage Vyas used to mediate in the upper section and to acquire knowledge in lower part. Sage Vyas used to do the same activities in two sections of the cave and it is believed that is why these two parts of the cave known one for meditation and another for recitation and worship.

Upper part of the cave abound with Siva Panchayan Temples, Fire-place for doing religious rites and the place where the sage had written Mahabharat and many rest houses contributed by assistance from pious devotees. This place is also full of the banana, and other variety of trees specially Siso and has enchanced the beauty of this place.

This cave has greatly personified the place which Puranas, Himabat Kunda (ancient, Hindu Religious texts) as Vyas cave, Parasar sages hermitage, Matshya Smarak pond, Chabdi Barahi, the confluence of two rivers etc. which now comes in an area of Vyas Muncipality resembling all descriptions with the narrations visualized by above religious texts.

This place is easily reached as it is located along the Prithvi Raj Marg. This sacred place has a shrine of Jal devi (Chabdi) Barahi, Dhor Barachi which are equallly famous religious places for Hindu devotees. It is for sure that Nepal is situated on the lap of Himalayan mountains and Himalayan regions have always been used by ancient sages as their places for meditations and religious researches and knowledge. So this Vyas cave is regarded as one of the prominent religious sites for the Hindus and all Hindus used to visit this place for salvation and worship.

Swargadari—This is also the most famous place of Hindu pilgrimage. This sacred place is situated in the western part of the district of Peuthan in Rapti Zone. The holy place is revered because of a sage who devoted his life to meditation in the region. The sage named Padma Giri, started the performance of Akanda Hom (Eternal Fire Rites) on a holy altar near his hermitage. Many pilgrims from several parts of Nepal and India visit here to pay homage every year on the occasion of Baisakhi Poornima (April-May) and Kartik Poornima (October-November) festivals there.

This religious place is located near about 450 kilometers west of Kathmandu Valley in Peuthan at an altitude of 2121 meters above sea level. The legend has it that Pandavas having completed religious rites in this place, entered heaven right from this place at the time of Mahabharat and so it is called Swargadwari. (Gate to heaven). Every Hindu devotee believe that by paying visit to this place one can reach heaven comfortably after death.

This place is located at the bank of Mandabi river. This

sacred hermitage is covered with dense forests and meadows. On the site of hermitage, there are temples of Swargadwari, rest houses for the pilgrims, police and health post along with places for education. There temples are architecturally small but are decorated with flags. There is the statue of Swargadwari great sage, images of deities, big fire place having Shiva Panchayan, Devi Panchayan, Vishnu Panchayan, Surya Panchayan, Ganesh Panchayana around it. Similarly, there are also places of religious worships for Gods, the hermitage site of Swargadwari Great sage and the route which the great Sage used to visit Mandabi river and the cave used by him for penance and the meadows for the grazing of the cows of the hermitage.

This sacred place has got its name as a boy named Narayan born out of Santu Ram Gautam his father and Swata Kumari his mother in a place named Rumti village in Rolpa district of Nepal. He went to Pevthan in remote area by his inner urge of devotion and established Swargadwari Hermitages in this place. This sacred place is always visited by the devotees and many devotees from India also pay a visit.

This sacred place is in the remote area. So the accessibility is rather difficult. It takes twelve hours or so by walking from Dang. There is rough road from Bhalungbang to Peuthan Migri market and the bus services are always available. But the road being rough, it is not comfortable usually, devotees from all over the country and also from India come here for devotion in the month of फागुन to कार्तिक . This sacred place is also equally honoured by all the devotees of different religious sects and denominations.

Ratna Nath Temple—This holy place is stationed in Dang in the Mid-western region of Nepal. Ratna Nath is considered to be a learned sage and this temple was constructed in his name. The holy place since then became famous after his name. Ratna Nath is traditionally remembered as a disciple of Gorkhanath, the founder of the Natha sect. So this temple is usually inhabited by sages and saints of the Natha sect and all religious worship and activities are managed by Pira-the head of the Matha (monastery) chosen every year on the auspicious day of Krishna Ekadasi in Falguna (Feb-March)

Gorakhanath is believed as the guardian deity of Nath sect. There is a temple of Gorakhanath on the way to Guheswhori on the eastern side of Pashupatinath temple. This temple is considered to be one of the oldest temples of Gurakhanath. This temple has contained the sanctum the Paduka (foot-prints) of Gorakhanath and it is worshipped by the devotees of the Nath sect. The famous temple of Gorakhanath is the outstanding features of Gorkha which is a headquarter of the district of the same name in central west of Nepal. The temple of Gorakhanath where from the town derives its name. The world famous Gurkha soldiers hail from this place.

The temple of Ratna Nath has a religious affiliation with Pataneshwori temple of Tulsipura in India. It is realised that this temple was established by Ratna Nath himself and the management and supervision of this temple are looked after under the authority of Ratna Nath temple. The attractive custom of bowl process of Gorakhanath which eight Ratna Nath temple and ends at Pataneshwari, is still followed leaving this occasion alive till the present time. A great fair is held on this occasion. Similiar temple of Ratna Nath was also located at a spot known as Falebang. Ratna Nath, being a great ascetic, used to visit different places such as Kabul, Kandahar, Jalalabad and other many places to propagate his dogma. There are existence of Mathas (hermitage) even in Rajasthan, Pesavar and Kabul at present. Dang Valley of Nepal always receive the blessing of Ratna Nath.

Baraha Chhetra—Another equally famous place of Hindu pilgrimage is Baraha Chhetra. It is located on the banks of the Koshi river, a few kilometres from the main industrial city of Biratnagar. The holy place is venerated where Barah, the boar incarnation of Lord Vishnu, preserver of the universe, conquered the demon Hiranakshya here. The main temple dedicated to Baraha, the boar incarnation of God Vishnu is here with other temples around it. This holy place of pilgrimage lies at the confluence of two rivers—the Sapta Koshi and Kokaha.

Hindu religious Texts—Puranas mention that Baraha Chhetra is the main spot. Where the Baraha from of word Vishnu onginated. The same reference is in the vedas. Though it is situated in a desolute and remote sight, it is a popular pilgrimage place from the ancient time. Hindus always regards two rivers Koka and Sapta-Koshi as very sacred rivers.

On the Haribodhini Ekadasi a great festival occurs here. Devotees from India, Bhutan and from all the parts of Nepal visit this place in large numbers. All pilgrims bathe in the Koka river and pay homage to Baraha Bhagvan incarnation of God Vishnu.

The temple of Baraha is considered to be a historical place as the image of Baraha enshrined here, is regarded as the masterpiece of the twentieth century stone sculpture. Baraha or the boar is the third of the ten incarnations of God Vishnu. Hindu texts Puranas have highly stated that Baraha Chhetra of Nepal is the authentic site where the Varaha avatar (form of Lord Vishnu) originate. The main temple of Baraha stands on the left side of the main entrance and on the right side by an old dharmasala.

The temple of Baraha is simple—a single-storey roofless stone structure. The main entrance door is notably artistic. There is a golden tympanum is laid on the ground and just above it there is a finial with the image of 'Garuda' carved on it. Both sites of it, are full of images of crocodiles, lions, and figures of gods and goddesses. The prominent carved image of Bhimsen with his Gada is noticed in many places.

This sacred site can be reached from the industrial city of Biratnagar in east Nepal.

20 *Monasteries in the Himalayan Regions of Nepal*

Buddhist beliefs and practices date back to Nepal since the time of its founder, Gautum the Buddha, who was born at Lumbini in West Nepal Terai in about 543 B.C. He was prince who relinquished luxurious life in search of enlightenment. He preached the Eight-fold Path for the liberation of human soul from worldly bondage and the endless wheel of existence. The Eight-fold Path included Right understanding, Right resolve, Right speech, Right action, Right living, Right effort, Right mindfulness and Right meditation.

In about 100 A.D. Buddhism split into schools of Hinayana and Mahayana. Hinayana does not practice idolatry while Mahayana worships the idols of Buddha. The Nepalese Buddhists are the followers of Mahayana School. One of the main beliefs of this doctrine is that man can liberate himself by "Bodhi" meaning essence. Very few other Nepalese Buddhists have adopted the Hinayana school of thought choosing rather to follow Mahayana teaching.

The Mahayana canon contains a larger proportion of the esoteric wisdom than any other religion and has always adhered more closely to the "Heart" as distinct from the "Eye" doctrine, the eternal life rather than the changing form of the Message.

Tantrism has greatly influenced Nepalese Buddhism by creating the path of Vajrayan "The Path of the Thunderbolt".

The main object used in Vajrayana Buddhist rituals is a small thunderbolt like sceptre that is said to represent the infinite in three dimensions.

Buddhism, as it appears in Nepal belongs also to a third "School" which has often been called the third vehicle—Vajarayana or Lamaism i.e. a school strongly influenced by Tantrism.

Lamaism, as the Buddhism of Tibet used to be called is a mixture of the best and worst of Buddhism and much that lies between. At its best it is a noble part of the Mahayana. Primitive Lamaism, may be defined as a priestly mixture of Sivaite mysticism magic and Indo-Tibetan demonolatry, ourlaid by a thin paint of Mahayana Buddhism.

Lama means the "superior one." It is a term which should be reserved for the heads of monasteries and the highest dignitaries but by courtesy is given to all of the fully ordained rank.

Before the seventh century the sole religion of Tibet was the Bon. The dominating figure was the Shaman, a sorcerer working on psychic levels to produce the right weather and the other needs of an agricultural population. This religion a form of nature worship with sacrifice to vaguely defined gods of the earth and sky, existed. These Bonpas are of two kinds—using "Red-Hats" as distinct from the "Yellow-Hats" of the later Reformation and having degenerated into Bon practices.

In the middle of the seventh century that Buddhism, became a force in Tibet. King Srongtsen Gampo married two chief wives a princess from China and another from Nepal. Both were Buddhists and between them they converted the King to Buddhism. The King at once begin to preach and to build temples. Bon reaction was immediate but the new religion has come to stay and Srongtsen Gampo is revered as the founder of Tibetan Buddhists.

By the sixteenth century, the various schools of Tibetan Buddhism were reasonably well defined. The established church, as it were, is the Gelungpa or Yellow-Hat sect. Next comes the Kargyutpa sect, founded in the Eleventh century by Marpa. This may be called the Semi-refomred sect and its members supply a large number of the "entombed one" monks who shut themselves in caves on the hills for a time or sometimes for life-leaving but a hole through which their disciples bring them the minimum of food and water.

Another is Nyingmapa or Red Hat order, the unreformed Buddhism of Padma Sambhava. Being now on the defensive against the Reformed schools its members justify places hidden revelations which they claim be the esoteric teachings of Sambhava. These discoveries are mostly concerned worth of the sect and add little to the religious worth of the sect. Beyond these schools, reformed, partly reformed and unreformed be the Bon-pa, who though affected by Buddhism are still the primitive nature-worshippers of pre-Buddhism days.

The Nyingmpa-Pa Gonpas in Nepal is Bodnath which belongs to the non-reformed order of the Nyingma-pa or "Red-Hat sect" which was first introduced to Tibet in the middle of the 8th century A.D. by Padma Sambhava, also called Guru Rimpuche. This Gonpa is headed by the chief abhot Chinyi Lama.

The Gelug-pa Gonpa belongs to the reformed order of the "Gelung-pa" commonly called the "Yellow-Hat sect" founded around 1407 A.D. by the mystic Tsong-kapa, whose statue stands in the centre of the wall opposite the entrance. This order is headed by Dalai Lama who, in other Lamaist Buddhists as their spiritual leader.

There are also the Sakya-Pa Gonpa which belongs to the "Sakya-pa" order founded in 1071 by one of the Tibetan disciples of the Indian mystic Nagarjuna an 2nd century A.D.

The Karma-pa Gonpa is recently build Gonpa. This Gonpa belongs to the "Karma-pa" or "Kar-gyud-pa" community to which belonged both the famous Tibetan mystic Marpa and his disciple Milarepa (1038-1122).

Tantricism is a synthesis of spiritual and material potential. Tantra does not advocate withdrawal or renunciation from life but it is the fullest acceptance of one's family life.

Tantricism is practised both by Hindus and Buddhists in

Nepal. Tantra is so much important in the religious beliefs that Nepal has preserved rich materials for the study of Tantrism.

In the second half of the first millennium Nepal came under the influence of a strange religious movement that incorporated ideas of simister spiritual power, magic forces, necromancy and a great variety of symbols. Named after its holy scriptures, the Tantra or "Warps.", it is known as Tantricism. The first period coming to the end of the 12th century A.D. was noticed by a deep religious activity of the Tantric variety, a left handed cult with its belief of sexual principles is worship. The unifying force in this seeming diversity is Tantrism. It unites Sakti, Shiva and Bhaisnava and known as Bajrayana in Buddhist terminology and its influence is pervaded all the religious practices relating to various sects. Bajra means immortality which is indiscriminable, indivisible, inseparable and incorporeal. The importance of Sakti sect rapidly increased with the development of Buddhism and Tantricism in Nepal.

Tantricism is an amalgamation of Hinduism, especially of Shiva worship and Buddhism, bringing about a kind of unity between the two religions. This syncretism is to be found even to-day in Nepal, where Buddhists visit Hindu temples and Hindus worship by visiting Buddhist places of worship.

So tantra is not to be described as a black magic. The term of tantra can be defined as a "scripture by which knowledge is disseminated" in providing all human beings the means to attain the highest aim in life even by passing a wordly life. Shiva and Buddhist tantras have been mixed up coining to a new type of esoteric worship in Nepal, thereby influencing the socio-religious life of the Nepali people.

Tantricism maintains that it is possible to make use of the powers of terrible gods and goddesses of one is initiated into certain magic rituals and practices. The master tantrist is able to conjure up deities at will and to be apply themselves to their powers.

The characteristic features of Tantricism is their mystic syllables (Bija), magic spells (Mantra)—significant gestures thinking on the oneness of everything, meditations between microcosm and macrocism. The contemplation of images and the absorption into them is of great importance. Strong emphasis is laid on the female element and on sensuality.

Buddhist Tantricism is known by the name of "Vajrayana"— 'Diamond Vehicle" after the Vajra—(magic dagger) or thunderbolt actually the word Vajra is also referred for the emptiness of nothingness which is Vajrayana is regarded as the absolute., In the sense Vajrayana can become a way to salvation by means of the sacred enjoyment of love like the Hindu Gods, Buddhas and Bodhisatvas are allowed female complements which act as their Saktis or female powers.

The most remarkable features of Tantrism are the importance given to symbolism, occultism, magic, image-worshipping, yoga etc. to a "rules of action" in opposition perhaps rules of thought. In such a way Tantric doctrine fully indorses without "outside action there can be no salvation." This principle supplies extreme complex and esoteric rites which gradually developed in what is now called Lamaism where importance is attached to certain rituals such as "mandals". "yantras" regarded as symbolic representatives of the universe and used at the same time as instruments of concentration and meditation.

Magic formulas called "mantras" and tools such as prayer-wheels, prayer flags, incense burner sounds produced by strange musical instruments "dorze", bells etc, ritual gestures such as Mudras which are prescribed movements of the hands used to please to the many benevolent deities or malevolent demons for asking with then their magic powers.

So there are also tantric streams both in Hinduism and Buddhism. One of the objectives of Tantrism which usually refers Śakti the female principle. It can allow the consumption of meat and liquor and the performance of esoteric sexual rites as well as scarifices is to go about all of these in a compassionate manner but with detachment. So the exercise of sexual contact can be done under tantric "laboratory" conditions which signifies performance on a purely mental plans and that which involves actual handling of the ritualistic "ingredients" including women, meat and wine.

Tibetan Buddhism is commonly called Lamaism. The name is given to the religious system which the clergy or Lamas play in it. Lamaism does not differ from Buddhism according to major principles of creed, it only posses more elaborate rituals. The main trait of Lamaism, that differentiate it from orthodox Buddhism is its strong belief in demons. Thus apart from gentle figures of various Buddhas and Bodhisatvas in Lamaistic iconography, there are many effigies of so-called "faith defender—who are the gods of demonical character. Goddess or female deities depicted as "air traveller" have human faces, other have heads of lions, tigers, bears and three-eyed demons. Sexual symbolism or unio mystica of the opposite principles of Tantric Buddhism is shown by the embraces of male and female images. Tibetan Buddhism finally ascribes the static function to the female principle..

Along the wayside in the northern mountain areas of Nepal, visitors come across many Chorten. This is the Tibetan name for certain monuments that correspond through the form of stupa. The above accounts are given to focus on the form of Buddhism prevalent in the Himalayan regions of Nepal. Even to-day, some of the picture of Buddhist culture can be seen emerging from Tibet. Such remnants of the flourishing Tibetan Buddhism can be witnessed far in the east from Tapleying to the far western region of Darchula and in the remote Valleys of Rolwaling Helambu, Manang, Kali Gandaki, Jumla Humla, Dolpa etc.

Many Gompas or Buddhist monasteries are located in various places of northern part of Nepal. Some of them have been built on isolated mountain tops. These Gompas are the rich treasures of traditional Tibetan art and crafts. These treasures are full of the hand printed old manuscripts, the sinning brocades silk thankas or Pauvas (scrolls), precious images made of gold and silver and wall paintings giving real representation to Buddhist legends. Along with these treasures, there are also frescoes and mural all providing scenes of the events of life episodes of the Buddha. There are many Prayer wheels which are of bronze or copper cylinders and on each is inscribed "Om mane padme hum", the jewel in the Lotus. There are libraries stocked with many kinds of books full of precious manuscripts. There are Prayer Hall which is scented with the smells of incense and butter.

The High Valleys of Nepal in the northern parts in the lap of the Himalaya Prayer flags are seen fluttering on the top of the monasteries, Chortens and even houses. One can notice even trail side rock walls carried with "om mane padme hum" devotional hymns to Buddha.

Taplejung District, the land of the Kanchenjunga in far east Nepal are covered with lovely monasteries dedicated to Lord Buddha. The people of Walangchung Gola Village are mostly Buddhists. Walangchung Gola has contained a very famous monastery known as the Diki Chholing Gompa. It is a centre of Ningmapa sect and this monastery is said to have been built by Chhyosar Dorchi Lama around the year 1895. This monastery has a rare assemblage of statues, hand printed manuscripts and geometrical Buddhist paintings. Side by side with these characteristics, this monastery has altar of an eternal flame that has been blazing for last two centuries. People belief has been centered on an idea as this flame is Satya Yug Ko Batti."

Kanchenjunga is 8,598 m. high and its dazzling peaks are of astonishing beauty and charm. The trek is equally enjoyable and memorable in the area. In this part of the northern Himalayan regions of Nepal, remnants of Buddhist culture are noticed. The glimpses of the rituals and customs of Buddhism are prevalent. Northern parts of the Kanchenjunga are covered with beautiful monasteries. As depicted above, the people of northern valleys of Taplejung especially Walangchung Gola Village are the followers of Buddhism. Khumbv region has been long associated with Everest, the highest peak in the world. The trail to visit this region passes through Phyphlu, a very beautiful Sherpa Village to Jumbesi, Salleri and to the Buddhist monastery at Chiwong. Lukla is another famous place and is popular as the gateway to the Everest region and Namche Bazar situated at 3,860 meters. The visit to this region also familiarize with the Buddhist culture and charmful Sherpa Village life. Sherpas, the people of this region are known as the tiger of the snow and mountain guide famous for their association with the mountaineers of the world. This region is a magnificent and fascinating spot. Here are the highest mountain in the world, snow-covered, rock-faced, they tower proud and are—inspiring, mass on mass. The Sherpas are very tough and very strong. Their staple food is barley and buck wheat. They tame Yaks their beasts of burden. These people practise Tibetan Buddhsim and there are a number of lovely monasteries in Solv and Khumbu regions where one can found the rituals and customs of Tibetan Buddhism.

The Buddhist monastery of the Tengboche or Thyanghoche is seen here against the background of Ama Dablam (68,12 m). It lies at an altitude of 3,860 meters. This monastery is among the most renowned monasteries and is an excellent feature of Sherpa artistry. There stands a 17 feet clay image of Lord Buddha has also enshrined inside the monastery. The chief Lama of the monastery is the second Lama incarnate Napang Tenjing Gangpo. This impressive monastery is situated near confluence of the Imga Khola and Bhole Kosi river. Its building looks like a medieval fortress and is painted white near the Sherpa Villages. This is full of handsome frescoes, Thanka painting and other works of religious art. It also contains a large collection of statues representing Sakyamuni Buddha, Maitreya Buddha, Manjushri, Vajra-dhara, Vajrapani, Avalokiteswara, Aparomita, Tara etc. But this monastery was firstly destroyed by fire in 1989 and by great earthquake of 1943. But this monastery built and renovated now. Commanding the panoramic views of the Himalayan mountains this monastery command scene and serene view. This monastery keeps alive the glorious heritage of Khumbu Valley. The famous Mani Rimdu festival is celebrated in the courtyard of the Thyangboche monastery in December, every year.

There are two other monasteries in this region as Palden Riu Gompa of Khvmjvng Village and Dekshen Chhokhor

Gompa of Thame Village. These monasteries are also worth visiting.

Thyangoche and Pongboche are two famous villages of Sherpa in the land of Sherpa-Everest Region. These monasteries have collection of fine pictures depicting various gods of the Buddhist religion. The Khumbu Valley, gateway to Everest looks like a Buddhist world.

The mysterious valley of Rolwaling lies couple of kilometres south of the Tibetan frontier, along the east bank of Bhote Koshi. It is remarkably one of the most remote and beautiful areas of Nepal. This area has known with many kinds of tales regarding the abominable snowman Yeti. Mr. Eric Shpton, the famous mountaineer is said to have photographed foot of Yeti on the Menling glacier regions in 1951. Also Sir Edmund Hillary preceded a Yeti Expedition in 1950 in pursuit for the elusive Yeti.

Visitor can drive to Barabise and start trekking and enter the Rolwaling Valley. This area is covered by vegetation and generally long tailed grey langurs are seen in many places.

The best way to visit monasteries is to trek a week from Charikot, headquarter, of the Dolakha District which provides rhododendron groves and green forested hills of the lower Rolwaling Valley to the Sherpa Village of Nangaon and Beding rich in monasteries. Bigu monastery is located in Dolkha district and this is singular monastery full of nuns and not monks. Nuns are seen there following their religious way of life which is very much interesting. This monastery contains 50 nuns and the village around it has scanty huts. This monastery has statues of golden Buddha and Avaloketeswara amidst many other images. There are also many thankas or scroll paintings seen hanging from the ceiling. The monastery can be reached by walking up the mountain from Chagu and takes four hours to arrive at the site.

After leaving behind Semigaon, the trail ascends steeply to Sambar Danda to cross the foot of Mahalungur Himal and grand view of Gauri Shankar (7145 m) is seen from the pass. The only settlement on the upper Rolwaling is the small village of Beding which is also a monastery famous for fabled story of Tantric saint Guru Padmasambhava is said to have mediated 2000 years ago.

Helambu is located near about 40 kilometres north of Kathmandu Valley. This spot is popular as a trekker's paradise. This place lies in Langtang areas and the inhabitants are of many ethnic groups. The Hindus live in lower valleys and Buddhists Tamangs and Sherpa in Helambu and Tamang and Bhotias in Langtang Valley. Rich temperate forests are another attraction of these areas. Helambu is an idyllic Sherpa village full of many Buddhist monasteries in the region amid rich and enchanting landscapes. The Langtang Valley populated by Sherpa and Tamang families over shadowed to the north by the high peak of Langtang Lirung (7,234m) on Tibetan border. Most of the area has been designated as National Park which is noted for its birds and flowers. Helambu has several Sherpa villages. Each village has contained a lovely monastery. The rich cultural heritage of Helambu resides in its monasteries. Tarke Ghyang monastery is very famous in the region. This monastery is known as Jhundup Dekchen Fotang Gompa—white-washed and has contained beautiful prescoes and idols of Buddha. Its collection of golden and terra-cotta statues, scroll paintings and hand written manuscripts are significant and is regarded as richest monasteries in the region.

Similarly Kyangjing Gompa is located at the foot of the Langtang Lirung glacier, eastwards to Langsisa. This monastery is also rich in statues of Buddha, scroll paintings and manuscripts. Another equally famous Gompa is Sing Gompa which is situated at 3,254 meters hill behind Syabru which offers views north into Tibet and west towards the Annapurna. This monastery has also a good collection of statues of Buddha, paintings and hand written manuscripts. Two other villages of Helambu—Melenchi gaon and Sermathang have got very beautiful monasteries.

To the north of Gorkha township stands Yangria Danda. There are beautiful alpine valleys of Sama and Chhekampar and also Prok village. These villages are stronghold of Tibetan

Buddhism. Sama village is located in green Valley in the backdrop of Ganesh Himal. Chekkamar is equally lovely. Both these villages have several monasteries. Sama village has a famous Karki Chyoli Gompa build about 1000 year back. This monastery houses the statues of Buddha and Guru Ringpoche or Padma Sambhava. Equally Kangyur Lakhang Gompa and Kanapungen Gompa are known monasteries in the region. The Prayer Halls of these monasteries are attractive with serere colour and there are statues of Buddha in the altar followed by Padmasambhava and incarnate Lamas. These monasteries contain rooms for monks and nuns to stay in.

The beautiful village of Chhekampar has many fine monasteries. The more famous are three namely Rachen Gompa, Dhechen Lhundup Gompa, Thukjeling Gompa and Chhefuk Gompa. Rachen Gompa is white and red coloured shrine and its inner sanctum is full of golden Buddha statues, Tara and Ambitabh. Equally Chhekampar monastery contains statues of Buddha, Padmasambhava and many other religious arts. The walls of these monasteries are painted with the images of Buddha. Chhefuk Gompa is dedicated to Ningmapa sect since 400 years and historically famous in the region.

Edging through the deep gorge flanked by Annapurna and Gorkha Himal groups, the green expansion of the Manang valley opens all of a sudden with forests, and river Marshyangdi passing through it along monasteries—crowned ridges. Visitors enjoy the bewitching view of imposing north face of the Annapurna range and glaciers on its top.

Manang is also one of the popular tricks in Nepal. The route follows from Kathmandu to Dumre on Pritivi Rajmarg (highway). The trek follows a few forests pastures, barren rocky slopes and rugged stone areas. The ethnic and cultural attractions are many as the Marsyangdi Valley is populated by Lama Buddhists. Many Gompa having art treasures are found along the way. The mystical valley of Manang is a portion of the Annapurna circuit which is the most popular trekking destination. The first adventurous trek from Kathmandu, Pokhara and Dumre—along the clear

Marsyangdhi Khola (river) and then to Bahundanda. After Bahundada the route passes through the villages of Magars and the Gurungs. The villages of Chamje, Tal and Bagarchap come across enroute. Their the houses are almost constructed of stone walls and their roofs flat. Stack of fuelwood are piled up on the roofs or hay being dried in the sun. Long poles by the sides of these houses are kept with printed prayer flags with the image of Buddha or the sacred Mandala written in the Tibetan script. The people here profess the Tibetan Buddhist. All houses are fully painted in white colour which provide a distinct look and colours. After Bagarchap arrives Chame. The upper Manag Valley is inhabited by Tibetan Buddhists. Everywhere prayer flags with the 'Mane mantra are seen in private houses, monasteries and Chortens. Not only in the private houses only, even hill tops flutter with prayer flags painted with prayers all over the Manang region. Almost all villages after Chame contain beautiful monasteries built apart from the stone houses. In the main villages of Braga, there is one very prominent monastery which stands high above the settlement having a look like a small fortress. This monastery is considered to be built five hundred years. This has been the seat to Kogyupa sect as well as the most important cultural centres in the region. The next big village after Braga is Manang from which the district takes its name. The people of this district are popular by the name of "Manangis". The beautiful Kali Gandaki river basin upland which has been a major trade route between Nepal and Tibet. This region is also known as Thak Khola Region which is one of the popular trekking destination of Nepal. Upper Kali Gandaki Valley is very rich with a number of Gompas. There is one prominent Saptelling Gompa in Marpha in the lovely Thakali village. This monastery is believed to have been built by Lama Renjen Chewang Norbu and this is considered to be of 200 years old. This is full of many kinds of artifacts and terra cotta idols of Amitabha, Avalokiteswara, Padmasambhava etc.

Kuchhep Terrang Gompa is located at the back of the River Gandaki Kali in Jomson. This monastery is full of excellent wall paintings and frescoes. It has prayer Hall full of terra-cotta statues of Amitabha Avalokeleswara, Manjushree, Vajrapani, Sweta Tara and incarnate Lamas.

The track to Manang through Marsyangdi Valley is full of unique attraction providing gentle and most comfortable route all along affluent and different landscapes and sceneries. Many picturesque villages and people of different ethnic stocks toiling on there fields of paddies on the lower south and the northern unusual habitation of which Barga makes out visible models of townscapes and architecture. The most fascinating village in Manang is Barga an ancient settlement situated in a pack of cliffs. As said above, racially and culturally, the upper Manang Valley is settled and dominated by devoted Lamaist Buddhists and Buddhism. Each village has its own place of workshop or monastery or Gompa which looks like a fortress standing detached in a cliff shielding the settlements and their inhabitants below as defender or guardian. Many of these monasteries or Gompas replenish with abundant store of assets such as statues of Buddhas, Bodhisatvas, mystical figures and Thangka—hand—printed scrolls with religious motifs. They also treasure significant and precious hand-written manuscripts which are very interesting.

Mustang's vast potential as a lovely destination is excelled for it has an exceptional wilderness, lovely scenery, snowy peaks, attractive 16th century monasteries and several other sights.

Mustang is situated in the Himalayan fold casted by the Annapurna Dhaulagiri massifs ward off rain bearing monsoon winds from the region which is in general, a wind swept desert. The 2000 kilometre interior that envelops the region makes up mainly of barren ridges, deep canyon, eroded cliffs and moraine valleys.

The most outstanding spot of Mustang district is Lomanthang village. This place is regarded as the ancient capital of Mustang and historical record amply proves it. It even now covered all around with a wall and gives a look as a walled city called to mind as a flash-back of the ancient

Greek and Roman city states. An imposing gate leads to the capital city of Mustang—Lomanthang from the eastern part. Near to this gate, five-storeyed and magnificent royal palace stands symbolising the true picture of this place. The features of the people, their culture and language look similar to that of Tibetans. The people known as lobas who are appeared to be pastoral nomads. The scenery of the Lomanthang is exotic. The Gompas of upper Mustang have a priceless collection of ancient scroll paintings. The Manyang Chhyoli Dakarling Gompa is located within the walled city of Lo Mathang. It is most sacred in Mustang. Along with this Zhyampal and the Thakchen Gompas which are very rich by history and culture in the walled city of Mustang. Zhyampal Monastery is the oldest and is in three storey made of mud and wood. It is said to have been built by Amgon Bzang Po in 1447 A.D. This monastery has fine paintings all over its wall. There is a huge and superb idol of Maitraya placed in the middle of it. There are sculptures of Dorye Semha Buddha and wooden Chortens. It is a treasure of Mandalas (paintings).

There is another Takachen Monastery is equally remarkable. The door of this monastery is engraved with the Ranjana script and the panel of it is carved with six lion heads. There are huge earthern images of Dhritarastra and Baisrawan on the right hand and Birudhak and Birupakshya on the left hand. A carved door leads into the sanctum. It has Chorten Lokeshwar, Buddha, Manjhughosh, Padma, Sambhav with consorts Hayagriva, Tara and Bagradhara.

Dolpa district lies in Far western Nepal. Dolpa is now becoming a popular trekking destination. This area is full of soaring mountainous forests of firs, pines forests. A three day's trek from Jufal airstrip takes one to Phoksundo Lake, one of the most attractive high altitude mountain lakes in the Himalayas. This region has been centre to a large number of monasteries. Each monastery has its own district characteristics. Ringmo village, on the southern end of lake Poksundo—a lake of beauty, there lies a monastery named as Tupte Lakharg Gompa. This Gompa contains Bon-po iconography which is ingenious. The nine mandalas (mystic circles) on its ceiling is regarded as one of the finest pieces of painting. Dolpa is located in its Tibet-like setting. This district is crowned by Kanjiroba Himal (6612m) which is one of the beautiful peaks in north-western Nepal. Tibetan Buddhist culture are maintained here as its heritage. This is still considered a "little Tibet. Some people of Dolpo still follow Bon, the ancient animistic faith of Tibet. The famous Shey Svndo Gompa stands above the right bank of the Sibu Kholat an altitudes of 4,878 m. There are many jumble of houses ringed by prayer walls and chortens. This Gompa is looked after by the head Lama, believed to be the reincarnation of the founder Lama Tendzin Ra-pa. This monastery hangs a great painting of the Karma—pa Lama. This Gompa is red painted building with prayer walls and chortens. This monastery founded by Tanjor Rewa Lama and contain a beautiful terra cotta and bronze statutes including that of the Vajradhara, holder of the Vajra or thunderbolt. The walls are painted with frescoes depicting Buddhist divinities. People of Dolpo travel to Tibet in the summer days and trade wools and salt in exchange for grains. The famous Shey Gompa and the serene views of Lake Phoksundo are writhin. Shey Phoksundo National Park, the largest National Park in Nepal having an area of 3,555 sq. kilometres. The village of Ringmo at the back of the Phoksundo lake has a monastery named as Namgyal Lakhang Gompa. This Gompa has also full of terra-cota statues and frescoes of Buddhist divinities. There are also monasteries in Phijor and highland settlements of Dolpo.

Nepal, being the land of birth-place of Shakyamuni Gautama Buddha, Buddhism, has spread in all areas of Nepal in the plain Terai, the southern part of Nepal as well as in the remote highland regions of Nepal.

21 *Mount Kailas and Lake Manasarovar*

PRECIOUS JEWEL OF SNOW

Mount Kailash lies 330 air miles from Kathmandu but nearly twice as far by land. The range of Mount Kailash expand from Kashmir to Bhutan. The significant peak of the range is Rakapast (7,788 m). The centre and the northern section of the range is surrounded by Lachu and Jhen gohu mountains and the northern part of the range is known as Kailash Peak. Mount Kailash main peak emerges in Ngari and this place in western Tibet is situated on one of the highest, coldest and most inhospitable places in the earth.

For western Nepal and its northern part, where the surrounding snowy mountains are being highest, a little way off from its boundary at Tibet towers sacred mountains of Kailash. The pious devotees of Lord Shiva of Hindu religion and Jain and Buddhists (Bon followers) devouts make pilgrimage to the top of the sacred Mount Kailash along with a deep bath in the Lake Manasarovar. Mount Kailash is located on the vast rolling landscape of desert like environs. It takes six days, difficult driving from Lhasa, the Capital of Tibet. The other convenient treks of 15 days duration across Humla (5293 m) in for western Nepal to Mount Kailash and sacred lake Manasarovar from Timmure into Kylrong and Kodari to the Dingri region. The convenient route, Simikot-Yari-Khoyarnath-Taklakot-Mount Kailash and Lake

Manasarovar. Trekking route via Simikot to Mount Kailash and to return via the same route is very exciting and comparatively easy than the Lhasa or Zangmu route.

The pious devotees to Shiva Mahadev come to worship the divinely carved representation of their God, stuck in the top of the mountain.

There is another of the amazing pilgrimages of Hindu sacred lake of Manasarovar.

Tibet, Autonomous Region of the People's Republic of China is a land in south central Asia. It is known all over the world as the Roof of the World. Its snow-capped Himalayan mountain and a wind-swept plateau known as the Plateau of Tibet is the highest in the world. It has an area of 1, 221,600 square kilometres and the high land of wilderness wraps up much of the land. Along the southern part of the plateau the snowy Himalayan mountains soar culminating the highest altitudes in the world. Many peaks in the north cover by the Kunlun range which hovers more than 6000 meters. Tibet has an average elevation of 4880 meters. Considerable portions of Tibet are waste land of gravel rock and sand. It has innumerable lakes and streams but a great number of them have stale banks and a high salt content. Some of the important rivers of Asia have their sources of the mountains of Tibet flowing out of it and crossing the Himalayas into India. These rivers are Indus, Sutlej, Ganga and Brahmaputra in India and Karnali in Nepal. All these rivers originate in the catchment areas of Mount Kailash—Lake Manasarovar in Tibet and the glaciers close to them. Karnali river of Nepal originating from Tibet embarks on Nepal at an altitude of 4499 m. Its head water is in Tibet and coming out of glaciers cause a perennial flow.

Mount Kailash is situated in wind swept and severely cold and arid region. This place is deserted except for small bands of nomadic tribes. It is a blank and barren waste-land. No public transportation exists in this remote desert. This area can be reached in five days from Lhasa, the capital of Tibet on vehicles. There stand a place named Tarchen small settlement of some habitation at the base of mountain. Mount

Kailash has dome-shaped conical summit. It is the only place of pilgrimage in the world where four powerful followers of Hindu, Jain, Buddhist and Tibetan Bonpas religions adhere to or redeem one's religious observances. The pious devovts of these four religions regard it as the supreme pilgrimage site. Mount Kailash is the venerated dome shaped peak and its dome looks strange and so it has seized the reverence of the Hindus, Jains, Buddhists all over the world since earliest time. Hindu mythology sheds light of Mount Kailash as the abode of Lord Shiva. Kailashpati as he is called the supreme lord of mountains. Lord Shiva, the destroyer but also the regenerator of the universe is considered to reside on its top. So Hindus worship it as the seat of Lord Shiva and the worshippers of Lord Shiva regard it the most sacred of all Hindu pilgrimages.

The Hindu religious scriptures such as Shiva Purana, the Shkanda Purana, the Himabat Kanda etc. have narrated the spiritual and religious significance of the Kailash. Hinduism refers God Brahma, the supreme post-vedic deity as a creater of all universe and originator of everything. Mount Kailash is contemplated as the earthy symbol of the emblem of Mount Meru, the sacred mountain created by the God Brahma at the centre of the universe. God Brahma has three main forms called Trimurti. They are Brahma, the creater of the universe, Vishnu its preserver and Shiva, its destroyer. Lord Shiva has been ascribed to reside in the Himalaya. Many Shiva temples exist all along the Himalayas. The great Himalayan mountain ranges are named after him and his consort Goddess Parvati. Hindus worship them as the seat of Lord Shiva and the worshippers of Lord Shiva regard them as their sacred pilgrimage site. Hindu religious text as the Bhagvat Purana has portrayed the account of "Naga Desha" with a saga of central south Tibet and western Nepal. The same holy scripture has also sketched the description of Holy Mount Kailash and Lake Manasarovar. This region is described as "Swarna Bhumi" and its internal part seems to comprise of Mount Kailash and the Lake Manasarovar area in the region of Tibet in the western part of the Himalayan range.

Similarly Jainism, ancient religion and philosophy founded by Vardhamana Mahavira, the great sage in the 6th century and the followers of this religion regard Holy Mount Kailash as the place where their first prophet Tirthankar Adinath Rsabhadeva attained salvation. They venerate Mount Kailash as Astha Pada or Padma Harada by being the place of their first Tirthankar who attained heavenly solace at this holy place. It is the most sacred of all of Jain pilgrimages.

Bon Religion of Tibet is known as Lamaist Buddhism of the Nyingmapa sect and is influenced by animism, totenism and certain rites dating from the old "Bon" religion. It is the religion prevailing in Tibet, Buddhism intermingled with Hinduism and Shamanism. The followers of Bon Religion consider Mount Kailash as very sacred for it is the place where its founder Shanrah is said to have descend from heaven. So Mount Kailash enjoys great popularity in the folk tradition of Tibet. The Bons circumbulate the Mount Kailash and consider by all Bon pilgrims to walk KORA or the Parikrama (circuit tour) around Mount Kailash as the most essential deed to come up with heavenly attainment. Pilgrims generally assemble at the ground encircling the mountain on all sides who come to observe their pious desires of walking the KORA or the sacred circuit. It is believed that a single day KORA permits the pilgrim to earn the highest reward of religious virtue. But usually a pilgrim can perform a KORA circuit by walking the first day and halting the next day for rest and can repeat the circuit the day after. The start of the Kora begins by walking westward, the sight of land appears with and bushes and deep gorges around golden colour dust. Mount Kailash is effaced all the time out of the pilgrim's route. The pilgrims trend on the border of foothills and then take the eastern route to reach at the valley of the Lhachu, famous as "River of the Gods". The elevated or tall point enroute named as Drolma Pass draws nearer enwrapped with saturated sandstone cliffs. A natural bowl shaped hole plunged into the rock with shaft is viewed as its lofty setting and the rock postulates the name of "Milarepa's food bowl" and the waterfall in the other side of it dignified by the specific name "Tail of the legendary horse of King Gesar of Ling". Two other peculiar phenomena notice in the rocks which give distinctive meaning as one is signified as Guru Rinpoche's big torma cake presenting to local deities reliefed into a chunk of a big rock and another rock stone beside it is known as the posture of the Hanuman, the monkey God of Hindu text Ramayana praying to God Shiva. At the sometime Tibetan Bon Buddhists venerate it as the place of twelve armed tantric deity DEMCHOG.

Along with Mount Kailash, Lake Manasarovar is equally famous as the sacred place of pilgrimage. Lake Manasarovar was also believed to have created out of the mental desire of Hindu Lord Brahma, the divine force that creates and sustains the Universe. South of Mount Kailash across the vast expanse of land space of Bharka at the base of the glittering Mount Gurlamandhatta, two water bodies of popular names as Manasarovar (Mapam Yumtso) and Rakbas Tal (Lhanag Tso) exist providing fantastic panorama of natural beauties and fantasies. These lakes are the highest bodies of freshwater in the world. Manasarovar Lake is situated at 4558 metres higher than Rakbas Tal. All the sources of the South Asia's greatest rivers are nearby at the base of the mountains surrounding these lakes. Lake Manasarovar, lying below Mount Kailash, is the sacred lake where a religious bath with sacred offerings will allow pilgrims to deliver a solace to the God's presence and panacea of all evil deeds.

For western Nepal and its northern part, where the encircling snowy Himalayas being highest in ethereal space, a little way off from its boundary at Tibet towers the sacred mountain of Kailash. The devotees of Lord Shiva of Hindu religion and Jain and Buddhists (Bon followers) devouts make pilgrimage to pay homage to the divinely representation of their god, suck in the top of the sacred Mount Kailash along with a deep bath in the lake Manasarovar. Mount Kailash lies on the vast rolling landscape that covers almost desert country. It takes six days hard driving from Lhasa, the capital of Tibet. The other three convenient treks proposed are each lasting 15 days across

Humla (5,293 m) in far western Nepal to Mount Kailash and sacred Lake Manasarovar from Timmure into Kylrong and from Kodari to the Dingri region. But arrangement as of present should be well and good for devotees to go to the region of Mount Kailash—Lake Manasarovar via Taklakot of the Autonomous Region of Tibet and facilitate them to trek through convenient route. Simikot-yari-Khoyarnath-Taklakot-Mount Kailash and Lake Manasarovar. Route to Mount Kailash via Simikot of Nepal in far western Nepal is very exciting and comparatively easy than the Lhasa or Zangmu route.

Kermi Village is also interesting halting place for making pilgrimage to Mount Kailash and Lake Manasarovar as it lies near about 28 kilometres from Simikot, headquarters of Humla in Nepal side just in day walking. This village is one of the lovelier place due to its specific natural and cultural peculiarities.

A week long trek from Darchula Khalanga is also quite interesting which goes through the scenic village of Chhangru (3354 m). Tinkar (3,963 m) a lovely village is situated at the northern face of Byas Rishi Himal about eight kilometres north from Chhangru. Most people of Chhangru and Tinkar journey across the high passes to Taklakot to barter wool, salt or other items from the south. There is another village called LINI VALLEY located at the base of Nala Nangkar (7,337 m) north of Humla is just alluring area rich of mountain scenery, pastoral panorama and rural life style of the people.

Saipal and Byas Rishi Himal are two major extreme western groups of the Nepal Himalayas stretch between the Karnali and the Mahakali rivers. The Byas Rishi Himal constitutes the western limit of the Nepal Himalayas. The two important groups are separated by the upper valleys of the Seti river. The western group is known as the Byas Rish Himal and the eastern as the Saipal Himal. North of the Byas Rishi Himal group, there are two groups of the border ranges such as Gurans Himal and the Lipu Lekh while in the south lies two minor ranges of Bankta Lekh and Surma Sarover Lekh. The two principal peaks in the Byas Rishi Himal group are

Api (7132 m), Nampa (6,754 m) and Saipal (7035 m). The whole of the southern part of the Api-Nampa-Saipal group forms a magnificent mountaineering area.

There is route to return back from Humla's Yari and Lini passes after visiting Mount Kailash. These passes at an altitude of over 5000 meters which can be utilized for monsoon as well. These routes are not viable during winter due to heavy snowfalls. It is also in practice that devotees wishing to visit Mount Kailash and Lake Manasarovar have been carried to Mount Kailash via Khasa. The motorable road from Khasa takes near about five days to reach Mount Kailash. But the best route for Mount Kailash and Lake Manasarovar starts from Simikot, the administrative headquarters of Humla district which is accessible by air from Nepalgunj. The north western Nepal Tibet boundary swings north of the main Himalayan axis and adventure begins in Trekking to Mount Kailash Lake Manasarovar through a panorama of changing scenery the rugged mountains, the barren slopes of the Tibetan landscapes to the wide sweep of the golden desert. The trekking in varied landscapes and experience is unique amongst all the travel discovery of the world.

22 *Stone Idols in Nepal*

Stone carving or sculpture has also brought about its share of fine works in Nepal since ancient times. It has really accomplished the glory and grandeur of distinction along with other fine arts. Stone carving or sculpture is an age old art that is still practiced throughout the country and has achieved the splendour of fine works. Using techniques and making processes slightly changed through the centuries, stone sculptors still employ most of their vigour as in olden times on Hindu and Buddhist images although they stand to turn out stone slabs, the figures of animals, temple guardians, the tantric symbols and other memorable tablets.

The hammer and chisel are the principal tools, even so, finer cutting instruments are used as the stone block presumes form with a buffer use to lay the last touches. A sketch is written firstly on the stone block as a model of carving in matching bold mark of black ink, after which sculptor chisels and chips until the final figure comes out perfectly. A big idol may take as long as many months to carve, a pagoda several months more. Nepal, having a mountainous country not only has plenty of stone but it also contains many quarries, granite, marble, sandstone and other porous rocks are also available.

Stone carvings or sculpture of Nepal dates in history more than thousands of years, back towards the 5th century. God and Goddess were introduced in Nepal as a mainstay to religion. Nepali carvers turned to wood rather than stone because it was easier to handle. Stone carvings were not so encouraged as wood carving. But even then, stone carvers turned out many admirable products. Images of both Hindu and Buddhist God and Goddess, however came to be regarded as object of worship rather than of art. The sculptural art of Nepal not only acted an important role in itself but also strived influence upon the art of neighbouring countries. Huan Chwang, the Chinese traveller who travelled through Nepal in 637 A.D. and his travelogue about Nepal which was full of admiration of the Nepali arts and crafts. In the same manner, Chinese account of Nepal, 643-651 A.D (History of the Thang Dynasty) highly praises about the Nepal and its arts including stone sculptural arts. A considerable number of ancient stone sculptural arts have survived up till now. The most important are the statues of the Kirat Kings and Verupaksha images situated near the Pashupatinath temple considered to be the images of Kirat age. So the Kirat dynasty rule in Nepal can be said to be the beginning of stone carving or sculpture in Nepal. However, early stone sculpture of Nepal can be traced demonstratively from the 5th century A.D. The early idols were carved after Gandhara, Mathura and the Pala schools of India. But these early idols or images illustrated intrinsic touch an origination of the Nepali carvers. There are some significant stone sculptures from Licchavi Period (5th-8th century) at Changu Narayan. Lichhavi age is the golden age of stone carving in Nepal. Images of Lichhavi age also tread close upon the Gandhara, Gupta and Pala style. Likewise the sculptural arts of 6th-10th century are also equally famous. Early Malla period (11th-14th century) also enfold most beautiful stone art treasures. Some stone figures of bygone ages as masterpieces can be seen preserved in Archeological Garden, Patan and National Gallery, Bhadgaon. Late Malla period is considered as the last phase of Nepali sculptural creations of Tantric images of violent appearance. The sexual symbolism "Parts of Opposites" of Tantricism represented by the love making component of male with female images is preserved in Nepal Museum. Stone carrying or sculptures of this period look simple, plain but decorative and lovely conspicuous in grace and appearance.

The range of stone carving of Nepal is varied and unlimited and they are demonstrated from the diagram or pictures to the attraction of the "Mandala" (signifying certain drawing of magical circles filled with some symbols and writings). These also enclose images of deities arranged in geometrical order as an aid to religious devotion. Such magical circles were seen drawn everywhere on the temple floors on stones, on the altars or walls etc. In the same way the Torana (the elaborate semicircular tympanum or torana placed above the door way of temple in Kathmandu valley) is found in the religious shrines everywhere around the Kathmandu valley. The people of Nepal are extremely religious and follow Hinduism and Buddhism. A remarkable feature of Nepal is the religious homogeneity between the Buddhist and Hindu communities who for centuries have cherished mutual regard and respect for one another. They observe traditional customs and rites. The exquisite architectural design of the Nepali pagodas and shrines that enshrine colossal bronze and stone images is an individualistic or exceptional feature of Nepal. The traditional shrines and stupas preserving images of stone sculptures add glory and grandeur to the artistic and cultural scene of Nepal.

The skill of the Nepali carvers are of high standard. The innumerable temples, stupas and viharas that were being built in Nepal in stone masonry gave place to essential stone cut sanctuaries unmatched due to their greatness. It is significant that the old stone sculptors of Nepal have also left behind examples of magnificent stone-carving works. Dhumbarahi, idol of Chendol a place is located near Harigaon, some two miles to the north-west of Kathmandu city and provides one of the best example of stone sculpture of high standard. The boar-headed incarnation of Vishnu the Hindu God represented as Dhumbarahi rising out of the disturbances of the serpent world (chaos created by Nagas) to rescue earth and sustain her on the elbow of his left arm which stands there in a temple testifying the best workmanship of Nepali stone sculpture. The whole sites of this place look as a treasure for the historians, archaeologists and art admirers.

This is six century stone sculpture which is a life-size in structure and is a remarkable piece of fine quality. This idol of Dhumbarahi is before in time to the bas-relief of Vamana incarnation of God Vishnu in Lazimpat and Trigunga dedicated by King Mana Deva to the memory of his mother dated 467 A.D. and the conception and execution of the image of Dhumbarahi is very simple and real. Similarly, the images of Vamana (God Vishnu Vikrantamurthi or Trivikrans) in his incarnation as the boar in disguise to destroy the demon Hiranyaksha who was pulling the earth under water) situated in Pashupatinath and Changu Narain are equally remarkable. Changu Narain about twelve kilometer east of Kathmandu and about eight kilometers north of Bhadgaon city. The temple is one of the most celebrated Vaishnav shrines of the valley. The temple is said to have been built by Vishnu Gupta and was later improved by Hari Datta Varna 323 A.D. But the earlier inscriptions belong to the ruler Mana Deva (5th century A.D.). The temple is elaborately decorated with sculptures and carvings and is considered to be the oldest pagoda style temple in the valley. The courtyard of Changu Narain temple is a storehouse of Nepali stone sculptures. The images of Garuda, Ganesh, Narsimha and Vishwarupa installed here are the models of representative stone images of Nepal. The images of Jamuna located at Deo-Patan near Pashupatinath and Satyanarayan at Harigaon (5th century A.D.) are also exemplary in execution. The best specimen of Shiva Linga known as Nepaleswara is placed at Harigaon and the big 4ft long standing image of Saraswati (the goddess of learning and knowledge) of 10th century. But the stone sculptures from the 5th to the 9th century belong to the Lichhavi period such as Dhumbaraha image of Chandol, Vishnu Vikranta images of Tila Ganga at Lazimpat and the Bhagavati image of Palanchowk and Budanilkantha image of Shivapuri are the outstanding stone sculptures of great repute. Budhanilkantha is located eight kilometers north of Kathmandu. There is a colossal idol of the God Vishnu sleeping on the bed of snakes (Anantasheshas) carved from a great block of stone. The idol is set in a pool of water thus giving it the appearance of floating. It is also believed to be the 5th century stone sculptural piece. The image signifies the God Vishnu asleep reclining on the bed of snakes as a result of having drunk as of poison. So the God known is Nilkantha which means blue throated one of the names of Lord Vishnu, the creator of universe. Then, the temple of Palanchowk Bhagavati which is situated seven kilometers north of the mountain of Panchkhaal on a top of a hill. The temple was considered to have been built dusting the reign of Mana Deva. The temple has a three foot long idol of Goddess Bhagavati in black stone. The black polished stone on which the figure is carved, proves the precious gem of Nepali craftsmanship of fifth century A.D. Another noticeable contribution of the Lichchhabis is the stone water spouts with engraved figures making as usual scene of Kathmandu valley many such water spouts are still seen at Garidhara, Satyanarayanthan in Harigaon etc.

Lichhavian period, a golden age so far as stone carving is concerned which lasted until 12th century. Then Malla period (12th century to 18th century) began and many Hindu and Buddhist images of various deities were carved. Stone sculptures dating from the eleventh and twelfth centuries are more frequent which are almost religious comprising statues of gods and goddesses, mythical beings, stone pillars, stone-memorial inscriptions, steps bearing pretty carved animals are noticed as decorations to the temples and temple courtyards. Malla period has produced an illustrious examples of stone sculptures like Royal bathing known as Shesnag. Sundari-chowk Dhara. Tushahity Kaliyadaman which are very reputed around the world. Among these above mentioned Royal baths of Hanuman Dhoka Palace, Kathmandu and Bhaktapur (Bhadgaon) Royal Palace "Tushahity" ancient Royal bath in the Durbar Square, Lalitpur (Patan) is lavishly decorated by minute figurines, statues and sculptures rescue medley which is one of the most noble and finest works on stone living for ever. In spite of inter-state quarrels, the Malla rulers of Kathmandu, Patan and Bhadgaon excelled with each other to beautify their capital with artistic palaces, temples, artistic creations on woods and stones which are considered to be the pride of Nepal at the present time. Durbar Square Kathmandu famous as Hanuman Dhoka epitomizes the grand show-piece of art and architecture. Famous stone sculptures to see there the image of Hanuman (monkey god) made of stone on the main gate of the Royal Palace signifying its name as Hanuman Dhoka kept by the Malla King Pratap Malla in 1650 A.D. There is a huge stone of Kal Bhairab, representing god Shiva in his destructive manifestation of the 17th century is fantastic in details. The stone idol is about forty feet high which stands in red and black and orange masonry, folding two hands over the breast, waving a spear and firebrand with two others and evading upon the head of a demon. Across his forehead is strings a row of human skulls and great pendants of them covered his neck. This image is of single stone. Such large images cut out of a single block of stone are very rare in Nepal. Bimaleswar Mahadev is a doomed shrine in Hanuman Dhoka as it is made of stone. Early Malla Period (11th -14th century confine a most beautiful stone art treasures in Kathmandu. Some of these places such as Mahankalsthan, temple courtyard of Lord Pashupatinath, Temple of Guheswari, stone elephant of Rani Pokhari and many others speak of the development of stone sculptures in that period. Other stone sculptures consist of the image of Lord Buddha in the courtyard of Swayambhu Nath Stupa, Boudhanath Stupa, Charumati Vihar and many other Vihars and Bahi such as Yatkha Bahal, Itum Bahal, Shreeghah Vihar, Kathisembhu scattered around the valley. Other places and areas in and around Kathmandu valley such as Kirtipur, Namo Buddha, Dakshinkali, Balajee, Panauti, Nala etc. also contain beautiful stone sculptures. Each and every temples have guardian deities, animals like lions, elephants etc. and more of griffins of stone before many door ways. Stone sculptures of Makara—(elephantine dragon) are seen in water spouts. The figures of Kinnara (figure of half bird half-man) angel are shown bearing the sacred water vessel. Those are also the figures of Nags (serpents) which are pictured around pillars, surrounding the base of chaityas, carved on beams window frames and doors. Likewise, sacred water vessel (eight auspicious symbols—Astamatrica), Gandarvas (celestial beings), Votive pillars, Yajna Mandala, Sila Patra, Swastica and star of David (specially sign of good luck noticed in Buddhist shrines). It is a usual sight to see stone lions guarding the entrance of Bahals in Kathmandu valley. Stone carvings dating from the eighth to ninth centuries are still to be found in Kathmandu city itself. But those dating from the eleventh to twelfth century are more easily found. The holy courtyard of each and every temple is worked into squares and terraces and it is frequently covered with stone images, shrines and religious symbols. Patan city or Lalitpur is known as the city of beauty. This city has stone sculptures of rare beauties such as Jagat Narayan temple, a shikhara-style temple of Lord Vishnu on the bank of Bagmati at Sankhamul and enshrines many dignified stone images of artistic values. Then, Kirshna Mandir holds a commanding position to be the first example of Shikhara style of architecture in Nepal. It is regarded as symphony in stone as it is only example in Nepal bearing 21 Shrines and is fully made of stone. It is said to have been built by Siddhi Narsingh Malla in the seventeen century. Most of the important scenes from the ancient Hindu epics the Ramayana and Mahabharat are engraved as bas-relief in stone. The quality of the stone work and the excellence of the carving are unusual. The minute details of this bas-relief work clearly show the high level that the art of stone carving has attained during Malla period. Then the Kumbeshwar temple dedicated to God Shiva is full with the stone idols of 5th century and earlier stone images. Eight stone images of Narayan, Ganesh, Sitala, Basuki, Gauri, Kritimukha and the Agama devatas of Buddha-margis are placed in various places in this temple courtyard. This temple is said to have been built by the King Jayasthiti Malla in 1422 A.D. Other temples like Bhimsen temple of Taleju also contain remarkable stone carvings. Lalitpur or Patan city is a marvel beyond the description due to its picturesque stone sculptures and carvings in its ancient Royal bath "Tushahity" in the Durbar Square. This Royal bath was made by the King Siddhi

Narsingh Malla in 1647 A.D. It is situated in the courtyard of Durbar Square known as Sundari Chowk and "Tushahity" the Royal Bathing Tank with engraved water sport is in the middle of this courtyard. The Royal Bath is octagonal in design signifying religious devotion to the eight Nagas (the serpent divinities or rain). The inner wall of the bathing tank are fully decorated with many stone-carved deities and the conic sections all are surrounded by a pair of sculptured dragons. It is masterpieces of artistic carvings on stone. It is considered to be one of the most dignified and finest sculptured works on stone. Then Rudra Varna Mahavihar, unique Buddhist monastery also envelopes fine and amazing collection of images of stone. The main Durbar Square of Patan are clustered with temples, shrines and sculptured stone works. It is enriched under the living brilliance by the delicate hand of stone carvers. The courtyards of temples are packed with pillars of stones, memorial inscriptions, engraved spells and prayers on stones, side by side entrance of these temples are all guarded all by a company of capricious beasts, phoenix and griffins. The whole city of Patan is a cluster of fine pagoda, shikhara stone temple and stone statues.

Bhaktapur or Bhadgaon is known as 'the city of devotee'. It is the home of medieval art and architecture. Its origin is considered to have been built in the time of Lichhavi rulers. It has also its Durbar square which is famous as the richest piece of art in Nepal. The Durbar Square and its main gate is adorned with the levely stone figures of Hanuman, Bhairava and Narashingha and known as Lion Gate. Batsala temple is equally famous for artistic decorations. This temple is made of stone with five architectural designs of a three stepped base with a colonnade of fourteen octagonal pillars. This shrine is dedicated to Goddess Bhagavati. This is also a Shikhara style temple in stone. This temple is the central land mark of the Durbar Square. This is equally famous for delicate profession of stone sculpture, beautiful design and graceful appearance. After Batsala temple, Nyatapola Temple, known as five-storied temple stands on a five tiered platform with figures of Jaya and Phattas Malla, wrestlers, elephants, lions, griffins and Goddesses Singheni and Bhagini perched on each side of the terrace posing ten times strength than the figures below them. This temple was built in 1702 A.D. by the King Bhupatindra Malla. The courtyards of the temples here too are really impressive and fantastic with stone sculptures. An ancient city of Bhadgaon is one of the most charming architectural show pieces of the valley highlighting the works of stone sculptures.

Nepal is the meeting place of the great civilizations of Asia and as such she is the cultural museum where art treasures and monuments of historical and artistic interests are preserved. The arts and traditions of Nepal inspired by Hindu and Buddhist religions are of an astonishing richness in Nepal. Many temples and shrines including stupas and pagodas are enhanced by the creative zeal of people with master pieces of stone sculptures. Nepal has population of 22 million and are divided into numerous ethnic groups. So Nepal is not only a geological mosaic but also a human mosaic coexisting peacefully following their own religions and tradition. There are many national cultural centres—Janakpur, birthplace of Sita and Lumbini world famous birth-place of Gautam Buddha. Likewise, Gorkha, Pokhara Valley, Khaptar, Rara, Itam, Bhadrapur, Helambu, Gosainkunda, Muktinath, Lamjung, Baraha Chetra, Nuwakot, Butwal, Dankuta, Palpa, Bhojpur, Shilgudhi Doti, Dailekh, and Jumal are equally famous in their own ways and are contributing major share in the development of Nepali art and culture. There are many national treasures in the form of religious centres, temples, shrines, mounds and sites of historical interests. Many exquisite stone images are found in all places of the country in temples and courtyard of shrines and forts. Nepal is equally known all over the world as the country of splendid Himalayan mountains with their number of high altitude peaks. Due to her singular mountain grandeur, she is known as trekker's paradise. So the trekkers come across the stone bearing the symbols in the trekking routes popular as the Mani walls. The stone is Chipped and the carving words refer, "OM MANI PADME HUM"—Hail! The Jewel in the lotus' sermons on stone. A trekker comes across in some place a great stone carved from top to bottom with these prayers. In the Everest Region, the Sherpaland as well as in the Thak Khola region, Kaligandaki Valley trekkers will very often see stone-walls covered with engraved slabs, mostly bearing the sacred prayers "Om Mani Padme Hum". Trekking routes are all covered with Mani walls composed of carved stones bearing prayers with sacred lotus flower carvings and a number of little pointed chortens symbolise monument of Buddhist religion with prayer flags. Many such chortens and a shrine are seen built over the trekking routes. Many Buddhist monasteries in different Himalayan regions contain unique idols of Gods and Goddesses in stone exposing a rich religious feelings and cultural heritage. Nepal has a testimony of the existence of spiritual and cultural treasures exposed by sermons on carved stone.

23 *Popular Symbolic Signs in Hindu and Buddhist Shrines*

Every Nepali temples and shrines are full of symbolic signs of devils, goddesses, serpents, vessels, flowers and plants. When visiting the reverend Hindu and Buddhist temples of shrines, any visitor is sure to be astonished by seeing small intricately carved scrolls, spirits, dwarfs, ghosts and many other figures. Now, some of the symbolic figures put as a common adornment in temples and shrines of popular deities and denominations are described below :

Makara : This is common sight at the water placed such as wells, spouts, ponds, and religious kund (pond) with a figure, of elephantine dragon with water coming out of its trunk. This sight of trunk and water coming out of it makes drink and bath in such place more energetic and refreshing. Such sight of makara is very ordinary in Kathmandu Valley and in all its ancient water places.

Purna Kalasa : Such symbolic figure represents sacred water vessel and one of the 'Astramatrica'—Eight Auspicious symbols.

Wheel and Deer : Such symbols are noticed above the door ways while entering Tibetan Buddhist Temples. These are common signs as the wheel denotes the Buddhist doctrine and the two deer are insignia of Deer Park in Sarnath, India where Buddha sermonised his first disciple.

Garuda : This is Mythical Sun Bird and as the vehicle and closest companion of Hindu God Vishnu—one of trinity of

Hindu religion. But this figure is also noticed with a snake victimized in its claws protecting a Buddhist shrine.

Kirtimukha : This is also the big mythical bird like Garuda which generally seen in Buddhist shrines which is placed to guard the religious places. Such features are not noticed in any Hindu temples but in Buddhist shrines with holding the victimized serpents in his mouth rather than the claws.

Kinnara : This figure of half-bird and half-man Kinnara looks like the Christian angel. Such figure is seen taking the sacred water vessel—Purna Kalasa.

Nags : Nags are regarded as the serpent kings of the valley. It is said that Kathmandu valley is a big lake in ancient time and the Nags or serpent is the king of the valley and there were many serpents inhabiting the valley. That is why serpents of metal or stone are seen put around pillars, oozing out of ponds, surrounding the base of Chaityas, carved on beams, window frames and doors. Kathmandu valley is for agriculture and so the people worship serpents in order to keep the rain in balance.

Gandarvas : These celestial beings are often noticed looking out of a nitch and were a popular theme in Lichhavi Nepal (300-900 A.D.) These figures are usually referred as nymphs who act being as one of the divinities for given salvation.

Mani Wheel : These wheels are generally noticed in relation with Tibetan Buddhism. These Mani wheels outside as well as inside the Buddhist shrines are put on a long scroll with prayers carved in small plates. It is believed that spinning these scroll clockwise reciting mantras or the names of god bestows success and prosperity to the devotees many times.

Swastica and Star of David : These two important signs are of good luck and generally in Buddhist shrines. An ancient and worldwide symbol + a cross with arms bent at a right angle which signifies the sun or good luck.

Chaitya is a small religious relic of the pre-Buddhist mounds called generally as "Stupa". They are found all over the Kathmandu valley and they are believed to be a reliquary for the dead.

Ankhijhya : An "Evil Eye Window"—a blind window with a celestial being peering mysteriously out. These symbols are placed in temples, palaces and homes. The mysterious figures are said to protect the temples and shrines from evils.

Torana and Tunals : Torana means decorative half-circle panels above the doors and diagonal struts that supports the roof are known as Tunals. Toran is considered as a Buddhist design and is generally used above doorways or niche of the Buddhist shrines. It actually gives meaning of keeping the Divine always above ones head. Tunals are supports of the temples which are generally full of artistic carvings and designs with these symbols. There are other religious architectures which are seen and to be known their names and values. These are specified below :

Mandala : The term "Mandala" means 'circle in Sanskrit'. It also applies to certain drawings of magical circles filled with some figures and writings. These magical circles were drawn everywhere on the temple floors, on the altars or walls etc. They have been used for sacrificial purposes expressing through its complicated symbolic composition metaphysical structure of the universe. This also refer to Yajna Mandala for places brunt offerings received in a fire pit (Homa).

Vajra (a Thunderbolt) : It is regarded as a divine symbol. It is a very important priestly symbol quite common in Vajrayana as well as Mahayana sects of Buddhism. It is a divine symbol of the changeless absolute : that is none other than Buddha himself and his enlightenment. Thus Vajra always stands for male principle whereas a bell for female. Vajra accompanied by a bell is a ritualistic requirement for every Buddhist religious ceremony.

Chorten : Along the wayside in the northern mountain areas of Nepal, one comes across many Chorten. This is the Tibetan name for certain monuments that is different to the stupa on the Square base, sometimes, made of superimposed steps, rises a sort of Cupola topped by a number of round discs held together by a certain axis which keeps them suspended. They may contain relics of saints or books or ritual objects no longer in use and are therefore honoured as sacred. But the Bonpo although accepting the Buddhist form in its architectural plan and for similar aims, carry out the ritual encircling keeping the chorten always on their left. One of the symbols of Buddhism is the Swastika with its arms pointing to the right that of the Bonpo is the same Swastika pointing left. But alongside the Bon, there is also Buddhism which has penetrated now through the work of a few Tibetan ascetics.

In this regard, it is useful to understand about the Bonpo religion. The Bonpo temples are seen in Nepal near the Tibetan frontiers. The Bon, the primitive religion of Tibet prior to Buddhism. The Bon religion has shamanistic beliefs over the long period of time but later on ideas and ceremonies have been borrowed from Buddhism. The Bon religion has developed the idea that the world is a continued struggle between good and evil. Good is a pure light that shines within us with any evils, and so it is necessary to defend goodness against the evils. The Bonpo do not expose their dead in the mountains where the wolves and vultures eat their fleshes without any traces in a very short time. Bon religion still in practice in Tarap and Mustong where Lamaism has been penetrating for centuries and which even now relate towards Tibet by tradition.

Tibetan Buddhism is commonly called Lamaism. The name was given to the religious system with the Lamas played in it. The creator of Lamaism Cang-ka-pa established a complicated system of monastrical hierachy worked out canonical law for Lamaist monasteries, introduced celibacy and allowed the monks to keep a limited property. Lamaist monks acquired strong ascendancy over simple folk. Higher Lamas became feudal rulers and lower lamas obedient tools in their hands.

Lamaism does not differ from Buddhism according to major principles of creed, it only contains more elaborate rituals. The main trait of Lamaism that separate it from orthodox Buddhism is its strong belief in demons. Thus leaving aside soft figures of various Buddhas and Bodhisatwas in Lamaistic iconography we come across many effigies of so called "faith defender"—who are the gods of demonical character.

Goddesses or feminine deities of Shivastic origins—they are shown as "air-travellers" with human faces, some have heads of lions, tigers, bears and three-eyed demons. OM MANE PADME HUM—The northern Himalayan valley of Nepal and the people living in these places are primarily Buddhists. As these valleys are isolated for a long period of times have followed nature worshipping faith of Bon-Po-of Tibet. Padma Sambhava was a great saint of Buddhism as his great influence is noticed in these northern valleys of Nepal. There are rock walls in the trails of the mountains which are caused with devotional words. These carved words refer OM MANE PADME HUM signifying "Jewel in the lotos" means the Great Buddha. While going on trekking, the trekkers can view such sights with carved symbols in various places in the Himalayan region.

Monasteries or Gompas : The Himalayan valleys are full of monasteries or Gompas. These monasteries and Gompas are really the heritage of these valleys. The international visitors will find out traditional belief and custom of the people living in these valleys. Prayer flags are seen fluttering in the air with the Buddhist prayer—Mane Mantra. These monasteries and gompas have rich idols of Gods and Goddesses of Buddhist pantheon. Many rich traditional objects of arts and crafts, hand written and painted religious texts, as well as silk brocade Thankas or scrolls are rich repositories of these monasteries or Gompas. The famous monasteries situated in the northern Himalayan valleys are Shey Gompa in Dolpo, Braga Gompa in Manang, Tarke Ghyang (Helambu), Thyangboche Gompa in the Khumbu valley etc. are the real treasures containing many kinds of religious objects and traditional ways of ritual worships.

Sexual Symbolism : Erotic painting and carving seen on temples in Hindu and Buddhist shrines are the ancient art. It is associated with tantricism. Tantric art, as it is known, is a visualization of the eternal cycle of creation, dissolution and preservation of the human race. The cosmic universe is seen as a harmonious balance between pairs of opposite forces. Tantricism is a synthesis of spiritual and material potential. Tantra, therefore does not advocate withdrawal or renunciation from life but it is the fullest possible acceptance of one's designs, feelings and situations. The creative process is possible only through the union of two principles and is subsequently symbolised as play and interplay between male and female.

Tantric images are given from the mid-fifteenth to the eighteenth century. The union cystic of opposite principles in the sexual symbolism of tantric Buddhism is shown by the embrance of male and female images. Male stands for Buddha principle which is compassionate throughout. The female image is Prajna or grosis, the knowledge and symbol of Absolute, Shunya-the void.

Polarity symbolism is represented both from a psychological and a mythological angle in man and women or rather man and women in their cosmicized version of god and goddess, Himduism assigns static aspect in the male principle and dynamic aspect to the female. Tibetan Buddhism finally ascribes the static function to the female principle.

Sexual polarity symbolism are originally Buddhist and the left handed Tantric schools derived their inspiration from them. Shiva without Sakti is a corpse—the great dictum of Hindu Tantrics.

Physical intercourse has been used as a comparative base to enable men and women to perceive the existence of the permanent fountain of happiness. Even to gain a momentary sensation of ecstasy, these must be complete mental, physical, emotional and spiritual education to the sex act. It is here that one has to retain consciousness of the self in the state of detached attachment.

It is said and believed that such symbols or partings in the religious shrines protect them from lightening.

Yaksha : These are often seen in the temples or shrines represented by benevolent deities related to the earth's production. They are beautifully shown in the form of a supporting pillar. The female is known as Yakshi.

24 Temple Struts Tip The Art of Love in Nepal

International visitors to Nepal come up with age old Hindu and Buddhist paintings and carvings set out in the temple struts of Nepal. These are intricately carved with myriad designs from both Hindu and Buddhist religions, dragons, twisted lizards, cherubim with tails, lions, elephants, god and goddess with innumerable arms. Along with them, the sloped struts of Pagoda temples are decorated with erotic and realistic manifestations of sexual intercourse with men and women and sometimes animals in a striking difference of postures. Each carving has a esoteric meanings. These art form that is referred "Erotic Art" in the western countries which verily is the time-honoured art of tantrism. Tantra is defined in a Hindu scripture giving religious teaching and ritual instructions including the use of incantations, diagrams, magic spells, significant gestures and mediation etc. So Tantrism is supposed to be a Hindu origin and to embrace some of the tenets of the cult of Shivaism. Tantric art, as it is perceived, is a contemplation of the eternal cycle of creation, dissolution, and preservation of the human kind. The erotic carvings in the temple struts of Nepal display the harmonious balance between opposites evolved into a system of worshipping male and female force as shown in the form of art depicting sexual organs and act of sexual contracts. These amatory compositions signify a cosmic universe as a harmonious balance between pairs of opposite forces. They show a synthesis of spiritual and material potential attached with the creative function of the consciousness coupled in male and female figures into a static and the dynamic powers. They reflect externalisation of the external cycle of creation with spiritual dedication.

In order to understand the true meaning or implications of erotic art, some knowledge of Tantrism both Hindu and Buddhist doctrines are necessary. Hinduism has a basic trinity of three gods: Brahma, the creator, Vishnu, the preserver and Shiva, the destroyer, Hindu Tantras and their fundamental doctrines refer absolute consciousness a God Shiva in the manifestation of the male principle and power as Sakti in female principle. The creative process is possible only through the union of these two principles. This doctrine is further crystalised in the form of Shiva Lingum (phallus, the symbol of generation—worship of the generative power of nature) in perfect union with Sakti-Yonis (representation of the female genitals, the symbol under which the Hindu deity Sakti is worshipped) given rise to the Shiva-Sakti cult. In the sakti-cult, female sexual energy is worshipped as Goddess Durga, Bhavani, Kali etc. wife of God Shiva (the third god of Hindu triad, destroyer and reproducer) as goddess of destruction. This cult was developed in the 7th century A.D. and gave rise to the concept of Sakti Pithas (Sakti shrines) and was associated with the worship of Sakti or the mother Goddess. The conception of Matrikas (divine mothers) was evolved as these were seven or eight female energies of the supreme Gods such as Brahmani of Brahma (supreme Hindu Deity) Maheswori or Durga of Shiva (Third God of Hindu triad) and Vaisnavi of Vishnu (the second God of Hindu triad, the benefactor of the universe) etc. Afterwards, the origin of 64 Yoginis (female counterparts with their 64 Bhairavs (forms of God Shiva) as male counterparts in their frightful aspects was created. Mahadevi, spouse of God Shiva presented with her superior powers in the Markandaya Purana with an interlude of 700 verses called Chandi Mahatmaya. These verses give static aspect to the male principle and a dynamic aspect to female. In the Tantric process, the female power of

Sakti forming active role of the authority and the female is to be worshipped rather than the male. So the Hindu Tantrism is regarded as a worship of force and the propitiation of female energies. Strong emphasis is given to the female force and sensuality. The power of Sakti is shown by play and interplay between women and beast as well. Dancing upon the male might not seem to be an act of more tenderness, the erotic sentiment copulation in which the female partner takes an active part. The Hindu Tantric tradition makes some distinction between the Sadhana (mortification) that is performed on a purely mental plane and that which also involves actual handling of ritualistic "elements" including women, meat and wine. Hindu schools usually refer to the latter as the left-handed, to the former as the right-handed. Tantrism can allow the consumption of meat and wine and performance of esoteric sexual rites as well as practices which is to go about all of them in a compassionate manner but with detachment.

Buddhism date back Nepal since the time of its founder Gautama the Buddha who was born at Lumbini in West Nepal Terai in 623 B.C. Buddhism gave birth to the two great schools of thought—the Mahayana and the Hinayana known as great vehicle and small vehicle, respectively. Buddhism as it appears in Nepal belongs to a third school which has often been called the third vehicle Vajrayana or Lamaism school strongly influenced by Tantrism. Vajrayana "diamond vehicle" is named after the Vajra "magic dagger" or "Thunderbolt" which represents indestructibility in the form of symbolized 'diamond'. The word 'Vajra' is also used for the emptiness or nothingness which is Vajrayanists consider as the absolute, in such a way, Tantrism is connected with Buddhism in Nepal by creating the path of "Vajrayana". Buddhas and Bodhisatvas are allowed female complements which act as their Saktis or female powers. There are eight major Bodhisatvas. Some of them are the most popular deities of Lamastic pantheon, namely Majusri, Vajrapani, Avalokiteshwara and Maitraya. Along with a masculine Bodhisatvas they are also provided with their female counterparts as Padma Pani, Tara etc. The most popular Goddess is Tara, the mystic wife of Avalokiteswara. Adi Buddha and the five divine Buddhas as their celestial Boddhisatvas have shown with their female energies. Vajra (Thunderbolt) and the Ghanta (Bell) are the Buddhist equivalents of the Hindu Lingum and Yoni, the male and female principles of life. For instance, the phallus is called "Vajra"—Thunderbolt or "Mani"—Jewel and the female organ is Padma i.e. lotus. In the sense, Vajrayana can become a way to salvation by means of the secret enjoyment of love. So the central Sadhaka (Mediator) of Tantrism, Buddhists like Hindus allow contact undertaken within "Laboratory" conditions. They are also allowed to use actual handling of the ritualistic "ingredients" including women, meat and wine. Buddhist Vajrayana puts emphasis on ecstasy or enlightenment which is reached when anyone learn to immobilize mind, breadth and seminal fluid. Solid example of above view is expressed with the figure of 17 headed or 74 headed Mahasamvara in sexual union with his Sakti—a vision of unlimited force that seems ready to explode the universe. There are goddesses or female deities of Shivaistic origin in Buddhism as Tulaja Devi, the special protector of the monarch, Vajra Dhateswari, fearful goddess, Devi Sitala, the goddess of smallpox, Singheni and Byaghini, the terrible etc. Many deities are air travellers and they have human faces, others have heads of lion, tigers, bears and three-eyed demons. They can be used as vehicles of demonic goddess.

The cult of Tantrism was developed to the 12th century in Nepal and was marked by a ardent religious activity of Tantric variety, a left handed cult with the focus of sexual principles in worship. The Malla Dynasty who ruled Nepal from the 13th to the 18th century and Malla rulers were ardent builders of temples, stupas and monasteries. These Pagoda temples and shrines all are decorated with erotic carvings in their struts. Both temples of Hinduism and Buddhism in Nepal have been strongly influenced by the beliefs and practices of Tantrism. Both the religions are worshipped by the people of Nepal in peace and harmony, temple of both amiably stand side by side with some practices of faith tending to mingle throughout the centuries. So the cult of Tantrism both Hindu and Buddhists spells have been mixed up giving birth to a new type of esoteric worship in Nepal, thereby, influencing the socio-religious life of the Nepali people. Nepal pictures a remarkable study of the interaction of Hinduism and Buddhism as social system. Shiva's vassals are the Bhairavs and they are also in Buddhism as for instance Bishwarup Bhairab the "Universal Form". So, it is in Nepal that the people practising both the religions Hinduism and Buddhism have assimilated each other's attributes and give rise to the development of a unique civilization and culture.

The erotic iconography carved in the temple struts are all teemed with philosophical and religious implications fostered by the Hinduism and Buddhism. These amatory union between two figures are not the manifestation of sex in its widest application for the production of erotic desire or gratification but are designed to bring back to the memory to the initiators the idea of union of two opposed yet complementary principles from whose united effort life evolves eternally. So the mystery of esoteric symbols is veiled in inexplicable theosophy and under an unravelled cover in Nepal. The Unio-mystica of the opposite principles in the sexual symbolism is shown by the embrace of male and female images and even by copulation or union in sexual intercourse in and around the religious places and astound the visitor by seeing such irrelevant and obnoxious exposition. But in reality, these symbols or figures indicating combination not alternative or adversative relation do not communicate unpleasing or obscene ideas, they represent deep religious meaning and profound theological notion. Regarding these esoteric symbols H.V. Glasenapps quite rightly emphasises in his Book entitled Buddhistische Mysterien (Stuttgart, 1940 , p. 158) that "those things should not be seen solely as records of a period of depravity, created by immoral priests for the gratification of their lusts. For behind all these teachings and rituals, though they do not fit well into their Buddhist framework, these stands and ancient popular religion, the belief in great Mother Goddesses and in the sanctify in the act of procreation. The ideas and pictorial representations of Buddhist Shaktism ares as inoffensive for anyone who has grown up with them as the Linga cult in India, which is condemned as immoral by Europeans who do not know it although the Hindus when they worship the holy Phallus stone, do not associate any lascivious ideas with it at all."

In the very intensification of explanation, love-making receives an indirect sanctification in all the esoteric symbols in Nepal. These esoteric symbols become an expression of salvation. Male stands for Buddha principle in Buddhism which is compassionate throughout. The female image is Prajna or Course in mind, the knowledge and symbol of Absolute, Shunya, the void. So the perfection in love can be attained only by the union of male and female in compassion not wishing for physical satisfaction but in sublime transmutation into the emotion of awe and veneration that which evokes deviation. Equally, Hinduism also puts emphasis on the spirit of principle of divinely love, i.e. attainment of love in compassion without any physical attainment. The esoteric symbols carved by those professing to communicate cosmisized aspect of spiritual love by visual means of expression. The cosmisized aspect of love gives the doctrine that spirit has a real existence apart from matter. The physical phenomena of love can allure only specially sensitive persons who consider worldly existence for their loves. The lively person has habitually nor naturally to look to things of the spirit i.e. spiritual love for his incorporeal living. The same essence has expressed by HANSUYIN in her book—*The Mountain is Young* (pp. 61.)

"These carvings at all, except to condemn this beautifully ribald and accurate observation of human behaviour with a tedious and in Kathmandu, a silly word obscene. The Nepalese themselves did not pay any attrition to them. For them they were as every thing else, sacred, they served a ritual function, they prevented lightening from striking the buildings. For the Goddess of Lightening was a virgin and fled before such depiction. And the act of love was as everything that was holy and of God, who found Himself in creation."

Esoteric symbols provide a very high meaning in Nepal that the burning lust of physical love is a brutish passion which caters lowerst tastes of human beings and not their highest requirements.

25 *Tourism and Cultural Cum Religious Heritage of Nepal*

Nepal has written its small territorial Compass singular tourist attractions including various sites full of art, architectural masterpieces and pilgrimage places in the background of natural panorama. Nepal has a most favourable position and as such helds exciting fascination owing to the vastness of natural attractions, the high standard of cultural achievements, pleasant, coolness of climate and uniqueness of its fauna and flora. It features attractions ranging from magnificent alpine scenery to the colossal Himalayan panorama. It is truly a betwitching land of contrasts, consisting of rugged mountain ranges, green valleys with various pilgrimage sites, cool and fertile flat lands, tropical forests and the pristine glory of perpetual snows.

Nepal in reality, is not only a geological mosaic but also a human mosaic. It has a population of 20 millions and are divided into various ethnic groups speaking different languages and dialects. Due to topographical differences they put different costumes and ornaments at different places. They peacefully co-exist and this character of the Nepali nation has created an astonishing Nepali culture. Hinduism and Buddhism are equally honoured in Nepal and the blending of the two religions in one entity has inspired and created the distinct culture of its own. The reality of these uniqueness can be seen in the everyday life of people and in the works of arts and architecture.

Nepal has the touristic heritage as she has the combination of elements to attract the attention of tourists and provoke a visit by them. This combination represents the supply of Nepal Tourist Market. Nepal has its source in a temple, stupa, a monument, unique landscape, lofty Himalayan peaks having abode of various gods and goddesses, living species of animals and vegetations or a piece of handicrafts. Active handicrafts (bronze, wood and brass idols of gods and goddesses made in Patan, pottery and clay images of different deities in Thimi, wood carving and painting especially scroll or thanka paintings in Patan, and Bhaktapur, pashmina wool materials in Jumla, Syangboche and other places testify that the traditional taste is still living.

Attractive festivals both gay and solemn are celebrated round the year. There festivals are elegantly displayed the traditional modes of the Nepalese people. These festivals actively have inspired a calendar of events which can be witnessed in age-old traditional festivals of Nepal. Some festivals such as the religious as the Indra Jatra festival, the chariot festival of Machhendranath, Mask dances during Dasain or Durga Puja, Ghanta Karna, Gun-la, Gai Jatra, Ram Nawami, Ghode Jatra etc. are celebrated with picturesque pageantry and religious solemnity. These conspicuous events are the heritage of an ancient culture.

The tri-city of Nepal, Kathmandu Patan and Bhaktapur are very rich in art and architecture. These cities are described as the seat of open air museums. These cities contain many historical monuments, temples, stupas, monasteries, galleries, museums, archives, memorials, the popular art, rural houses, handicrafts production, folklore and popular religious and civil festivals.

There are many other historical and religious places outside Kathmandu Valley. Just to mention a few, Lumbini, the nativity of Gautam Buddha, the prince of peace, Janakpur the birth-place of Sita, daughter of the King Janak and consort of Rama, mentioned in the great Hindu epic Ramayan, many other temples, stupas, gompas and archaeological places of interest scattered all over the country.

World Heritage sites—seven cultural wonders of Nepal include within 20 kms of radius around Kathmandu Valley. These cover religious and cultural sites as Swayambhu Boudha, Bhaktapur, Changunarain, Pashupatinath, Kathmandu Durbar Square and Patan Durbar Square. These areas are included on the World Heritage List upon approval of the working body of the World Heritage Conservation, which was negotiated in 1972 under the auspices of the United Nations Educational, Scientific and Cultural Organisation (UNESCO) and which has now been ratified by 38 nations. Thus the preservation and sound management of these areas are important to inspirational, educational and recreational welfare of the people of the world, to scientific progress and to the economic advancement of the country in which they remain.

The imposing religious and cultural heritage is the Swayambhunath stupa and the Boudhanath Stupa. They are regarded as a religious monument showing a typical example of Stupa architecture. The Buddhist Stupa of Swayambhunath is situated on top of hillock three km. west of Kathmandu amidst of lovely and quite environ. Swayambhunath means "the self-born word" and the Stupa's great sanctity for the Buddhists of the Mahayana (the great vehicle) sect is due to the fact that once the Kathmandu Valley was a lake in the middle of which bloomed a lotus. And Swayambhu nestled on the lotus flower. This Stupa is a symbol of Mahayana Buddhism with a fifty feet high hemisphere representing the sublimity Nirvana and enlightenment. This hemisphere is surrounded by a golden square projection which in turn is capped by a Chudamni, conical canopy of gilded rings. From each of the four sides of the dome a pair of large painted eyes look out at the world. These eyes represent the all-seeing eyes of the Buddha. There are five meditating Buddhas known as Akshobhya, Ratna Sambhava, Amitabha and Amoghasiddhi. The courtyard of the Stupa contains many Chaityas, Shrines, sacked pillars and so on. There is also a pagoda temple of Harate, the guardian deity of the valley's children of smallpox and other epidemics. Such a blend of

Buddhist and Hindu divinities at one particular religious site reflects the unique religious harmony in Nepal. The Stupa represents the essential unity of the Buddha and the universe. At the top of the Stairway, there is a big Vajra of thunderbolt lying upon a Mandala.

Another Buddhist Stupa of Boudhanath is situated eight kilometres east of Kathmandu. This Stupa is one of the largest Buddhist Chaitya in the world. This Stupa is a hemisphere on a four-stage plinth. It is built on an octagonal base. The dome is set on a platform in the shape of a mandala and supports a beautiful proportioned pinnacle. The hemisphere of this Stupa represents the word of wisdom which contains the relics of Kashyapa Buddha. It is built on an octagonal base and about eighty small recesses each containing an image of Buddha. The Chudamani supports an umbrella. The four sides of the Stupa are inset on four sides with the all-seeing eyes of Lord Buddha gazing in each direction. The dome and its base are adorned white and coloured with yellow paint in the form of petals to signify the lotus. The wall around the Stupa is studded with hundreds of prayer wheels that are spin by the devotees as they walk around the Stupa. The origin of this Stupa is a little obscure. However, it is considered to be built by Lichhavi King Mana Dev in the fifth century A.D. Around the Stupa are various small shrines and the houses of important Lamas (Buddhist priests) and monasteries. The Stupa assumes a gay solemn appearance at all Buddhist festivals when Buddhists visit from all over the country, India, Bhutan, Tibet etc. to take part in the sacred rituals.

Bhaktapur as represented by the Durbar Square with shimmering pagodas decorated with exquisite figures and religious symbols. It is a conglomeration of pagodas and shrines. These temples—Batsala temple, the Pashupatinath temple, Bhairabnath temple, Nyatapola temple, Dattatraya temple and many others. It had the origin in the time of the Lichhavi ruler. Later on 889 A.D. it was expanded in the shape of conch shell by the King Ananda Deva.

Patan is also equally famous. The ancient name of this city

is Lalitpur (city of beauty). Here too the Durbar Square is full of Buddhist shrines and Hindu temples. Hindu temples, guardian deities and endless carvings. It is an old city built during the region of Veer Deva in 299 A.D. there are many pagoda-styed temples as Hiranya Varna Mahabihar, Kumbeshwore temple, Jagat Narayan Temple, Machhendra Nath temple, temple of Bajra Varahi, Krishna Mandir and Mahabouddha.

Kathmandu Durbar Square is also complex of varied attractions as well as for experiencing some of the greatest sites of South Asia's cultural heritage. The Durbar Square is full of temples, palace buildings constructed during Malla period (12th to 18th century). There is triple-roofed Taleju Temple. These are also number of other famous temples are Gigantic Shrine of Kal Bhairab (God of terror), Jagannath temple, Temple of Deotale, Sweta Bhairab Shrine, Shiva Parvati temple, Trikokya Mohan Mandir, residential building of Living Goddess Kumari in pagoda style, Kasthamandap etc.

Most famous double-roofed pagoda temple of gold-gilt brass dedicated to God Pashupatinath. This is the holiest of Hindu God Shiva Shrine in Nepal. Lord Pashupatinath is the guardian deity of Nepal. The doors of the temple are plated with silver. It is situated on the western bank of the Bagmati river about five km. north east of Kathmandu. It contains the Lingam of Pashupatinath. The holy place is a mosaic of other temples and shrines. This temple is visited by thousands of devotees including large number of visitors from India.

Other Buddhist sites and monuments in Nepal Lumbini, the birthplace of Gautam Buddha and one of the four major poles of Buddhist pilgrimage is in Nepal. Lumbini lies in the south-west plain of Nepal in the Terai where the Buddha was born to Maya Devi in 623 B.C. It is a sacred place for Buddhists all over the world.

Nepal houses innumerable holy shrines of Hindu and Buddhist deities. The places of Hindu pilgrimage Janakpur Muktinath Baraha Chhestra, Gosainkunda, SwargaDwari Gorkha, Manakamana are very famous and many devotees make a visit or pilgrimages to these places annually. In the same way, Buddhist places of pilgrimages such as Namo Buddha, Kapilvastu, Niglihawa, and other important Buddhist shrines and monasteries are scattered all over the country and many Buddhist devotees pay visit and make homage to Lord Buddha.

By going through the details given above, it is clear that Nepali culture is a mixture of two different civilisations of Asia-Mongoloid and Indo-Aryan culture. Hinduism and Buddhism are both equally honoured in Nepal and the assimilation of the two religions into one entity have created the distinct culture of its own. The fusion of Hinduism and Buddhism has given cementation of the spirit of religious tolerance. Any visitor can see a mixed breed with Buddhist stupa or monasteries and Hindu shrines or temples clustered close to one another in the courtyard of religious places. Nepal is really a Dev Bhomi (the land of gods and goddesses) and religion has played an important role in moulding the outlook, attitude and custom of the people.

Bibliography

— TUCCI, G. "Tibet, Land of Snows." London : Eleck. 1967.

— WALDS CHMIDT. E.and ROSE I : "Art Treasures from the Himalayas". London : Eleck, 1969.

— BHATTACHARYA, B. "The Indian Buddhist Iconography", 2nd ed. Calcutta; Firma K. Muhopadhyaya, 1958.

— SINGH, M. "Himalayan Art", London, Macmillan, 1971.

— STANLEY JEEVES. "Land of the Sherpa", University of London Press Ltd., Great Britain, 1962.

— EKAI KAWA GUCHI. "Three years in Tebet" Madras, 1907.

— TONI HAGEN. "Nepal : Kingdom in the Himalayas." Berne, 1961 and Kathmandu, 1998.

— KUNWAR, RAMESH RAJ, "Fire of Himal : An Anthoropological Study of the Sherpas of Nepal Himalayan Region." Jaipur, Nirala Publications. 1989.

— DUNCAN FORBES. "The Heart of Nepal." Robert Hale Limited, London. 1962.

— K.P. JAYASWAL. "Chronology and History of Nepal". M.N. Barman & Co. Patna. 1937.

— Professor CECIL BENDALL M.A. University College, London. The History of Nepal and Surrounding Kingdoms (1000-1600 A.D. Compiled chiefly from MSS lately discovered. - 1898-99.

— HUMPHREYS Chr : "Buddhism," Harmondsworth-England, 1952.

— KAZAMI TAKEHIDE : "The Himalayas—A Journey to Nepal." Kodansha International Ltd, Tokyo. 1968.

— RUBEL, MARY: "The Gods of Nepal". Bhimatan Harsharath, Kathmandu, 1971.

— SEN, K. M. "Hinduism" Harmondsworth-England, 1961.

— SNELLGROVE. D. : "Buddhist Himalaya"—Oxford, England, 1957.

— SNELLGROVE. D : "Himalayan Pilgrimage"—Bruno Cassirer-Oxford-London, 1961.

— WADDELL. L. A : "The Buddhism of Tibet or Lamaism." Cambridge. 1967.